UNSUNG HEROINES

Women's Life Histories from Tanzania

Magdalene K. Ngaiza
and Bertha Koda (eds.)

WRDP PUBLICATIONS
P.O. BOX 35108, DAR ES SALAAM

Published by WRDP,
P.O. Box 35108,
Dar es Salaam
Tanzania.

ISBN   9987   8820   1   3

CONTENTS

Chapter One: Background to the Project
Project Team Members

Chapter Two: Life History of Bibi: A Woman in Urban Tanga
Bibi with P. Mbughuni

Chapter Three: My Life is a life of Struggles — A Young Barmaid
Anna x with A. Nkhoma – Wamunza

Chapter Four: A Migrant Peasant Woman in the City
Eva with A. Nkebukwa

Chapter Five: The Life History of a Housewife
Mama Koku with M. Ngaiza

Chapter Six: Grassroot struggles for Women's Advancement
Rebecca Kalindile with M. Mbilinyi

Chapter Seven: From a Peasant to a Worker in the City

Mwanaidi with Asseny Muro

Chapter Eight: Overcoming Cultural Barriers to Modern Life

Paulina M. with B. Koda

Chapter Nine: Conceptual and Legal Issues

M. Ngaiza, B. Koda, F. Temu

Chapter Ten: Lessons Learned 221

Project Team members

List of Tables

Abbreviations

C.C.M.	—	Chama cha Mapinduzi (The Party)
CHAP	—	Chapter
I.D.S.	—	Institute of Development Studies
ILO	—	International Labour Organization
NORAD	—	Norwegian Organization For Research and Development
SIAS	—	Scandinavian Institute for African Studies
SIDO	—	Small Scale Industries Organization
SUWATA	—	Shirika la Uchumi la Wanawake Tanzania (Parastatal for Women's Economic Activities)
TANU	—	Tanganyika African National Union
T.N.A.	—	Tanzania National Archives
T.P.H.	—	Tanzania Publishing House
UMATI	—	Tanzania Family Planning Association
UNICEF	—	United Nations Children's Fund
U.W.T.	—	Tanzania Women's Organization
W.R.D.P.	—	Women's Research and Documentation Project

MIGRATION MAP OF 7 WOMEN IN TANZANIA 1920s–1970s

International boundary
Railways
Major roads

NAMES	MOVEMENTS
1. Mwanaidi	From Ugweno → Arusha → Dar es Salaam
2. Mama Koku	From Bukoba → Tabora → Kasulu → Kibondo → Newala → Morogoro → Masasi → Musoma → Maswa → Mbulu → Arusha → Moshi → Dar es Salaam
3. Bibi	From Tanga → Moshi (Nyumba ya Mungu) → Tanga
4. Kalindile	From Masoko Kasyeto (Rungwe rural)
5. Anna	From Mtwara → Dar es Salaam → Mbamba Bay → Mombasa → Songea → Dar er Salaam.
6. Paulina	From Songea → Ifakara → Kilosa → Morogoro → Dar es Salaam
7. Eva	From Tabora → Dar es Salaam.

2. Mama Koku : From Bukoba → Tabora → Kasulu → Kibondo → Newala → Morogoro → Masasi → Musoma → Maswa → Mbulu → Arusha → Moshi → Dar es Salaam

3. Bibi : From Tanga → Moshi (Nyumba ya Mungu) → Tanga

4. Kalindile : From Masoko Kasyeto (Rungwe rural)

5. Anna : From Mtwara → Dar es Salaam → Mbamba Bay → Mombasa → Songea → Dar er Salaam.

6. Paulina : From Songea → Ifakara → Kilosa → Morogoro → Dar es Salaam

7. Eva : From Tabora → Dar es Salaam.

Foreword

The Women's Research and Documentation Project (WRDP) is proud to be associated with the production of "UNSUNG HEROINES". WRDP contributed the idea of writing these life histories through its learning process. The Project aims at promoting study, research and documentation of women's lives and gender issues. The underlying objective is to provide a study forum, to inform potential researchers about the gaps which need to be filled as well as the need for new data which is required to step up women's struggles.

The Tanzanian women intellectuals have just come of age, many fellow feminists who have argued that publications from Africa are few and less accessible will now find Tanzanian women who are ready to write and present a variety of research findings on several themes. WRDP is proud to have had the opportunity since 1980, to provide a forum for the researchers who have brought up this book. It is indeed a great effort for one to write history if one does not belong to that discipline. The co-authors were faced with two challenges: one relating to the missing voices of rural and urban women in the records of history, the other was the accusation that intellectual women speak and distort other women's lives. WRDP felt obliged to provide a supportive forum through which the authors and co-authors were able to give first hand accounts of the lives of women who needed to be heard so that their counterparts could be helped. Indeed, they have used few words so that the readers can have a moment to think and judge.

Magdalene Ngaiza
Bertha Koda

Acknowledgement

This book has a long history. It was started in 1986. We would like to acknowledge all the women and men who helped to make this book possible.

We thank the life historians first and their families whose words are the life blood of this book. In Africa, life is not of an individual, but of a family and even the clan, and so one does not disclose much about himself/herself lest the others feel offended. These women have disobeyed and we would like to acknowledge that this is a form of resistance well intended to further women's liberation.

Our particular appreciation go to WRDP for the sisterhood which never failed us even when we felt tired. We cannot fail to acknowledge the seminar and workshop organized to give meat to the skeletons of the chapters in 1987. Here we would like to single out Dr. Pat Macfadden, Professor Wamba-Dia-Wamba, and Mrs Theresa Kaijage for their inputs which strengthened the respective chapters. Professor S. Geiger of the University of Minnesota is also remembered for her encouragement.

In the process of authorship there are many others who seem equally concerned, like the author, in ensuring that the book finally comes out. In that spirit, these papers were painstakingly read by Dr. M.M. Mulokozi, Director in the Tanzania, Ministry of Culture & Youth, Dr. Mpangala from the University of Dar es Salaam, Institute of Development Studies and Professor R. Besha from the Department of Kiswahili, University of Dar es Salaam to whom we owe many thanks and much appreaciation for their valuable contributions. As we shared the stories we bacame part of them and in this way we could not be judges in our own cases.

We also solicited the participation of a lawyer Mrs. F. Temu from the Ministry of Community Development, Women and Children who came in handy to write a section on legal provisions. We thank her for her enlightenment on legal intricacies. Mr. C. Kamugisha of the Institute of Development Studies proof-read the manuscript with much interest. We appreciate his cooperation.

Funding for the research and publication was provided by NORAD without which this book ᵈ have been impossible. Their patience for thⁱᶜ book is highly appreciated as we slowed down for two years. Finally, we want to thank our families for understanding the complicated roles of academic women, but for sure they have learnt a lot in the process together with us.

The Secretarial skills of women who typed several manuscripts are appreciated and we would like to mention only a few, Mwajuma, Rukia and Sarah who put the final manuscript out. Much as we owe everybody thanks, the responsibility for shortcomings remain ours.

The life Histories co-authors.

CHAPTER ONE

INTRODUCTION AND BACKGROUND TO THE PROJECT

Towards a definition of "Life History"

The idea to launch this project on Women's life histories arose from the realization that the gender question is fundamental to a proper and fuller understanding of the historical development of our Tanzanian society, and of the social contradictions and struggles that have characterized it todate. One felt that the concept of *class* alone did not fully explain the nature and extent of the social differentiations and oppression in different modes of production of different levels of social development. Hence an additional analytical category, that of *gender,* has to be employed.

By definition, a "Life History" is an *extensive* record of a person's life told to and recorded by another, who then edits and writes the life as though it were an autobiography. The Women's life histories, which are the focus of this book therefore, emphasize the experiences and requirements of ordinary women rather than of those in power or of men. Indeed, there is need to relate the story of over half the population, that is, the story and experiences of women. Women do not often appear in standard history books; one can read accounts of prehistorical man, of the political and economic changes during the slave era, or colonial empires and the Zanzibar Sultanate or, more recently, the history of TANU and CCM in building the nation of Tanzania. But women, either as individual actors in this large historical stage or as a gender affected by and affecting changes, do not often appear. Standard histories belong to the public domain where women are not immediately visible participants in war, politics, trade and matters of state.

Another reason for studying women's history is to gain an understanding of women's past and therefore gain knowledge of how to bring about change. If we can understand what forces, for instance, were brought to bear on women farmers during the periods of intense labour migration and what varying strategies women utilized to manage or accommodate changes in their social relations, we will come closer to understanding how an oppressive gender division of labour was perpetuated. If we wish to examine the nature of women's subordination, its roots, origin and tactics, we can start

1

by looking at the tactics used by the colonial government to strengthen male dominance, authority and control over women and other producers such as the youth. These are just a few of the topics of current interest to women researching their history in Tanzania. The list of possibilities, as most of the history pages are so far blank, are endless.

Still another reason for studying women's history is to gain new strength for women currently struggling for their own progress and equity. The examination of the past through new eyes can posit alternative images of women and the impact they have had on history, both as individuals and as a gender. One easily forgets that there were women who ruled and consolidated societies in Africa, or that many played heroic roles in various wars, both internal and colonial. Yet one need not only look for heroines in wars or political strifes; the strength of women can be portrayed in their struggles for the survival of themselves and their families in the face of varied forms of domination and opposition.

Finally, the study of women's history offers a new perspective on changing social relations. Women's history is told from the point of view of the oppressed or dominated section of society. Usually history is written for and about the dominant members of society. At any given time it will tend to justify, legitimize or rationalize the status quo. This tendency is quite evident in histories such as those taught in the colonial era legimitizing the colonial expansion. But it should also be clear that male dominance can also inform the perception of history and women can be left out or portrayed as marginal supporters to man's efforts. Women's Voicelessness on the other hand gives the impression that women are consumers rather than producers and shapers of history. Indeed this is a wrong impression. Women have contributed handsomely in both socio-economic and political development of their societies and these contributions are extremely important historical facts worth recording and preserving for future understanding and analysis of social change. In short, women's history offers a perspective of an oppressed people, a situation which links it to the history of colonized peoples.

It has been demonstrated elsewhere that the misconception of women's role in the making of history is invariably a reflection of the system of gender oppression and female subordination guided by both patriarchal and capitalist ideologies which have governed both the research work and the writings of many male and female historians and scholars. In seeking for clarity on the roots of women's voicelessness in history, therefore, one is necessarily forced to trace the material basis of women's oppression and subordination, i.e. partiarchal and capitalist relations of production.

Patriarchy as it influences the recording of 'history'

In many of the pre-capitalist social formations, especially in Africa, patriarchal relations were the basis of women's invisible and voiceless status in written history. Under patriarchy, women are politically, economically and socially subordinated and powerless as a gender group. Patriarchal relations have also contributed to class formation and hence social differentiation. This has also led to the creation of a dominant culture of the upper class and a subordinate culture of the disadvantaged social groups. As economically sub-ordinate group, the majority of women belong to the latter culture and thus their interests and role as contributors to history was submerged. Women of the upper classes too, were and still are unnoticed and taken for granted as supporters of important men and so are unimportant, while reality has proved that such women very often deserved the credits. It should also be pointed out here that those men belonging to the lower classes were also denied the chance to record their particular experiences in written history, for it was the dominant culture which was reflected in historical records.

Patriarchal relations

In analytical terms patriarchal relations which developed prior to the emergence of capitalism are constituted at the household level with the male head of the household being a patriarch. The patriarchal ideology influences gender division of labour institutionalized at the household level and transplanted at the community level.

At both the household, community and even internationally, the division of labour is by gender, age and status (family or class or both) and it includes access to and control of resources including major means of production (e.g. land, forest, cattle), labour and even the products of labour In many areas women's access to resources have to be mediated through men, depending on their status as wives, daughters or sisters. In any households, women are disadvantaged in resource allocations including land, labour and leisure time. Women are for instance found to have lesser rights to mobilize the labour of others either within their own households or at community level for use in both productive and reproductive spheres including the writing of their own histories.

Time use studies worldwide also reveal that women have longer working hours and less leisure time than men of the same households. The assumption that the household or family is a combined unit of production, consumption and reproduction with a corporate access to resources or indeed that it has any one of these as universal characteristics has been

3

demonstrated to be empirically in-accurate in Africa. It is within these very institutions that there is increased control over wives. Household units have never been egalitarian institutions.

While patriarchal relations refer to the way production and reproduction is organized within households, peasant production systems are not reduced to the household level. With the introduction of colonialism pre-capitalist social relations were subjected to capitalist relations and the patriarchal ideology was also perpetuated. Likewise, households are not isolated units but are part of broad processes. The inter-relations among households, between households and other structures and processes including kinship systems, commoditization, the nature of the state, international economy, cultural/ideological constructions of personhood, masculinity and femininity, need to be analysed with a gender perspective. It is implied here therefore that historians should become gender-sensitive; hence they must integrate relations between men and women to other processes to be able to reflect class and gender relations in their historical analyses.

The oppression of women under capitalism

Women subordination is a fundamental aspect of capitalist relations of production and reproduction. The oppression which takes place both at home and in the productive sphere is necessary for the reproduction of capitalist relations, since the work done by women in the domestic sphere is a vital part of value of reproduction of labour power. Just like patriarchy, capitalist relations allocate men and women to different positions both in production and reproduction. These positions are very well reflected in the way both relate to production resources and remunerations.

Women's oppression is fundamental to the exploitation of peasants as well. In peasant production systems, female labour isn't only vital to domestic labour process, it is also a major component of food and export crop production. The way in which those productive and reproductive systems operate is highly profitable to capital in that prices paid for marketed crops do not reflect the real value of labour power expended on it. Female labour subsidizes the production of exchange value yet it never enters into the calculation of prices of commodities. In purely economic terms, female contribution in this way is rendered unimportant and thus not reflected in national statistics to the extent that women's work has no cash value. Women have thus seldom been allowed to influence the dominant public records even when such records have a great bearing on their lives.

It was therefore partly in recognition of these basic facts that as far back as 1983 seven members of The Women's Research and Documentation Project took the initiative of writing women's life histories.

Why Life Histories

Women's history tends to bear the stamp of their particular struggles. It arises out of the documentation of specific concrete situations which may often challenge the accepted generalizations of the dominant ideology. Examples of such generalizations are many and not limited to women's history: the African continent was 'underdeveloped' and stagnant until the arrival of colonial interests: women's place is (and was and shall forever be) in the home (kitchen, field). Women's history, documents the varied places and strategies of women in specific situations which reflect both her class and gender. It begins with the specific and the person, at the grass roots.

A life history, as a form of personal documentation, is thus particularly suitable for women's history. Like any history, it is selective but deliberately so, told from the women's own point of view. Life histories are embedded in the social relations of class and gender which dominate women's perception of the course of their own lives. To them the most important points of reference may be their relationship with their husbands, their children of kin, and these play a large role in women's narration. In telling their stories, the women reproduce their own images of themselves and their relations with others. This is a type of data often ignored in conventional histories as too individual, too specific and atypical. But it is this very specificity and concreteness which gives it strength as a challenge to long standing generalizations. In particular, women's life histories offer the possibility to examine the interactions of classes and gender in specific historical situations.

On the theoretical level, there have been several sets of objections to the use of the life history data. The first set of objections focuses on the issue of the truth or validity of life history data. In contrast to the empirical, representative data of conventional historical narratives, life histories are said to be non-representative, atypical and eclectic. Life historians have several answers to this objection; some seek to circumvent the charge by recording group rather than individual life histories, seeking the safety of 'representativeness' in numbers. A second tactic is to record a number of life histories and then search for the general pattern, in which case the recorder becomes the analyst of the life histories. A third tactic is to relate an individual or a set of individual life histories to various forms of macro-data such as demographic or economic surveys or other 'empirical' data such as that found in archives and records. A final tactic, is to recognize and embrace the atypical or specific nature of life histories. History must always be selective and the recognition of such selectivity and subjectivity is also a fact of history and a permanent motivating force to individual action and perception.

A second set of objections also relates to the issue of subjectivity, but focuses on the reliability of the narration itself rather than on its representativeness of typicality. The women's life history is a personal account which relies on the woman's memory as well as her conscious selection of what material should be narrated. The narrative or data itself will therefore be biased to reflect her desired self-image, often linked as well to her relationship with the recorder of the life history. But rather than invalidating the narrative as a historical document, such subjectivity reveals the woman's perceptions of herself and the social relations which are important in her life; it reflects her own consciousness. For example, a woman who represents herself as a faithful and supportive wife, who plays only a marginal role in family maintenance is reflecting the consciousness promoted by patriarchal ideology which states that women must support their husband's endeavors but are by themselves ineffective. Such consciousness also reflects the middle class ideology of the supportive home-bound wife. A woman who presents herself as having overcome various obstacles such as husband's failure to support the family, long absences from home, her struggles to obtain food, shelter and clothing for the family, is also speaking from a consciousness which is particular to her class as well as her gender. Thus the women's subjectivity can be seen not as a drawback to validity, but as an asset in the search to reveal changing and varied patterns in social relations and consciousness.

In summary, the women recording and analysing the life histories in this collection have adopted a variety of approaches to deal with the issues related to subjectivity. Most have looked for patterns which reflect specific gender and class issues. Furthermore, this collection is regarded as a beginning to the documentation of women's history in Tanzania which will challenge accepted generalizations about women's participation in the shaping of Tanzanian history. We note for example that in this collection women have not made any reference to war and famine situations, yet many women given a chance will bring to the open a lot of such stories. Peasant women who are the backbone of the nation deserve proper representations in economic history, health care, household economics, transportation and social reproduction

II. METHODOLOGICAL APPROACH

Choice of Area of Study and History Makers

The choice of urban women was not accidental; but it was a conscious reaction to the tendency by researches on women-related issues in the last decade to concentrate on rural women under the assumption that urban women have lesser problems. The interest in urban women has also been aggravated by the fact that although the sex-ratio in urban areas has dramatically increased since the 1950s, there is very little record on the different forms of struggles they engage in. Of course there is data, for instance, to show that the majority of urban women work in the informal sector in food processing and preparation, house keeping, beer brewing and trade, petty trade, prostitution etc. and that a few are also found in certain formal wage occupations like nursing, teaching, secretarial work and retail * .de. How ever, very little is known about their real personal struggles

Although no specific location within Dar es Salaam region was intended to be covered, efforts were made to select history-makers from both unsurveyed, squatter areas like Mlalakuwa and Kawe, and the surveyed areas like Oysterbay, the oldest residential area used by the white population during colonialism and later by the African ruling class.

Selection of history makers, on the other nand, partly depended upon personal contacts with the researchers except in two cases where the researchers were introduced to the history makers one by a former student of hers in Mbeya, and the other one in Tanga. The main objective was to identify "knowledgeable" persons who are willing to share their knowledge. The sample, however, was supposed to include young, older and middle-aged women who could articulate their views about the colonial period, the changes they have observed and experienced over time and their own role in historical changes. It was also important to include in the sample young women with specific experiences of a set of circumstances in the city, especially single women who are heads of households.

As far as data collection is concerned, two techniques were adopted. The first task of the researchers was to identify interviewing procedures which would put them and their research partners on a common plane. They thus started off with the most important step of explaining the project to their partners, making sure the objectives and end results of the project are well understood and also accepted. Some of the history makers grasped the importance of the project, that it was meant to contribute to the correction of gender-biased historical records in Tanzania. It took others a little longer to realise the importance of the project and what they stood to gain, but they finally came round and co-operated fully in the research. Thus the role of the researcher as an educator and consciousness raiser has become very clear to the researchers, perhaps more so in this particular project than in their other researches.

7

Having assured themselves that their partners understood the importance of the project, the next step was to programme the interviews at the conveniences of both participants, but especially of the life historians who had no fixed schedule of daily activities but had their hands already full with their daily activities and struggles for survival. Both reached an agreement to be flexible.

Having agreed on the time, the other aspect that emerged during the research was how to regulate the interviews to avoid getting into emotional entangles, over excitements and boredom or disillusionment. This can be a problem depending on how the two research partners relate to one another. Too close intimacy can lead to emotional constraints, especially given the sad episodes emerging in almost all the histories. Boredom and disillusionment can occur due to the nature of the research questions themselves, the principal researchers' approach to given issues and the time taken to respond to questions. Quick dismissals of certain questions as being unimportant and dwelling on others can both lead to the above negative developments in oral history research. Making the interviews too business-like can also distort the responses. The researcher, thus, had to learn to adjust to her research partner and be able to ask relevant questions and guide the responses without dominating the conversation.

Closely related to the above is the decision on how much of the history is to be included in the final document and how much is to be left out. This decision is guided by how well the research partner understands the objectives of the research and the issues at stake. The answer on how much to include therefore comes from the owner of the story, who is the one who has lived the life that is being documented. It was agreed that often the personal interests and biases of the researchers have to be subdued to accommodate the personal and public interests of the owner of the story. The final decision on anonymity or open identity were also made by the owner of the story.

However, this whole process of telling, listening and discussing necessarily cements mutual trust and a personal relationship between the narrator and the recorder. This does not mean however, that problems of confidentiality will not arise. In fact this is one reason why the use of tape-recorders was very much limited in this project, not only because of limited supply of the equipment to WRDP researchers, but also because the narrators were suspicious of the outcome of their use. With the awareness that their opinions are stored in their own words, the narrators tend to be too conscious of what they say and thus limit the freedom to discuss issues intimately and express personal opinions on delicate or political issues. This limitation is

8

aggravated by the fact that the narrators are usually not very sure of who is going to read or listen to the recorded data and how that data is going to be interpreted and used. Analysis of data recorded on tapes also needs very careful interpretation because the interviewee is usually absent at this stage and cannot therefore be called upon to clarify some of his/her statements when need arises.

The literature surveys were carried out in the national archives, libraries and documentation centers. There were other rich sources of data. Files, books, journals, published and unpublished papers, dissertations, newspaper articles and other works were consulted to enrich data collection especially for background information which proved to be very useful indeed.

After having written the first drafts, the researchers organized two workshops to discuss the drafts. The first workshop aimed at getting academic input and expertise from learned scholars, while the second one, which involved the life historians themselves, aimed at reaching points of agreement before the life-histories were published. After each workshop the researchers did the necessary revisions. We are happy that several male scholars made a lot of input in this collection and shared our concerns.

Limitations faced by researchers

The main limitation was time. It took the researchers more time than they had planned for, due to the nature of the work itself. Sometimes the narrator was not in a good mood that affected the discussions to some degree. There were times also when the researcher would walk into the narrator's house only to find the latter too busy with other tasks which could not be postponed. Sometimes the planned meeting schedules did not meterialize due to other equally important commitments for the recorders.

The general method of pen and paper recording used by researchers also tended to be very slow and tedious, culminating in the double task of listening and recording at the same time. Interviewing the old people also tend to take more time than expected because much depended on the memory of the narrator and sometimes there was need to counter-check some of the narrated information in order to clear some of the contradictions which seemed to crop up in the accounts.

III. CONTRIBUTIONS MADE BY THE VARIOUS LIFE HISTORIES AND THEIR SETTINGS

The life histories contained in this book are either biographies (third person narrations about the subject) or autobigraphies (first person narratives). The stories were delivered in Kiswahili and/or in the subject's mother tongue and later translated by the co-author into English.

Generally, all the stories focus on women's life struggles for social and economic justice. They all touch on various factors that influence the women's stature and situation in society, such as upbringing and socialization (including schooling), traditional attitudes and practices, marriage, motherhood, infertility, divorce and widowhood, economic subordination, religion, politics, health, unemployment and gender oppression in general. Furthermore, they all attempt to delineate a process – the process of gradual self-awareness and self improvement that almost all the women in the study have experienced as they struggled to overcome the socio-economic obstacles placed in their way.

Each story, however, focuses on a given central theme characterising the life of its subject, for instance: adult education as a form of gender struggle (ch.7 and 8), women as wage slaves and victims of sexual abuse (ch.3), the urbanization of women and their search for economic independence (ch. 2, 4–7), women and "modernization" (ch.8); etc.

The seven stories make independent chapters which vary in length, focus, organization, subject matter, conceptual and ideological emphasis. Nevertheless, they all share a clear "feminist perspective, the perspective of the struggling woman as an oppressed and exploited member of society. They all reveal a deep commitment to gender struggles, and they are, we believe, written with dedication and genuine feeling. As such they are dramatic, gripping and unfogettable. Together, they give us a non-flattering but engaging portrayal of the experience of being a woman in both the past and contemporary Tanzania and Africa. A brief summary of each contribution is as follows:

Patricia Mbughuni and *Bibi* present Bibi's life history in Chapter two. *Bibi* was born near Tanga, 15 km away, moved into Tanga town when she was a small girl and has lived there ever since, leaving it only for brief periods to seek her livelihood or to follow the husband. Bibi is, thus, essentially an urban woman.

She received a thorough informal traditional education and attended the Koranic school (but no western type of schooling). Later she educated herself as an adult. Bibi married several times, often in polygamous households, and divorced several times allegedly because of ill-treatment by her spouses. She was unable to have children and raised relatives' children. Eventually Bibi became a widow and struggled and succeeded to achieve economic independence as a petty trader.

This pattern highlights the problems of *infertility* and *polygamy*. Apparently, many a woman's life has been ruined or changed by these two prob-. lems. Education (both traditional and "modern") is seen throughout as a positive factor which help the woman to find her place in society. The article furnishes data on traditional education given through oral literature, children's games, etc. It appears that on this point there is not much difference between the urban and the rural people. This is a very valuable section as it reveals how traditional societies socialized the new generations: the ideology is hidden in the songs and games. The article is interspersed with historical and sociological accounts about Tanga town, these help to situate Bibi s life into the concrete context.

In Chapter three, a life of struggle as presented by *Anna, x* and *Alice Wamunza* depicts *Anna,* the youngest person interviewed by the researchers. She was born in Mtwara, went to school but quit before completing primary school because of pregnancy, married and went to live with her husband in Mombasa. She was maltreated by the husband and deserted with her children after some years. At the time of the interview she was self-employed as a petty bussiness woman. Her story illustrates the common trends of school girl pregnancy victims, deserted wives and the lives of barmaids: These are struggles which demand our attention.

A migrant peasant woman is presented by *Eva* and *Anna Nkebukwa* in chapter four. This chapter recounts the story of Eva. She was born in Tabora 60 years ago, grew up in the village, was married to a spouse she did not like, divorced, married again, divorced again due to alleged ill-treatment, and finally moved to the city, where she still lives, striving to earn her living through various projects, including petty trade.

Her story illustrates well the beliefs of the society regarding virginity, bridewealth, polygamy, fertility and choice of spouse. The *unyago/kufunda* rites are shown to be negative institutions (at least partially) that serve to domesticate the woman. The emphasis on virginity before marriage is explained in economic terms – the virgin fetches a better "price". Like Anna, Eva moves to the city in search of personal freedom and economic independence, although originally she followed her husband.

In chapter five the life of a housewife is underscored by *Magdalene Ngaiza* with *Mama Koku. Mama Koku* who at the time of the research was a widow, is now deceased. She was born in Bukoba in 1938, attended school up to class eight, and married in 1955. Her husband, who was a teacher, changed his profession twice, ending up as a magistrate. By virtue of his job as a magistrate, he was transferred often. *Mama Koku* moved about with him so that by the time he retired she had lived in most of the regions of Tanzania. Eventually, they settled in Dar es Salaam in 1969.

During their sojourn in Dar es Salaam, Mama Koku was maltreated by her husband but refused to divorce him because she was a "Christian and a mother". Upon the death of her husband she inherited nothing. She convinced the government, through the personal intervention of the former President, *Mwalimu Julius K. Nyerere,* to give her a "pension" and a building plot. Mama Koku lived with her husband until he died. Unlike *Anna* and *Bibi,* she refused to divorce but earned her freedom and economic independence as a consequence of her husband's death.

Her life illustrates the role of three factors in subjugating the woman i.e. marriage within religion which forbids divorce; children who inspire women to suffer indignities rather than abandon their offspring; and economic dependence.

Grassroot struggles for women is presented by *Kalindile, M. Mbilinyi* with *T. Sambulika* in chapter six. This chapter narrates the life history of *Rebeka Kalindile,* a Nyakyusa lady who was born in 1914, and grew up to become a housewife, a mother, a farmer, a Christian educator and village midwife. The story tells of her childhood in the village, her schooling, her conversion to Christianity, puberty and the accompanying rites, her marriage (including details of the accompanying, now defunct, ceremonies). The second part of the story is about Kalindile's married life. We are told about her yearning for offspring and her first painful experience of childbirth. This part ends with a description of Kalindile's activities as a church elder and women's leader and educator. The final part of the article focuses on the theoretical issues arising from Kalindile's life experience and the ideological and theoretical conflicts she had with the researcher in the course of recording and writing the story. There are also comments on the significance of the story for other women and for society in general.

The article succeeds to highlight the nature of the oppression suffered by women during colonialism. This is characterised by being colonial, racial and patriarchal. It is complicated by the causal labour relations on the level of the family. *Kalindile* wants to illustrate how the women reacted to this oppression, the methods she adopted in the struggle, and the successes achieved. Her life highlights the women's contribution to the history and struggles of the country.

In chapter seven *Asseny Muro* with *Mwanaidi* explore the shift from a peasant to a worker. This is the story of Mwanaidi, a Pare Woman who was born in 1934. She attended school up to Standard III, underwent the initiation rites and learned the traditional chores under the guidance of her hostile step mother. She first married in 1944 Mwanaidi worked very hard in her husband's farm, but was disturbed by her failure to have children. She assisted her husband to get a second wife, who proved "fertile". She cared for her step children until her co-wife's harassment forced her to seek a divorce. Mwanaidi moved to Arusha, and later to Dar es Salaam as a baby-sitter. She worked for many years as a househelper until she secured a job at the University of Dar es Salaam, as a cleaner in 1966. In the meantime, she managed to acquire building plots in different areas and build several simple houses before she retired from the University service in 1985. She now lives in Dar es Salaam.

Mwanaidi quit school because of health problems, married, divorced her husband because of domestic problems (infertility) and decided to move to the city and shape her own life through wage employment and investment in petty projects. It is important, however, to highlight the fact that *infertility* was the decisive factor in her selection of future options for her life: She divorced because she could not bear children. This fact underlines the fundamental role played by fertility in the life of an African woman as seen also in Bibi's life (ch.2). Other factors affecting women that are revealed by this study are: Bride wealth; the value placed on virginity; polygamy as a potential wrecker of homes, divorce as a source of economic loss for the woman, and the plight of house maids.

Finally in chapter eight, *Betha Koda* with *Paulina Makarios*, present a theme on overcoming cultural barriers, This is the life of *Paulina Makarios*, a strong-willed woman who managed to shape her life in her own way after a long struggle.

Paulina was born at Peramiho in Ruvuma. She attended school up to Std. IV, assumed adult responsibilities early in life because of her mother's death and married at the age of 20. After living with her husband, Francis, for a few years, the latter ran away and came to live and work in Dar es Salaam. Paulina travelled to Dar es Salaam looking for Francis, and discovered him at Kawe. Thereafter she lived with him at Kawe and later at Mbezi and had two children and several grandchildren. In Dar es Salaam, Paulina became a women's leader and adult educator, in addition to her other chores as a peasant and a housewife. She managed to fulfil all the tasks and turn her village, Mbezi, into a hub of development activities. She still lives at Mbezi with her aging husband and her grandchildren.

One important element that affected her life was the belief in witch craft/superstition. As her children died, and she herself almost followed suit her husband ran away. Paulina and her people believed in witchcraft and did not seek medical help. This factor should be borne in mind when talking about the problems of women and health services in Africa today.

CHAPTER TWO

A Life History of Bibi: A Woman in Urban Tanga

Bibi with Patricia Mbughuni

Introduction

A story usually tells its events in a single straight line from beginning to middle and to the end. But this story has three lines and they do not always run parallel, in an even flow, nor do they start at the same point in time. The three stories are like three skeins of wool, each with a single thread of a different colour. Sometimes one thread gets in the way of another, sometimes they will touch in perfect harmony. For the knitter, myself, these skeins are my basic materials, sometimes unrully and obstinate, inpenetrable maze, sometimes easy to handle.

The first story is the story of Tanga town, the backdrop for Bibi's life. This story is by no means complete, as facts and records are missing and even the data available is sometimes questionable. But the story is incomplete for another reason as well. I have chosen those threads of the town's history which seem to touch on and illuminate the second story, Bibi's life history

Her history is a life history told by oral narration in a series of interviews and discussions.[2] I have kept to her own words and sequence as much as possible. As such, her life history is a rough recounting of this elderly woman's memories of her life, and is informed by her own perception of herself and the meaning of her life. Her narrative is not a strictly chronological biography. It is more like a clothes line with bundles strung up here and there with gaps in between. Each bundle, or memory, or set of memories, was important to Bibi, but the framework or chronology of the vast set of personal relationships which make up these bundle are not always clear.

The third thread wound into this narrative is my own narrative voice, my own subjectivity in relation to Bibi and her story. My own values and priorities permeate the analysis and evaluation which couches Bibi's story. I have tried to demarcate my own voice as well, making it clear when I am speaking, evaluating and analysing.

The narrative therefore has a number of voices or threads. The story of Tanga town told by historians, demographers, planners, economists. These are often colonial officers, politicians cum administrators. Then there is Bibi's voice. She loves a good rounded story or vignette, filled with conflict, character and plot with beginning, middle and end. Finally there is my own voice trying to unravel, link, connect. By allowing all these voices perhaps we can gain a portrait if not a picture of a woman's life in Tanga.

Tanga town

Tanga town squats on the edge of the Indian Ocean. It is a port town with a natural harbour of calm, unruffled waters. It probably sprung up around the sixth century A.D. along with other coastal communities, but does not figure in the history records until the time of Omani domination of the coast. For centuries the limelight focused on Tanga's elder sister, Pangani. Pangani lost her bloom when the Germans discovered her lacking – she had a sandbar which hindered large ships from entering her port. At this point around the turn of the century, the Germans decided to shift the commercial and administrative centre in the area to Tanga, which soon took centre stage in their colonial enterprise.

The story of the Tanga coast and its settlement thus begins at Pangani. This town was first known in historical records as Rhapta, a flourishing seaport mentioned by Periplus Maria Erythraei, a shipping gazette written in the first century A.D. At the time Rhapta was a commercial centre under the suzerainty of an Arabian state, dealing in the export of ivory, tortoise shell, coconut oil and rhinocerous horns. At least two historians[3] regard Pangani as the Rhapta mentioned by Ptolemy who wrote in the second century B.C., and assume that it had been a hub of trade since sometime in the 5th century B.C.

With the fall of the Roman empire there is a hiatus in the records mentioning Rhapta. It surfaces again as Pangani by the 7th century A.D. when the Persians dominated trade on the East African coast, importing mainly slaves and ivory. By the tenth century Arabs had established large coconut plantations around Pangani and inland along the Pangani River for a length of 25 miles. Shirazi controlled the coast by setting up an administrative apparatus in a series of small cities or enclaves. Each city had a governor (Liwali) who held authority over a number of Jumbeates or chiefdoms. These cities had appointed officers, Waziri (Minister), Tajiri (Treasurer), Kadhi (Judge) etc. This structure served to collect taxes or tributes and facilitate slaving and ivory expeditions. The apparatus also had cultural, legitimatizing activities. It organized dance festivities and competitions, ruled over successions, quarrels, and officated at the resplendent installation ceremonies for new chiefs. The smaller city, towns of the coast were thus amalgamated

16

into Shirazi administrative structure. Robinson[4] puts the colonization of Vumba, a town to the North of Tanga, at 1199–1216, while Baxter[5] dates the beginnings of Mkwaja-Saadani colonization to the South of Pangani two centuries earlier.

Thus the Shirazi expanded the colonization process along the coast, setting up frontier posts geared to milking the resources of the African hinterland. Their "stone towns" were in an ambigous position; perched on the Indian ocean, their focus on Persian motherland, yet dependent on the "hinterland" for trade and subsistence goods.

This pattern of colonization continued throughout Shirazi, Portuguese, Omani, German and British domination, and Tanga town became one of these city-states caught in the web of coastal rivalry. In 1824, the Sultan of Zanzibar sent troops to secure Wasin Island. The inhabitants were driven off, plundered of their ships and slaves. The population of nearby Tanga town dropped to 300.[6] In 1939 the Mazrui resistance to the Sultan's dominance reached Tanga. Mazrui supporters under a woman leader sacked and burned Tanga, and the Sultan quelled them only by setting up a permanent garrisson there.

Thus the maintenance of colonization required tactics of violence and plundering to maintain the authority over this flow of slaves, ivory and coconut oil from the frontier ports. While the records are not clear on the exploitative details of earlier Shirazi and Omani colonization, with the coming of the Germans the exploitative base of these frontier towns becomes vivid. For the Germans opening gambit was the bloody quelching of the Bushiri uprising. They continued to develop exploitative channels, choosing Tanga as their centre, until the devastation of WWI (First World War) sent them out of East Africa.

The Germans, like their colonial predecessors the Shirazi and Omani, set up a "fortified" or walled town in Tanga. At the turn of the century they sliced off their own European section of the town by building a railway. On one side, of the tracks facing the ocean, were the European quarters with German administrative fortresses, hospitals, churches, gardens and monuments. On the other side of the tracks was Ngamiani, planned along for the African population. It was laid out like a grid with straight streets with numbers for names. Here there was little room for gardens or trees, but coconut plantations surrounded this central grid. There was a mosque and later, under the British, another section near the railway was sliced off and given to the Christian immigrants for their sole ownership. Asians were scattered throughout Ngamiani, living above their shops which serviced the population.

Thus the Germans established their segregated fortified town. According to records, the crossing of the European-African barrier was dangerous. Violators were dealt with brutally:

Kama mwanamke hana cheti cha kuuza tembo, mleteni bomani. (If a woman doesn't have a permit to sell palm wine take her to prison). People aren't allowed to dance near European houses. Everyone has to keep the area in front of his house raked and sprinkled, and whoever doesn't is taken to prison. If one who is chained in prison tries to escape, the police may shoot on sight. And in the afternoon, at 4 p.m., a soldier blows his trumpet... and after the trumpet is blown, anyone found in the European part of town is arrested and taken to prison, and if he tries to run away he is beaten.[7]

German violence was the basis for relations with the "hinterland" as well. The Germans initiated forced labour on public works or plantations. This system is remembered with hatred today, for it bred degredation as well as famine and disease. By 1911 German companies had alienated large tracts of land in Tanga district for a total of 54 estates, mainly of rubber and sisal. Taxes were added to the forced labour system to ensure a smooth flow of workers. But the conditions on the plantations, like these in the town, were dehumanizing. The German Secretary of State and Director of the colonial office wrote the following after an inspection tour in 1907:

Nearly every white man walks around with a whip... and almost every white man indulges in thrashing any black man he wants.[8]

World War I climaxes German exploitation of Tanga, and it is here, that Bibi's life history begins, touched from the beginning by colonial devastation. She was born in 1919 in Segeju village a few kilometres south of Tanga. Her father was a tailor, but Bibi said nothing of his education or family, probably because she never knew him. For he, like thousands of other Tanganyikans, disappeared during the First World War. He was conscripted sometime in late 1917 or 1918 and never appeared again. Tens of thousands died in the porter corps, and as the army moved accross Tanganyika, disease and famine followed in its wake. Cameron wrote:

Chiefs were without people and people without chiefs. Thirty thousand natives were said to have died of famine... Amongst these remainig great numbers had pawned their children for food, husbands had left their wives, mothers had deserted their children, family life had very nearly ceased to exist.

Bibi's Life History

Bibi was the last born in a family of four sisters. One of her sisters was blind. She mentioned only her mother's side of the family, as, no doubt, with the death of her father it was her mother's family who took over and helped in raising the four sisters. She spent the first seven years of her life in this coastal village outside Tanga, and recalls her childhood years in the following manner.

We girls used to go gathering crabs and clams on the shore. When the tide was out, we would pick over the tidepools, rocks and sand for them. When we brought them home, mother or grandmother would boil them in a pot. We girls would peel cassava and add it to the pot. In ten minutes, the cassava is done and it is removed and put on a rock. We then removed the meat from the shells. We ate a bit of it right then and there while the rest we return to the pot. We add spices to the pot, buyu or unripe mango, to make it into a sour sauce. Finally, we throw the shells back into the sea.

Or, if we don't have any fresh cassava, we would make millet ugali. We take bran from the millet and pound it and place it in a mortar to sour. This souring is added to the millet flour when the ugali is being cooked. Mother would divide out the portions. Grandmother would be given hers first, then we girls. We would take a small ladle and make holes in the ugali. We then put soup and meat in the holes. By this method, we were ensured that neither ugali nor sauce would turn cool before the end of the meal.

After the meal we would wash the dishes and rinse our hands. The night's work is games. If there was a full moon, we could continue our games until midnight.

These are the games Bibi remembers:

Monkey game: One child is 'it.' She stays by the goal until the others run and hide. They call out ohh ooh, iih. The one who is it moves out looking for them. If she finds them, they scatter and she chases them. If she touches one, that one 'has been slaughtered' and become captured booty and has to stay at the goal. The others are to hide again and the game continues until all are captured. If a child can touch the goal, she is 'free.'

Kifura. One child makes an "0" with her fingers. The others dip their finger through the "0" but the one who misses out is "it" "anabaki na kifura" and chases the others until she tags one who then becomes "it".

Ulingo. The children hold hands in a circle and one starts the song. She mentions by name a child who comes to the centre and slowly dances to her knees. Once she has reached her knees, a second verse begins asking her to get up dancing.

		English
1st verse	Ulinge baiyoyo	Ulinge baiyoyo
	Binti fulani	Daughter of……
	kita goti	Bend your knees
	Tukuone maringo yako	So we can see your swaggering graces.
2nd verse	Ulinge baiyoyo	Ulinge baiyoyo
	Binti fulani	Daughter of…
	Nyanyuka	get up
	Tukuone maringo yako.	so we can see your swaggering graces.

Buyaye Another song-game imitates the courtship process. The group starts by singing a refrain which mentions one child by name and asks her to state who she wants. After she mentions "hers," the boy whom she wants, the others sing in actions, "he doesn't want you."

Chorus:	Buyaye milele
	Chanyatia
	Na bi fulani sema wako
Child	Na mimi wangu Bin fulani.
Chorus:	Bin fulani hakutaki
	Anataka mwana na kwao
	Amwendee kuni na maji
	Na kikombe cha msio.
Chorus:	Buyaye milele
	Chanyatia
	And so and so state yours
Child:	And me, mine is son of….
Chorus:	Son of… doesn't want you
	He wants a child of his own name
	who will fetch firewood and water for him
	And a rubbing stone.

Kibumbu: The children are covered with a blanket. One child stands aside and touches and feels the children until she recognizes and calls the child out by name.

Tambo: The children form themselves with 2 teams which sit down in a line placing their legs in front of them. Two poles, one for each team, is placed about 20 feet from the end of the line. One team passes a small stone down the line, hiding it as much as possible. A member of the other team then passes down the line reciting "kichanga – kipevu, kichanga–kipevu" touching

20

each child on the head. If she is able to discern who has the "tambo," the last child in the teamline moves over to the line of the other team. Thus each team moves slowly towards the pole, its goal. When one team reaches the pole, the first in line has to pass the 'tambo' around the pole without touching it. If she succeeds, her team has won. If she touches the pole, she is jeered "mgumba mgumba hana mwana" "that sterile person – has no child."

Dolls Let's play dolls!

If we hear that we know we'll play with dolls. We made our own dolls. We take two strips of fibre and place them together like a cross. If the doll is to be a girl we take two small stones and tie them to the cross with fibre, on each side of the arms close to the chest. We take black thread for hair. We pick up old scraps of cloth, fan the dump pile and wash them clean to make clothes, blankets and other accessories. We take cottonwool silk to make small pillows and matresses. We can keep one doll for a mother or more. We hide the clothes we have made for it. These dolls are loved and cared for just like real children. They are fed and scolded and dressed up. We can even hold a wedding for our dolls. Say I have a girl doll and yours is a boy. We decide to marry off our children. We scruplously follow all the wedding procedures.

All right bring the suitors.

All right bring money.

The money itself is fragments of a broken plate.

For my child I want two hundred. The father goes to look for a cow. The cow itself is a dried palm branch, and is slaughtered.

All right let's have the wedding.

Today there's a wedding at my place!

A drum is brought and dancing and celebration take place. The two dolls are placed side by side in bed.

War games. The boys make guns using *msisi* and *papaya* leaves. The leaves are cut into small pieces and placed in the whittled *msisi*. They are catapulted like bullets. When the boys play war games, the girls run and hide, snatching up their children, pleading with them to keep quiet.

If we pause for a minute in this life history to reflect on these games, it is clear that many reinforce and are based on gender relations and social values attached to gender relations. The "ulingo" song encourages a form of subdued sexual ostentation, "Let us see your swaggering graces." The 'Buyaye' song imitates courtship and jokingly voices a competitive rivalry of the sexes: "So and so doesn't want you; He/she wants a child of his/her own home; who will fetch water and firewood for him/her; and a rubbing stone. "The final jeer at the loser in the 'Tambo' game points out the high value placed on fertility; the loser is compared to a sterile person. The games with dolls reinact the courtship and marriage process with as much detail as the children's imagination can master. Sexual as well as economic rivalry runs through the play. Girls and boys tease each other about their sexuality. It would appear the gender is a major base for distinguishing and defining behaviour in this society. Sexuality and rivalry appear to be the basis for social relations. Bibi herself pointed out that most of their childhood activities imitate adult roles, are based on gender and work. We can expand on her statement to say that these are adult roles rather than class or age differences. She describes the following play as an example of adult imitation:

We girls taught ourselves to cook in the sand. The boys made as though going to the sea to fish. They take leaves and teach themselves to fish.

We girls take a coconut frond stem and make a small pestle. If we decide to pound dried cassava, we take clay like earth for making pots. If we want to pound paddy, we get sand. One girl will scrape the cassava, another may winnow the husked rice. So we teach ourselves to twist the winnowing tray in the right manner, to winnow millet, "kuchunga unga" etc. When a girl takes over a task from another there is a lot of testing: "oh ho, you think you know how to pound rice – how come rice is not all clearly husked?" The men (the young boys) come now with their leaves. We make like we're a family. That is, we call out "Father over there! go receive him and take his bag". A young child will be sent. "Take this relish", the father will say. Or another time the women (girls) will take korokocha – "I want to cook ghee sauce today". She takes the korokocha and scrapes it with a clean shell to get fine flour. Then she takes an empty coconut shell and puts in water then adds ashes or lime. She puts it on her three stones and after 10 minutes the sauce is done and you would think it is real sauce!

The girls make all their own utensils for cooking: the large flat spoon for stirring ugali; another type for dishing out rice; ladles, and tin for winnowing trays.

Cooking rice is another game. If a girl decides she will cook rice today she takes some sand that is slightly damp and mixes it with dry sand. She will say "bambo nipe maji yangu" (bambo give me my water.) She looks at her rice to see if it is dry. If it isn't done yet she will add more dry sand. Finally she will add a bit of damp sand to the top of her rice to serve as crusty top.

Now the rice is ready for serving. The crust is now removed and the men are served first. Then the teasing starts.

"you don't know how to cook!"

"Ah ha, today the food isn't done"

"How come the food has no flavour?"

The girls chase the offender away,

"How come you're hitting him so!"

Another activity Bibi recalls is plaiting:

On days when the women go to gather *ukindu* we girls are told to stay around the home. We are kept at home to plait.

Each girl is given the same number of strands.

"Ok, give them to us now"

"Well, how many a piece?"

"I have 10."

"I still need one more"

"Has everyone got 10?"

"Ok., let's begin."

We begin the competition now. We all start at the same time and the girl who finishes first wins.

Bibi also recalls how children made up and sang songs to one another. Those songs, she said, were like a school of good manners and taught proper behaviour, cleanliness and respect. She stated that through songs children can often correct one another's behaviour.

She remembers:

We teased one child about her tattered clothing. The next day the mother of the child made her a dress.

This is the procedure: one child says she will sing about so and so today. Then she sings satirically about some habit or an article of clothing:

"you have no clothes. Your clothes are in tatters and your buttocks show."

"you are a thief. One day I saw you.

You thought it was a secret, but I saw you steal a doll at...."

"you don't brush your teeth, your mouth stinks."

I asked Bibi about daily tasks and activities in the village, and it became clear from her description that most activities were gender-assigned.

She described daily tasks as follows:

Girls might start out the day by gathering tiny shrimps or *duvi* with their khangas. When they return they accompany, along with small boys, their mothers to shamba. The main crops were rice, cassava, millet, cowpeas, graham peas and some maize which does poorly. The first meal of the day takes place at around two. The mother comes home from shamba around 12 or 1 carrying water and firewood. The noonday meal is prepared and, if the men have returned from fishing, all eat together. The afternoon brings tasks of fetching water, washing clothes, processing rice or cassava, plaiting mats until evening. After the 8 oclock prayers the evening meal is eaten.

Girls' tasks included guarding the fields against birds, planting, washing, sweeping, fetching water. Boys of the age of 7 to 8 started to learn to fish with hook and line and would be taken out in the boats with their fathers. They also learn to tend and harvest coconut trees and prepare palm wine.

Men carried out all tasks of fishing including making various types of traps and nets. They were also responsible for roofing the house. All coconut tree cultivation and the processing of nuts up to the cooking stage – was the work of men. Fish and coconuts in their raw or processed state were sources of income. If he was ready and able, a man could also help his wife in farm work.

Bibi left the village when she was about 7 years old to join her uncle on her mother's side. He was a fairly high ranking civil servant in Tanga town. She did not state why she left the village, but such fostering by relatives is quite common, almost normal rather than odd; rarely do you find a house with only a nuclear family. Bibi also stated that she lived in town with her male cousins, the sons of her uncle. Perhaps her uncle had no daughter and wanted a girl in the house as well as wanting to help his sister of the burden of raising 4 daughters.

Bibi's Adult Life

Bibi spent about 12 years with her uncle in Tanga before she was married around 1938. She had little to say about this period except that she lived peacefully with her uncle's family – he had 2 wives. There were no harsh words, quarrels or mistreatment. She does remember that she was eager to learn to read and write. She recalls:

I used to listen to my friends recite. I got hold of a board and spread it with ashes. I whittled a pen and took some soot from the pots and started to learn the letters. My uncle and elder brother (cousin) helped me to learn when they saw how eager I was.

After marriage I went to the teacher to join his classes. The children laughed at me but the teacher agreed to teach me. I began to learn roman letters with the help of a friend. My uncle asked me where did I learn Arabic and English? I joined the Koranic school and learned to read 3 of the Koran's books before my husband left me and I stopped learning.

There are only a few glimpes of Bibi's life in the 40s. Her first marriage broke up as the war arrived in East Africa. She did not not get along with her first husband. Once she gleefully quoted a Kiswahili proverb: "the bad husband takes you out of the house; the good one you will come to know yourself." She explained that you are given your first husband by your parents and he takes you out of the house. Since you did not choose him yourself, you are often incompatible. But later, after the first marriage has broken up, you can choose your own husband and you will find a good one for yourself. Considering the humour with which she explained the proverb, it probably related closely to her own experience.

What did Bibi do after her marriage broke up? She dismisses the next nine years with a wave of the hand and the sentence "niliishi maisha ya kihunihuni," (I led a life of vagabondecy). She says she spent some time in Arusha, around 9 months, and the remainder of these years in Tanga.

We know, from the story of the Koranic school, that Bibi was bright, full of initiative, and not afraid of breaking new ground. Probably she lived as did many other women in Tanga, through petty trade which at least helped one to eke out a living from the cash wages of the sisal labourers. For despite the world economic depression, Tanga had been growing steadily throughout the thirties and by the forties it was the most prosperous town in Tanganyika. The reason for this was sisal.

If Tanga had a population of 300 in 1824, by the time the Germans had left migrant labour and neighbouring migration had swelled its population to 86,666 (estimated in 1921). The population would continue to increase with a high immigration rate of migrant labourers who then stayed on in Tanga. In the 1930s Baker[10] estimated an alien labour population of 50,000, and by 1940 it had reached 50% of the total population of the District. In addition, Indians, Arabs and Europeans continued to move to Tanga especially during the years of the Second World War. In 1967 Tanga town still had the highest number of non-Africans of any Tanzanian town.[11] In 1957, indicative of the sisal boom, 25% of the town was non-African,[12] and although it had dropped, along with sisal prices, to 16% in 1967 it remained the highest.

This growth gave Tanga town a special nature. With outlying plantations to feed and service, the town became a commercial centre for trade, food processing, services, and agricultural products. This commercial activity attracted and sustained a large population. Tanga had the highest percentage of employed persons, as high as 37% of the total national wage earners, up until 1961.[13]

Although high percentage of wage earners means cash to swell commerce, life was nonetheless hard for the average family. Baker[14] estimated that a family of 5 needed 26/- a month just to maintain subsistence level, but the monthly wage was 10/- to 12/-. Besides daily subsistence needs, a town dweller needed 10/- cash for hut tax, 10/- for municipal tax, and, if he rented a plot 6/- a year for plot rent. In his analysis of 2 streets in Ngamiani area, Baker concluded that unemployment was high; there were a large number of bachelor male immigrants, and the number of females who headed households was high. Therefore despite increased labour force and increased circulation of cash, families continued to live at subsistence level.

With the advent of the second World War, the European plantations continued to flourish but the average Tanzanian family remained poor. When there was a subscription request for the Tanganyika Territory in 1943, almost half of that subscription came from the Europeans of Tanga Province (£4,122 out of £9,608).[15] Sisal had become a strategic product. Rubber plantations started up again. A sisal Labour Board was set up to ensure a smooth influx of workers. By 1945 the labour population had increased another 50% and stood at 77,000.[16] The European population increased by 35% in 1943.[17]

But for the average African in Tanga town, life was not easy. Added to taxes were new army conscriptions and food cultivation quotas. Problems of tax defaulters and difficulties in fulfilling food quotas overburdened "the administration". Ration coupons began. Labour strikes began to upset production. The war effort had drawn a clear line between the exploiters and the exploited. The 'benevolent patronage' of the British had changed into exploitation.

The Provincial Commissioners reports show some hint of this change. In 1940 the Provincial Commissioner could write that assistance given by the population to war efforts and volunteer service was due to "The general appreciation of British methods of government."[18] But in the same report the PC could write that "the most important duty trusted to the Native Authorities is the collection of Native Tax."[19] It is no wonder that the British optimism as to their benevolent reception was soon undermined. At the end of the war the PC observed that conscription duties had made the government unpopular and had "adversely affected the personal touch with the African population."[20]

The post-war period ushered in the sisal boom of the 1950s. From 1941 to 1947 there had been an approximate 50% increase in the population of the province. Over roughly the same period the value of exports from Tanga rose from £1,550,431 (1943) to £6,882,439 (1948).[21] In 1949, 95% of this value of exports came from sisal.[22]

Along with population growth and increased sisal productivity came price rises and shortages of food and basic consumer items. Smuggling, particularly from Zanzibar, was rife. The African population was still under continual pressure to comply with food cultivation quotas. Even as late as 1947 court cases concerning non-compliance with food cultivation ordinances were increasing.[23] Wages remained low despite increased exports

26

and the rising cost of living. Strikes broke out again in the late 1940s, but the drought of 1949 still brought sufficient labourers to the sisal fields.[24]

What had happened in Tanga town over the last decades? Large scale immigration, escalation of exports, increases in commerce, service and food processing sectors to maintain the growing population. But none of these meant an increase in wages or the standard of living of the average African.

Bibi started off the new decade of the 1950s with a clear state, having divorced her second husband after one year's marriage. It had been an unhappy marriage. She states:

I remained with him for only one year. He was quarrelsome. He fed and dressed me well but he had the habit of beating me up and was always quarrelsome.

Sometime in 1950 she got married again as a second wife to a trader, who had made his money out of smuggling goods; foodstuffs and clothing from Zanzibar. She recalls:

But I left him for his stubborn pride. He was mean. He had a smuggling racket from Zanzibar. He would bring his goods and I would sell them at home. If he bought a khanga for 10/- it would be sold for 15/-. When I began selling, my husband said he would give me a wage. I refused saying wait to see my work first then I will ask for a wage. I sold goods for 6 months and asked for clothing as a wage. My husband refused. I left him in the seventh month (of our marriage). His relatives urged him to keep me as I did good business for him but I refused to return. He was a mean husband. He refused to let my relatives come home or eat there.

In another version of this ending of a marriage, Bibi relates how the return of her husband's first wife followed her own departure. The first wife had said Bibi had brought him misfortune and was a jinx. But as Bibi explains, the man's fortune turned from bad to worse after she left him:

After 4 months the man began to have problems. He fell off his bicycle; his money from cigarette smuggling from Mombasa was confiscated. He drank vinegar and his mouth got sores. His business associates stopped bringing him goods. He was bitten by a dog and developed a sore and he was in a bad state. His trade in khangas fell off completely. Then his first wife quarreled with him and they went to court and the wife forced him to return her to her home (in Somalia). This is when he asked me to come back to him but I refused... He had one misfortune after another until he returned to Mombasa where he became insane.

1953 started a long new chapter in Bibi's life when she became mistress to the man who would eventually be her husband for 23 years, until his recent death. She had finally found the "good husband", of the proverb. We will call him Omari.

When they first started life together in 1953, Omari lived with his first wife, we'll call her Amina, and a child of Omari's brother. Bibi also had a young girl, the child of her cousin, with her. Bibi kept up her trade, living separately, from her lover's family.

In 1956 a crisis occured when Omari lost his hospital job. Bibi increased her business efforts. In the morning she would put her buns and prepared chickpeas on the varanda, -/50 a cup for the cooked food. She resolved that she would not leave him now, but would help him. He was not to be tossed out just because he had no income now. She spoke quite proudly of how she would buy the children in his charge clothes for Idd, or how she would be the one to make contributions to funerals in his name.

One year after he was fired, Omari got his termination benefits. This money was divided up among the family and her share was 500/-. She bought khangas and a big lot of firewood. She was fortunate. Heavy rain had made dry firewood scarce, and she was able to make a good profit.

Now Bibi, a good businesswoman who was supporting herself and any number of children, decided that it was high time Omari married her. She asked him to marry her so that "her spirit would not be troubled." Omari agreed. She asked for 300/- dowry and was given it. They were married secretly, although a few months later Omari informed his first wife that he was moving to live with her co-wife. From then on Omari stayed with them in turns.

Bibi had often had trouble with housing; for some time she had been renting a room in the Ngamiani area. But now financial strains – a death in the family, the expenses of Ramadhan, had left her broke and she moved to her sister's in Usagara, which was at that time a squatter's outskirts. She continued her business of firewood and prepared food.

In the mid sixties her husband got work again with the help of his relatives. He got hospital work on the Muheza–Usagara road. This job kept him for 3 years and he moved Bibi into his brother's house on the outskirts of town. After the road job was finished, he worked with the railways around Wami for 3–4 years.

Bibi must have been tired of not having a place of her own, and there was also friction with her brother-in-law. She has vivid memories of how she struggled to obtain a plot and eventually build a house. She relates:

My husband looked for a house. After bargaining over the price with the owner, they agreed on 600/-. I put out 300/- for the house which belonged to my brother-in-law. He was sick with TB and had gone to Muheza for treatment. I followed him there so he would write out the ownership papers.

28

We signed them. I agreed to pay my brother-in-law's debt of 300/- for the plot and house. After returning from Muheza I went to the woman who owned the plot and told her I would pay the 300/- debt. We agreed that she, the owner, would take 2 khangas every month until the debt was finished. Each khanga was worth 20/-. So she sometimes took 2 or if my business was good even 3 or 4 a month until the debt was finished.

I looked for poles and twine. There was only one room. I expanded the house – now it has 3 rooms. I took one man and put him in the house to keep goats. I bought stone and lime. I built one room – then put in cement. I gathered my resources and got stones again. I built a second room and put in a renter. I gathered my resources again and hired a workman who made major errors. At night it rained and the roof caved in!

But soon the place was finished and, she stated, she had a secure place to do her business and a source of income from rent.

Now in the late sixties, Bibi started looking for work for her husband again, the work on the railway at Wami being finished. She was still caring for the young girl she had reared since childhood as well as Omari's sick mother. She recalls:

Now at this place, my husband has no work. I was selling clothing and buns I even got the courage to ask his relatives to help him get work.

The employer asked me if my husband could live in the bush. I said, wait, I will ask him. He said he could and he agreed to start work. He was sent to Moshi where he worked as a hospital dresser at a station near the electric dam 18 kilometers from Moshi town. My husband held this job for 9 yaers in Moshi.

But Bibi foresaw difficulties in moving to Moshi. Her husband's mother was ill and needed constant care. Her husband should have a second wife so they could take turns between Tanga and Moshi. He took a second wife, and Bibi stayed in Tanga to look after his mother. When she died, Bibi related with pride how she "Stood in place of (her) husband and did all the work for the sake of (her) husband's relatives." But this only strained further relation with her brother-in-law.

Two months after mourning had finished, Bibi was called to Moshi to take the place of her co-wife, to 'relieve' her. The young girl in charge was by this time married, and Bibi took in to her care 2 of her brother-in-laws grandchildren aged 2 and 4. When she arrived in Moshi her husband was mad at her. As she describes the scene, her husband said "Why did you bring these children? Who will buy clothes and food for them? What is your real intention in bringing these children?" I replied, "It's true, I have my own reason for bringing these children. I took the children so you would not leave me. Is that bad? I actually have 2 reasons for taking the children. First of all, I love you and I am protecting myself by bringing these children. Secondly, I am protecting you and your family. You have not had even one child. Your relatives say you are sitting around iddle and that's why I took care of your sick mother and took these children. Now your relatives will recognize you as a real relative. Furthermore, these children will know you as their father, their grandfather. Your relatives will know that you raised these grandchildren. When you are old they will take care of you. If you don't take good care of them, your relatives will ask these children, how come you refused to look for your grandfather and it is he who raised you?

You say I took the children so you wouldn't leave me, and it's true that's one reason, but my intention is to protect you and build up your respect. I am protecting you and your family should now stand up and take notice of you.

"Even recently, just now", Bibi continued in the present, "when my husband was so ill (before his death) I called for these children and they came. I told them to disparage their father and they refused. I told my husband, do you see the real gain of raising children now? He saw, and laughed."

Bibi had no children, but she always kept children with her. In the early fifties, she raised two girls to maturity until they married. She continued to take in and raise children or serve as a long time caretaker. When I met her in 1986, she had at least 4 young ones. Two were children of unmarried mothers, one child was left with her by his father after his divorce, one child was staying with Bibi during his mother's pregnancy. She also had under her care her kindly but senile elder sister.

Her attitude towards children, as stated to her husband to defend herself, to some extent an economic one – they are investments. But also they are part and parcel of her own self-image. She never bore children, but was proud to be a responsible and loved stepmother. Her ability and willingness to take care of others built her own self-respect and her respect in the eyes of others.

Bibi also spoke often with pride of the care she took of her husband and his relatives. Witness, for instance, how she proudly looked for work for her husband, took care of his sick mother, provided for his family when he was out of work. Although she loved her husband, her relations with his family were not always smooth, as mentioned by her when she defended herself for bringing the children to Moshi. The economics of living on a shoestring coupled with the traditional ethic of sharing what one has makes a fertile field for such jealousy, envy and quarrels. Nonetheless she regarded herself as having fulfilled her role to satisfaction in the family.

Bibi often mentioned her various co-wives in her narration, sometimes with relish and sometimes with reticence. She enjoyed her victories over her co-wives, as when she spoke of the moral victory over her trader husband's first Somalian wife. In the end it was Bibi who was a valuable asset, the Somalian only brought him trouble. The request for remarriage vindicated her.

She tells a similar tale of her last husband's second wife. But the petty jealousy, meanness and ill-feeling the tale provoked in her went against her feelings for justice, and she asked me not to tell it. I will only say that it was with some laughter and glee that she told of how her co-wife on return from Moshi, found her house in Tanga too poor in amenities, too lacking in modern furniture for her taste and went off in a huff to live with her mother. Afterwards, Bibi and Omari had a good laugh over the woman's pretensions.

Aside from problems with relatives, children, co-wives and a place of her own, the 70s were years of expansion and education for Bibi. She was eager for all forms of learning and she generously shared her knowledge with others, even her co-wife.

In Moshi she joined a "Bibi Maendeleo" group. She learned again to read and write. She got a certificate in Domestic Science and taught her Tanga specialities to anyone who would come to her house during Ramadhani: cakes, buns, doughnuts, flat cakes, rice flourbread, sambusa, meatballs and all the Ramadhani specialities. Evidently the Moshi women were not too familiar with fish preparation. While she was cleaning and probably filleting a fish, one woman called out "Come! and look! The Doctor's wife is performing an operation on a fish.

Their group also cultivated a shamba and raised money through handicrafts – they used their proceeds for home consumption.

Bibi shared her knowledge. She held adult education classes in Tanga, up to the third stage and even had her picture taken with her group. She taught her *renter,* who knew, she said, nothing from nothing to read and write. She had a small Koranic school as well, which she kept up until 1979 when she became a court accessor.

The late seventies saw her with a number of responsibilities. She became a court assessor in 1979. She was a ten cell leader and a UWT chairperson. She is active still in all UWT functions and belong to an income-generating group.

Now she still lives in the house she built a bit on the outskirts of Ngamiani area. She makes her living in a variety of ways which recall her colourful past. She sells charcoal on her porch. She sometimes makes buns for sale. Often she is called in to be master-of-ceremonies at celebrations. She composes and sings poetry for religious, Ramadhan or Iddi and mourning festivals. She is paid to wash corpses for burial. She is an absolute necessity at marriage celebrations. She also admited, with a shrug of her shoulders, to selling black market cigarettes. What is an old woman to do, she laughs.

When I asked Bibi about women's life in Tanga in general, she stated that there had been great changes since her youth. Nowadays, women can "marry themselves" to men. "Their condition is better economically, because they are engaged in trade in salt, buns, cassava, beer. Also in the old days a woman couldn't go to the market. It would be a great scandal. Nowadays she can go even without a "baibui". She can be independent." When I asked her of women's major problems, she said "having things taken away from us all the time ('kunyang'anywanyang'anyw'a) – that's what sets us back. We do not have any good opportunity to advance ourselves." I asked Bibi, at the end of our meetings, what was most important in her life. She said that education and cooking were most important to her. Her choice of priorities reflects the contradictions and struggles in her and other women's lives. On the one hand, one whishes to fulfill the traditional role of nurturer – cooking, rearing husband and children. On the other hand, Bibi had a great desire for self advancement through education. Since childhood she searched for knowledge and later in her life she shared her knowledge as a teacher. But as she stated herself, the major difficulties facing women are their subordinate or secondary place in society. Women have little opportunity for advancement and moreover, are often pillaged (kunyang'anywa) of the few resources, educational or economic, which they have secured for themselves. Bibi's struggles to get education and property bear witness to this difficulty.

Conclusion

Bibi's life as a woman in Urban Tanga also bears witness to the struggle for economic survival of many men and women in that town. As stated in the survey of the 1930s, most inhabitants lived at subsistence level. This still held true in a Pilot Survey done in preparation for the second 5 year development plan in the early 1970s, despite the "relative prosperity" of the region.[25] The reasons for this may be complex and manifold, but if we look at the patterns of colonization perhaps we can get a clue.

Since the first historical records available the coast around Tanga has been an export frontier. While trade prospered, it was in the hands of a few who then exploited the resources of the hinterland. Thus, although, for instance, the Tanga European colonialists could raise a high percentage of contribution funds, the average Tanzanian stayed at subsistence level throughout the period, with perhaps, an exception in the boom of the fifties. Similarly in the early seventies, we still find a situation in which 10% of the households of the town earn 42% of the income, while 50% of the households earn only 15% of the total income.[26].

Given the large number of female-headed households reported in the 1974 survey (25%), this means a great deal of women are struggling alone to break out beyond subsistence, much as Bibi struggled throughout her life. Most women are at home (65.3% of female labor force)[27] Although the survey did not specify their work one can guess that they were involved in chores of family reproduction, and many, like Bibi, made an income from petty trade. They are thus dependent on the fluctuations in employment market, for people without income do not buy buns and fried fish. As such, they are marginal, susceptible, not in control of the forces which govern their economic lives.

In conclusion, it would appear that the Tanga woman was fighting two colonialisms.[28] They had to struggle against the colonialist economics geared to export exploitation of the region and subject to its vissitudes. At the same time, woman's resources, economic, sexual, educational, emotional, are subject to pillaging or subordination to male patriarchal dominance. Her secondary status in society means she is exploited twice over. It is in this sense that we can understand the meaning of Bibi's formulation of the major obstacle to woman's advancement, to be allocated little opportunity and to be pillaged (kunyang'anywanyang'anywa and "hana nafasi kubwa").

FOOTNOTES

1. Bibi has asked to remain anonymous, therefore I am calling her by the Kiswahili term which can be variously rendered as Ms, lady, mistress or grandmother.
2. Interviews took place in Tanga town during a series of visits in 1986. I used pen and paper as tools. We usually sat together for a few hours and shared a meal at my mother-in-law's house.
3. A.M.H. Sheriff, "The East African Coast and its Role in Maritime Trade" in G. Mokhtar, ed., 1981 *A General History of Africa II*. Heineman: Unesco, pp. 551–567, and H.C. Baxter, "Pangani: The Trade Centre of Ancient History". *Tanganyika Notes and Records* 17 (1944), pp. 15–25.
4. Arthur E. Robinson, "The Shirazi Colonization of East Africa: Vumba"., Tanganyika Notes and Records, 7th June 1939), p.92–112
5. Baxter, op. cit.
6. CCS. Nicholls, 1971. *The Swahili Coast: Politics, Diplomacy and Trade on The*

East African Littoral 1798–1856. London: Allen & Unwin, p. 313.

7. Karl Velten, Prosa und Poesie der Swahili, pp. 165–66, quoted in Ben Pike, "History and Imagination: Swahili Literature and the Resistance to German Language Imperialism," unpub. mss.

8. Hassan Omara Kaya, 1985 *Problems of Regional Development: a Case Study of Tanga Region in Tanzania:* Spektrum 7: Breitenbach, p. 107.

9. Zoe Marsh and G.W. Kingsworth, 1961 *An Introduction to the History of East Africa:* Cambridge: Cambridge University Press.

10. E.C. Baker 1933 *Report on Social and Economic Conditions in the Tanga Province.* Government Printer: Dar es Salaam.

11. United Republic of Tanzania, Ministry of Lands, Housing and Urban Development, Urban Planing Division, *Tanga Master Plan, 1975–1995.*

12. Ibid.

13. Kaya, op.cit.

14. Baker, op. cit.

15. Provincial Commissioner's Report, 1943.

16. Provincial Commissioner's Report, 1945.

17. Provincial Commissioner's Report, 1943.

18. Provincial Commissioner's Report, 1940. p. 59.

19. Ibid, p. 63

20. Provincial Commissioner's Report, 1945, 91.

21. Adolfo Caridade Mascarenhas, 1970 "Resistance and Change in the Sisal Plantation System of Tanzania, "unpub. Ph.D. diss. University of California at Los Angeles,.

22. Ibid.

23. Provincial Commissioner's Report, 1947.

24. Provincial Commissioner's Report, 1949.

25. United Republic of Tanzania, *Tanga Master Plan,* op. cit.

26. Ibid.

27. Ibid.

28. See Stephanic Urdang's *Fighting Two Colonialisms* on the struggle of the women of Guinea Bissau.

CHAPTER THREE

My Life is a Life of Struggles: The Life History of a Young Barmaid

Anna, x with Alice-Nkhoma-Wamunza

Introduction

The employment status of women in Tanzania is characterized by many features. While the majority are in the unpaid family labour either in the agricultural or service sectors, a small minority found in the formal labour market is either employed as unskilled or semi-skilled labour-force and is predominantly in the service sector. One such area where female labour is concentrated is the selling of drinks in beer stores and bars, which can be a very hostile environment.

It takes a woman extreme courage to work as a bar-maid. In the first place the job is tough in the sense that quite often one has to deal with both oppressive employers and nasty customers. To many bar-maids it means accepting abuses and oppression with much perseverence. Many bar-maids are so poorly paid that a good number of them is forced to enter into prostitution. The social attitude of both men and women in our society tends to look down upon barmaids either as prostitutes or potential prostitutes, a behaviour which is socially unacceptable.

Whereas barmen are respected, on the contrary, barmaids are not respected, first by the employers, their counterpart barmen, the patrons they serve, and society in general. They are not protected by law. In a way it is contradictory in that the patrons they serve often treat them as objects, while on the other hand, the barmaids offer them consolence and take time off to listen to their problems and frustrations. These are brave women, they are where they are, not by choice but because something somewhere went wrong in their background and there is a lot one can say about society's contribution to their status. Usually barmaids are forced by circumstances to work in such hostile environment. As they are desparate for wage employment, employers on their part take this advantage and stipulate dubious contracts which give the employee no extra benefits apart from being paid a small wage.

The plight of bar-maids however, has not been well documented since very little research has been done in this area. The oppression, exploitation and dehumanization of women as employees in bars therefore needs a critical analysis as it is a unique and extreme form of exploitation which operates under the distortion of the relationship between capital and labour which assumes a sociological rather than an economic form.

As an attempt to respond to this call for more documentation of the lives of barmaids, this chapter narrates the life history of Anna, X a young barmaid, her struggles for survival in both formal and informal employment; and her struggles and determination to bring up and educate five children as a single parent.

Although Anna is originally from Mbaba Bay, she grew up and has lived most of her life in the urban areas and has been influenced by urban life style. Like many of us who live in urban areas, we are still tied or have strong roots with our rural villages which offer refuge in time of need and peace.

Anna became pregnant when she was only fourteen. Ignorant of the changes taking place in her body and her own sexuality (due to lack of exposure to sex education), she was made pregnant by an older man. As a result she was expelled from school and was unable to complete primary education. Hence, the chapter also touches on school girl pregnancies and expulsions from school and notes that many more girls have fallen victim to sexual abuse by older men and yet there is no legal provision to protect the victims and punish the culprits. Whereas girls are held responsible for their sexuality, boys and men on the other hand do not take responsibility or control for their sexuality.

Lastly the chapter highly commends the government's efforts to introduce family life education to both girls and boys in schools and the on-going Law Reviews exercise which started a few years back. The Law Review Commission has for the last couple of years been looking at the various laws and the Marriage Act is among them. What is significant is the fact that the Commissioner has been seeking views from all the people, male and female, and it has also involved women lawyers in the committee.

Early Childhood and Adolescence

I was born in Mtwara (where my parents had moved to, from Mbamba Bay for wage employment) in the month of February, 1955. My parents are from the Wanyasa tribe living on the shores of Lake Nyasa, in Mbinga District. I was the youngest of the three children. There were two girls and only one boy who later died. I didn't know much about my mother until I was about fourteen. My parents separated when I was about three years old and after divorce my mother moved back to Mbamba Bay. We were brought up by our father and step mother. From what I can remember we were a happy family and we lived comfortably. Both my parents were workers, my father travelled a lot. His job as a trade unionist demanded long and extensive travels; we did not see as much of my father as we would have liked to. He was a good man but strict, and he provided well for us. I do not remember us going hungry, we were a happy family. My step mother on the other hand was quiter. She looked after us and fed us well. She did not talk much but she gave us all the freedom and she loved us, we got on very well. In 1958 my step mother gave birth to a pretty baby girl and I loved my little pretty sister very much. I carried her on my back as I played. My mother worked hard; she woke up early in the morning, prepared breakfast for us and made sure we had breakfast before she left for work. She had a full day, working from morning and coming back late in the afternoon. While she was away we were left in the care of a young ayah, we used to play with other young girls in the neighbouhood, we had great fun together.

As I was growing up I usually played with the neighbours' children of my age. Some of my play-mates were slightly older but we got on well, the older girls sometimes sent us away but as I grew up I was accepted and played with them and the boys. When I was about thirteen I had my first menstrual period. It came as a shock to me, as I did not know what it meant. I rushed to my elder sister, she saw my distress and told me not to panic. She calmed me down and took me to my step-mother. In the evening I was taken to my aunt's house by my stepmother. It was from her I learnt about the new changes taking place in my body. I lived with my aunt for two weeks.

Among other things my aunt explained to me was that what I had seen was a sign that I had now become a woman. She taught me how to behave and respect older people and she also emphasized body cleanliness and personal hygiene on my part. She told me about what I could and what I could not do, for example she insisted that I should not play with boys otherwise I could get a baby. Looking back, years later, I realized this must have been my first lesson in sex education. But at that age it was not easy to understand such deep matters and as a result I did not understand my aunt's sermon or the implication. I wish I had known what I know to-day! Things are different today, for, there is a lot of information in written form which one can read on her own. In the past, most people were still conservative and you could not find such information in newspapers or hear them on the radio so openly There is more openness now and people can be heard discussing these things. However in some ethnic groups for example among the Yao, young girls, even before they begin menstruating – went through the initiation ceremony (Unyago) – where girls are taught good manners, respect for elders, kindness and being generous to people etc. Young girls were also taught sex education as they were being prepared to take up adulthood and family responsibilities as wives even though they were so young. This is something which did not often happen in urban areas. The introduction of formal education meant that a girl could not be kept in the house for a long time as it would interfere with her schooling. So while staying with my aunt I was only taught the basics and a few facts of life which I did not even understand; and I went to school as usual.

I became pregnant when I was fourteen and in Primary school in Dar es Salaam. I do not remember what happened. It was such a long time ago; but I know the man was much older. He was in his early twenties, between 25-28 years old and was working and living within our neighbourhood. I remember that I played with my friends who had boyfriends and sometimes they discussed their adventures. I don't think that they knew that they were playing a dangerous game. They regarded it as just a game. Perhaps it was just curiosity on my part, I do not even remember what happened and I went to bed with the man. It was not until after I was six months pregnant that I realised something was wrong. I missed my periods but I took it to be normal because I had irregular periods. I was never sick. I attended school normally and played with my friends as usual. I was very healthy and plump and nobody noticed that I was pregnant not even my step-mother or neighbours. A few months later my step-mother did notice; and she began to ask questions. I was frightened but she was even more frightened because she did not even have the courage to tell my father. When I was in my eighth month my step-mother picked up courage and went to see my uncle and told him the "bad" news. My uncle in turn went to see his younger brother and together with my step-mother they discussed the issue and decided to tell my father. They planned it in such a way that they sent my step-mother to tell my father to expect them the following evening. They also informed my two aunts, my grandfather who was sent for from Dodoma, a few elders and the ten cell leader. You see, when a girl becomes pregnant out of wedlock it is not only shocking and unacceptable; it becomes a matter of family concern. Often parents especially fathers became emotional and hot tempered. The mother suffers silently because people turn their anger on her and accuse her of not having taken care of the girl because the responsibility of bringing up children and disciplining them is often regarded as her major responsibility. As a woman she suffers more because she understands what it means to be pregnant, she has been through it. It was therefore important and significant to have all these people present in order to calm my father and to protect me from my fathers' anger.

The meeting (baraza) which constituted my aunts, uncles, my grand-father, my sister, myself, and my parents took place in our house one evening. My poor father had no clue as to the reason for the meeting. My uncle started the discussion in a round about way until my father deducted that they were talking about me. It was a shocking revelation. My father was so angry that he threatened to throw me out of the house but my aunts and uncles calmed him. I was made to reveal the name of the man who was responsible. The next day a message was sent to his home and he came with his brother. Naturally, as is usual, the man refused responsibility.

I could not believe my ears. I think I began to grow up from that day. He did eventually give in and accepted the responsibility. The anger in my father had disappeared; he explained to the man the graveness of the matter and calmly told him that he would not prosecute him. The man was also informed that he would not be forced to marry me as he had behaved irres-ponsibly. The next thing my father said was that he himself would take care of me until the child was born. The man was told to keep away from me and my father swore that he would take him to court if he ever came to our house. That was the last I ever saw of that man. The next day my parents took me to the hospital for a medical check up and to verify beyond reason-able doubt that I was already eight and a half months pregnant. Silently we walked back home. I know my father was angry with my step-mother. He felt that she and I had let him down and that she should have informed him earlier.

I don't really blame my step-mother for what happened; although I feel that had she taken a keener interest in us and our doings perhaps she could have disciplined us more. On the other hand we must understand that she was a busy woman working and trying to take care of us. We spent most of the time by ourselves. She gave us so much freedom but I think we needed more guidance and counselling from both our parents. As mentioned earlier, my step-mother did not talk much and I wonder if perhaps being a step mother she was afraid to control us! It is difficult to say but I know she was very good to us.

As for my father I had disappointed him very much, but he gave me a lot of support and has been the pillar of my strength. He told me that as soon as I delivered he would see to it that I completed my primary education. I could not believe my ears. My mind had been in so much turmoil all this time and I needed the reassurance my father gave me that day. At least I felt hopeful.

I stayed with my parents until 1969 when I gave birth to a baby girl. My parents bought clothes for the baby and took care of both of us. Meanwhile my father was making plans to find me a school so that I could continue with my education. He found me a place in a private school. He was sent application forms and filled them in and was preparing to submit them to the school. But "Luck was not with me." Something happened in our family which shuttered all of us. My father was arrested either in 1968 or 1969 and put in detention on political grounds.[1] The sheltered life we had led was disrupted. We were searched, and everything in our house was turned upside down. It also meant I could not go back to school for the forms were misplaced. My uncle was also arrested and detained. There was no body to make the follow-up. My step mother was shuttered. Apparently my mother had been informed about my pregnancy, explusion from school and subsequently my having given birth. She also heard about my father's arrest and travelled all the way from Ruvuma to Dar es Salaam to see us. That was when it was decided that I should go and live with my own mother in a small village in Ruvuma.

I did not know my mother quite well. I wondered what my reunion with my mother would be like. She remembered me as a child and now I was going back to her as a mother. It was a long and tiring journey, especially with the baby. The journey took about four days. When we reached the village we went to my mother's house and one of my aunts received us calmly and took the baby. She wept and I wept. I didn't know what to say as we settled down but my mother made me feel at home. She did not scold or condemn me, she calmly accepted the reality and we began life afresh. We began to get to know each other. She taught me many things for example, child care, and encouraged me to do a few things such as cultivating, fetching wood and water. Village life was a new experience for me and I found it tough for there was so much work to do. I learnt how to go out and collect wood, how to go down hill and collect water and how to work and till the land. Child care was not so much of a problem. In the village there was always someone to take care of the baby while I was pounding or out in the field. I began to mature and to fend for myself. My mother never re-married but she had her own house and there were a couple of grand-children and relatives to whom she devoted her life.

I often thought of Dar es Salaam and my father and step mother as well as my other sisters and brothers I had left behind. I kept hoping that one day I would go back. I thought life in Dar es Salaam was less taxing than in the rural areas. I had and still have a lot of respect for people who live in the villages despite the tough conditions. One did not need much money in the rural areas because you ate what you produced and food was very cheap, we got enough fish for the whole family for less than ten shillings. But neverthe-less I thought village life was hard especially for someone who has spend all his/her life in the urban areas. I realized life was equally tough in the urban areas unless one was employed and has a regular income. I however pre-fered town life. I stayed in the village for about two years, before I met a young man and we got married.

Marriage and Life in Mombasa

I had now lived in the village for two years and I was beginning to cope with the demanding rural life. My daughter was growing up and she was in good health. My mother and relatives continued to give me all the moral and material support I needed. I made friends in the village.

In 1971 I met a young man in Mbamba Bay who later in the same year became my husband. The young man had come to visit his parents and he also came looking for a wife. So you see, this trip was an important trip for him. He had travelled all the way from Mombasa where he lived and worked. He had to come home and marry a girl from his own ethnic group. This was expected of him and I think he must have been under pressure to get married to a girl from his village, for he had attained the age which it was automatically expected that he should marry and begin to set up a family.

His family took up the task of looking for a wife for him. His sisters who were my friends approached me and delivered the message that their brother wanted to marry me. In fact they said they had decided to ask me because they felt I could make a good wife for their brother. I had in me the qualities of a hardworking, good mannered, young and good looking girl. Of course it came as a suprise to me. Apparently there had been discussions bet-ween his family and my family. My family, i.e. my mother, grandfather and uncles had no objection. In fact they were happy that I was going to get mar-ried. I am sure they must have felt that this was a good opportunity for me to put right the shame I had brought to them. There is still a lot of prejudice against a girl who gets a child out of wedlock. You become the scarlet woman, and in some social settings it also means the door to marriage is closed. In my own case I do not remember being shunned for having had a baby out of wedlock, but perhaps I was too young to see through people's attitudes towards me. All I remember was the friendly atmosphere and the supportive family and friends I had, and the love that was bestowed on my baby.

I had not thought about marriage, so when the proposal was made my mind had mixed feelings – I cannot remember if I was happy or unhappy about the news. I bet I took it for granted and accepted marriage as a matter ot fact. The idea of going away to another country and starting a new life seemed to be exciting. It meant a new experience and I looked forward to going to Mombasa, and starting life a –fresh.

Essentially this was an arranged marriage. It was not love at first sight. In many of these arranged marriages it is taken for granted that love is not important. It is assumed that it can be developed and cultivated in the course of living together and reproducing children. Arranged marriages have been known to last and work out well. I think there are many factors for this. I wonder if perhaps the fact that two families of close friends whose children are united in marriage help to keep that marriage intact! I also wonder if the age difference between the couple has anything to do with the stability of a marriage. Normally the man is older than the woman and most often she has a minor or subservient role. Anyway, mine was an arranged marriage. We got to know each other before marriage – although it was such a short time. I think he had an extended leave of about two months. I think we liked each other and perhaps even loved each other. However, perhaps two months was too short a time to get to know someone well. The wedding preparations were made and all the traditional marriage customs were performed. The traditional bride wealth was given to my family – that is my uncles and grand-father. Each member of the family – the uncles, grandfather and brothers got a little share of the bride-wealth. The females normally do not, except for the mother and perhaps the grandmother. Compared to other ethnic groups the bride wealth in our case is not exorbitant. In fact it is just a token. In addition there are symbolic gifts which go to the mother and father for example a hoe or an axe, which symbolises hardwork, a blanket to keep the old people warm and literaly emphasizes the importance of looking after the old parents. There are also a few goats for the uncles. You can either pay in cash or in kind.

My husband to be was aware that I had a baby but he nevertheless accepted me with my baby. After we married and were preparing to go to Mombasa my mother insisted that I leave the baby behind in her care. I did.

We were married in Church in 1971. It was a nice wedding, both families prepared food and drinks. There was dancing and joy. Within a short time I had been transformed from a young teenager to a mother and finally to a wife. I think that was a heavy responsibility within a short time and all of it coming at the same time!

We left the village and travelled to Mombasa via Tanga by bus. We spent some time in Tanga with my brother's family before finally going to Mombasa. We reached Mombasa in the afternoon, and for the first time I had a home of my own. My husband had a house of his own which he bought after having lived and worked in Mombasa for so long. I also discovered that he had two young children born from a woman with whom he had been living but had left her. So I began looking after the children and all household matters while my husband went to work. With my education I did not think I could get a job so I didn't even try. My husband too expected me to stay at home and look after the children.

Mombasa was not very different from Dar es Salaam. Being a coastal town, it reminded me very much of Dar es Salaam. A few months later I discovered that I was pregnant. I gave birth to a baby girl towards the end of 1972. This time there was only my husband, myself and the children. It was a different atmosphere. I did not get the supportive reassurance I had received from my parents and relatives during my first pregnancy. The only support I got was from my husband. I had not yet made friends in Mombasa. Looking back I think it was an exciting but difficult experience. I learnt to be self reliant.

When the child was hardly one year I discovered that I was again pregnant. I had been worried about getting pregnant. I did not know about family planning and I did not know about modern contraceptive methods. I could not even ask my husband for help. I found it difficult to discuss the subject of child spacing with him. However in 1973 – my third child was born; he was a boy. I was about eighteen, yet I had a lot of responsibilities and I did not get much help from my husband who took it for granted that it was a woman's responsibility to look after children.

I have said earlier that I knew nothing about modern contraceptives: but I knew a little bit about traditional child spacing method. When I first went to my home village in Ruvuma, among the friends I had, there was an old woman who treated me like her granddaughter. We had a kind of joking relationship. In her presence I felt free to discuss anything. She told me I should be careful and abstain from sex if I didn't want to get another baby! In the course of our discussion she told me about various traditional contraceptive methods. She mentioned how in their days they were able to space children well and how both men and women worked together to prevent unwanted pregnancies by strictly observing various beliefs and customs, for example abstainance during lactation. One other method she revealed to me involved wearing a specially woven waist band made from a bark of a tree. The band has special nots and normally the traditional specialist tied this around the waist of a woman who did not wish to get pregnant. I remember I asked her if she could prepare this medicine (dawa) for me and she did and I wore it until 1972 without getting pregnant. After I married I untied it and took it off. I remember I conceived soon after taking off the band. Looking back I felt sorry for myself, and the children and my husband for these subsequent pregnancies over which I had no control. It meant a lot of hard work for me, especially as I did not even have a house helper. I had to do every-thing myself

I used to think about the old lady and wished she was near so as to give me her wisdom. I did not even know from which type of tree this medicine was made. There is something interesting about traditional medicine men – the waganga (doctors). They do not show you the plant or tree from which they make the medicine. It is a safely guarded secret, which is inherited from generation to generation by certain members of the family, so they don t reveal it to their patients. Another reason is that it is a source of their liveli-hood and revealing it to many people may cut off their source of livelihood. My friend did not get much money out of this, intact what she received was a mere token. Anyway the old woman was too far way to be of use to me there in Mombasa.

I lived in Mombasa until 1974. After four years of married life and child rearing my relationship with my husband turned sour. Before the children were born we often used to go out, to see films or just taking walks along the sea, but with the coming of the children I hardly had time for any of these activities anymore. My husband began coming home late each night and I noticed that he had begun to drink. Previously he had been a teetotaller! but now he came home having reeking smell of local beer (pombe!) When I tried to talk to him and protest about this new behaviour of coming home very late at night he used to become angry and sometimes beat me. Matters went from bad to worse. He didn't care about the children either. "Maisha yalianza kuwa ni ya matatizo tu (life was becoming tough). One of my daughters was always sick and the youngest needed all my attention. I realized I could not take it any more and my husband's behaviour did not improve matters.

I did not know of any elder I could discuss my problem with. Eventually one day I just packed a few things and took the youngest child with me and took a bus to Tanga. I called on my brother and his wife. I wanted to discuss my marital problems with my brother. I told him everything and do you know what advice I got? He advised me to go back to my husband. You must learn to persevere, all marriages have problems "inabidi kuvumiliana" (you have to persevere)! I could not beleive my ears. I had gone to my brother for advice and yet all he told me was to persevere and literally pursuaded me to go back. I did not know who to turn to next, so after three days I boarded a bus and went back to Mombasa and to the house. If I had thought my going away would have improved matters then I was wrong. Matters had gone from bad to worse. On reaching home I found that a woman, who was a lodger in our house, had moved in while I was in Tanga. I was bewildered and sought for an explanation. Anyway he walked out of the house with the woman and they lived in a hotel to-gether, and he rarely came home any more, and I was very unhappy. I made a decision to leave him and go back to my village in Tanzania. I packed and without saying goodbye to him I left with my two children. I did not take anything from the house except a few personal belongings, and by this time we had bought a second house. I left all the property. We first went to Dar es Salaam where I stayed with my sister in Tandika for a few days. I could have gone to my step mother but I refrained because I knew she could never understand my decision. She could have told me to go back to my husband.

A few days later we took another bus to Ruvuma. Before reaching Njombe we had an accident. Our bus overturned and some people were injured. I was injured and had to be rushed to Njombe hospital, where I got stitches. I was in hospital for about a week. I was discharged and we left. That was a hard time; being in hospital with the children. The weather was cold and quite different from Mombasa, the children had a hard time.

When we reached the village I explained to my mother what had happened. All the same my mother insisted that I go and live with my in-laws because according to our tradition once a woman gets married she moves to her husband's home and even on holidays she cannot stay with her parents but must stay with her inlaws. I tried to explain to my mother the fact that I had left my husband but she still said as long as there was no legal divorce I still belonged there. As a matter of fact my mother, in accordance with our custom was right. If I stayed in her house she could have been found guilty of breaking up my marriage. So I took my children and went to live with my in-laws. They wrote to my husband and requested him to come and fetch me, he never answered and he never came. I stayed with my in-laws for a couple of months then I left.

Meanwhile the children were growing up. My first daughter was growing bigger and she started school. I realised I could not stay in the village. I began thinking about getting a job in Songea to support my children. I was not getting financial help from my husband. I decided to look for a job in Songea. There was nothing like wage employment in the village, and I did not feel like working on the land. I had tried it before and found it too demanding. I was worried about the children and how I would support them, although my mother provided both the moral support, food and care for us all. Still I felt it was too much for her for she was already supporting my daughter and my sister's children.

Single Parenthood and my Search for employment

After living in my home village for a few months I made up my mind to move to Songea town – in search of any type of job. My dream was to save enough money and eventually go back to Dar es Salaam to be near to my father, who was still in detention. I still thought about him and what he was going through.

To begin with I lived with friends and immediately began my search for a job. I had no skills so I knew I had very little choice. There were very few opportunities for the unskilled such as sweepers, and cleaners, and Songea is a small town. I came back home disappointed each day. Eventually I got a job with the TOBACCO Company as a clerk. The job was not difficult; we mainly did the counting of the sacks of tobacco and registering them in a book. I worked here for about two years from late 1974 – to 1976. I sent money to my mother to support the children. I met a man in Songea and we became friends. He gave me a lot of support. But I found myself pregnant again. In 1976 I gave birth to a baby girl. I took my maternity leave and was paid. Unfortunately I lost my job when the company had to reduce the number of its staff. So I stayed home and my friend supported me. I found another job with a construction company, as fuel pump attendant. I worked there for one year but lost my job again because the Company finished its construction work and they moved to Singida where I did not want to go because I found myself pregnant again in 1977. By that time I was twenty I had already given birth to five children.

With the little support I got from my friend I was able to support his two children. My friend could only give me limited support. I learnt later that he was married with a large family. I realised I could not depend on him only. I had to look for a job again. This time nothing was forthcoming. I kept thinking about the other children I had left with my mother. I had been unable to send back any kind of support to my mother for the children. I felt guilty and helpless. Meanwhile I was doing a bit of petty trading but the returns were not enough.

The Barmaid and Job security

A month later I decided to work in the bar as a waitress or barmaid. At least they didn't ask for a certificate or high education. Some of the girls I came to know were bargirls and they made enough money to live on. It was not much, but it kept them going. It was not a decision I made on impulse. It took me weeks before I gradually accepted my situation and plucked up courage and applied for a job in a bar. I did not like the idea but the odds were against me. I was determined to bring up my children myself and support them too.

I approached one of the bar owners about a job. He wanted to know if I had any past experience as a barmaid. I said no. He said "I wonder if you can do it. It is a tough job". I said "I could try". So I was offered a job. I got my first orientation on how to attend customers and take their orders. Some customers were nice but others were not. It was a traumatic experience with all these men around you each one trying to catch your eye or paw you. Eventually I got used to it. The job involved serving drinks to customers, talking to them, being pleasant and polite, that is, creating a condusive atmosphere for customers to spend their money and ensuring that they came back. Some of the customers were very good, but occassionally we got customers who after a drink or two turned nasty or misbehaved, and as a barmaid you had to take in the whole scene silently. It was expected of you, if you wanted to keep your job. So most of us stood the test and silently accepted the abuse and oppression with much perseverance.

I was not earning much, my salary was meagre but I got enough money from tips. Most barmaids make a lot of money from tips for some customers are very generous and especially the regular customers. Somehow there develops some kind of bond between the bar girls and customers. I cannot explain what it is. If you are good, well behaved and pleasant they like you. Of course a lot other things happen in bars, some women earn additional income through prostitution.

In 1979, after working in Songea as a barmaid for a few years, I found myself a bigger house and bought a few households, and went back to the village to collect my other children. I wanted to be near them. I was used to having children around me and I missed their joy and laughter although sometimes they were naughty and difficult but this is normal with young children. We had a long discussion with my mother about the welfare of the children and the job I had taken. My mother tried to persuade me to give up the job and stay in the village. I explained to her that she needed not worry, I had made up my mind to work and support my family. I explained to her that I could not cope with shamba (farm) work and since my ambition was to educate the children beyond primary education I did not see how I could raise enough money by growing crops. There was no market in this part, not even the co-operative authorities came to buy crops from peasants, and from what I could see, people did not produce for the market but mainly for their own consumption. Sometimes they sold rice or nuts, cassava and maize which are stapple foods through barter system, but normally people do not sell such crops. A lot of fishing goes on but it is on a small scale and this is normally a male dominated occupation. So I had limited choice for generating cash to support my children.

I convinced my mother that I could take care of the children but she refused to let me take away the three children I had left in her care after I moved to Songea. Eventually, she agreed to let me take away the third born who was then about six. My eldest daughter and son continued to live with my mother. I was happy that she agreed to let me take away at least one child. She helped in looking after the other two children and to run small errands for me. She also helped the ayah in a number of other cores.

Towards the end of 1980 I decided to move to Dar es Salaam. I had resigned from my job on a matter of principle. You see, the owner of the bar was a very scrupulous man. He cheated us on our salaries. For a long time we were paid less than our actual salaries. This is what he used to do on pay day. He would call you in his office and pretend to count eight hundred and fifty shillings, but first he made you sign the receipt for the money and then he only peeled off two hundred and fifty which he gave to you. We used to protest but not loudly because we were afraid of losing jobs. We knew he was exploiting us but we also knew that by signing the receipt of 850/- even though we did not get the money, we knew it would be very difficult to prove that he was stealing from us, no one would believe that we did not actually get our full salaries if he saw that we had actually signed the receipts ourselves.

But one day I just got fed up. I got drunk and told him off, the next day I reported the matter to the police who came and questioned him. He denied, but I told him to ask the other girls. He was finally told to pay me my full salary. He paid me two months salary and I left! I took all the children back to my mother except for the youngest one and I told her I was going to Dar es Salaam to look for a job.

In Dar es Salaam I lived with my sister in Tandika for a few months before I finally decided to look for a job. In 1981 I got a job at Silent Inn. It was interesting but very tiring. We worked for long hours. This was the time when Kamanyola – (Marquis du Zaire Band), one of the best bands in town used to play at Silent Inn. The weekends were full and we worked very hard serving customers. It was backbreaking. On saturdays for example we worked from 5 pm to 4am in the morning. You could not go home at that time because transport was not provided. So we normally stayed on until the early morning hours. We complained to the management about our security, so he provided a room within the bar where we could stay if we were unable to get home. Sometimes, if it was your turn to prepare food for the customers (food was also served at Silent Inn), it meant you continued to work until the beans or meat was ready – so you just rushed home for a short nap and at 5 pm you were back again working. The management was mean. Do you know how much we got paid? Five cents per bottle! But one could sell up to 50 crates of beer during weekends. But you did not get much money still. All of us got more from tips than from our salaries as you can see and that is why we stayed. I had already sent for my other children by then. Two of them came. So I had three with me and my mother kept the other two.

Mlimani Park bar had by this time been opened and we heard that they were paying decent salaries, that is the official minimum wage. Most of the girls left Silent Inn including myself and we joined Mlimani Park. For those who were not officially employed, they were paid by the bottle like at Silent Inn except that here they paid one shilling instead of five cents per bottle. I was employed and received the basic minimum wage. Because of my long experience and satisfactory work performance I was promoted to position of supervisor. My schedule of duties as a supervisor included supervising all the barmaids, to maintain discipline, settling disputes among fellow workers and generally seeing to it that everything was going on smoothly and bringing up any issues of importance to the attention of the manager. I liked my job. My salary was 650/- per month on top of money from tips I received from customers. That way we managed to lead a decent life and the children had enough to eat; my second daughter was already in Class three by now. I found someone to look after the youngest child so that the others could attend school properly and regularly.

Working as a barmaid has its prons and cons. First there is no job security, you can be hired and fired at a moment's notice. Second, there are no fixed salaries as most of the bars are owned by individuals who unilaterally decide how much to pay you. The women who opt to work in a bar are in any case desperate and do it at their own risk so they accept the arbitrary conditions and terms of services as stipulated by the owner. There is the "take it or leave it" attitude because they know you must be desperate, and so they take advantage of your situation and offer you employment on their conditions. For example when I was employed at Mlimani Park, as a Supervisor I got a fixed salary of 650/- monthly – but the rest of the ordinary barmaids did not. They got paid by the number of bottles they sold. The amount one took away home therefore depended on one's skills and wit as a sales-woman, although in the final analysis the employer got more out of one's skills. For example if you sold 25 bottles you got 25/-. This is very exploita-tive relationship. The barmaid's real money comes from tips which we get in cash or kind. On average a barmaid can make between 400/- and 800/- a day from tips alone. You see it is like this, some customers give you cash for good service or if you are one of their regulars they offer you beer everytime they order beer. "Sasa hapo bwana akili kichwani mwako" (it is up to you to make the best out of it). Most of the women who come to work in bars are often single parents with children. These are either divorcees or widows, deserted wives and sometimes young school girl dropouts. They are not stupid, because at the back of their minds they are thinking of their children and how to support them. So if you are offered a beer, you will accept it, while you sit and chat with the customers. For the second offer and many others, you will ask the barman to keep them for you. If you happen to get "Konyagi" or any other hard drink you deposit it with the barman. Instead, you fill your glass with either water or soda and lace it with a bit of whisky or konyagi and sit with the customers pretending to sip your drink. At the end of the day – you reconcile the number of bottles with the barman and either you sell them back to the bar or customers and collect your money and go back to your children, thus life goes. Being a barmaid one has to be intel-ligent and sharp.

However there is no security of employment as mentioned earlier, you can be hired or fired at a moment's notice and there is no compensation. There is no Pension or Insurance either. In other organizations they have the "Akiba ya Uzeeni" (National Provident Fund) to which both worker and employer send monthly contributions in cash-form. However, there is nothing like that in our case. After termination or dismisal you leave as empty handed as you came and if you decide to terminate your services before the end of the month you don't get paid-so you stay on until the end of the month. You get leave if you ask for it but it is unpaid leave. The same applies to maternity leave. So if you get pregnant you get leave but most women come back to work a month or less later to earn money to support their families. Most women do not get financial support from their partners. No woman likes to leave a young baby in the care of another young child – but it is a risk we take – and leave everything to God. Everybody knows about our working conditions and our rigid working hours, 5.00 p.m. – 11 or 12 mid –night or even longer on week-ends. Like any other woman – we worry about our children and about ourselves as we work so late and the chil-dren are by themselves, or with neighbours or young ayahs.

I have told you about job security. I must say something about personal security. We get all kinds of customers coming into the bar. Usually when they come in they are gentlemen but after a couple of beers some of them begin to misbehave and mishandle you as if they own you! And all along you are expected to remain calm and not loose your temper, and keep on smiling. Some will insult you or paw your ass, shoulders, etc. and you just pretend it is Ok. Sometimes you loose your temper but often you shrug and have a good laugh, or pretend you like them. You have to acquire the techniques of diplomacy and survival.

There are times when a man will try and force himself upon you or decide to take you home against your will. We also develop defence mechanism about how to get away from such a situation. Sometimes it works but often times it does not. You see you can always get rid of him if you don't like him. Our customers also apply different and sometimes mean techniques if they want to get their back on a woman. For example he may try to hit you and accuse you of having stolen his money. Others seem to think that once they have offered you beer then they have bought you. Although the management always intervenes, they always apply the principles of a "customer is always right". They are interested in their money and therefore it is important for them to maintain good relations with the customer. They can always get another barmaid! So often they will calm the customer and if he says you stole his money the management will offer to refund him but you know it is not the end, you know at the end of the month they will get it out of your salary! So we end up paying for money we did not steal and that means hardship for you because they have taken away your hard earned cash. It can be very humiliating.

Not all the customers who come to the bars misbehave. You see, there are different categories of people who come to the bars: there are those who come to have a good time and peacefully go home after closure and there are those who come looking for excitement and women, some come to socialize and meet friends, or pass time. Couples too come and go. You also have some customers who come because they are lonely and feel they can find comfort in a crowd, away from home. Some have family or marital or employment problems etc. So they come to the bar looking for company and a sympathetic ear. They often find a sympathetic ear in a barmaid. So you listen to their problems, sometimes you discuss with them but often they want you to sit and just listen, and sympathise. It makes them feel great. You relieve them of their tensions and anxieties, and you reassure them and make them feel confident! Most barmaids are good listeners. You learn and develop these skills with time. Being a barmaid is also an art – it requires a lot of patience and tolerance, and I think you can cope with so much because you yourself have gone through a difficult time. Not every barmaid sleeps with everyman, and not every drinker comes looking for women. Many people cannot understand this, I know. They think that just because you are a barmaid then automatically you become a prostitute. I am not saying that there is no prostitution. It is there, of course most barmaids do not have a choice so they combine prostitution and their job as barmaids. But you must understand that women do not do this for pleasure. It is all a question of economics! It is often not by choice that a woman becomes a prostitute. I am sure most people believe that we are all prostitutes just because we work in a bar. Some of us have one permanent boyfriend and don't just sleep with any man around.

I must say, not every woman who works in a bar is a prostitute. Some women are decent and being a barmaid should be considered a job like any other although the job carries with it a degrading social stigma. The woman bears most of the blame and the man who comes prowling into bars looking for a good time is regarded as doing just the normal and accepted practice. He is never branded as a prostitute even though he entices and pays for sexual favours. His money and status and power over those who do not have gives him the power to dictate the time and terms of the relationship even when we know the sexual act is an act of equals.

On the terms and conditions of employment, the privately owned bars are the worst. Those who work in big hotels or government owned bars like the Dar es Salaam Development Cooperation, are much better off in terms of salary and job security.

I think one could take legal action against the owner of a bar for unfair dismissal, or even for denying you your maternity and other employment benefits. But it would take so long a time that you would only get frustrated, and in the end you may get nothing. You see the owner has money, "Mnyonge hana haki!" (a poor person has no right). The man with money can use it to speak for him; and they always use your reputation as a barmaid against you. Society looks down on barmaids because most of us do not live according to conventional expectations, so they say. So you can imagine what it would be like to fight against your boss! Today some bar owners pay a regular salary to their barmaids, but I know a lot more women are exploited and are paid less. However at least you can move on to another place if the conditions become intolerable. Currently the salary of a barmaid is between 700/- – 1,000/- a month. Perhaps Dar es Salaam Development Corporation (DDC) barmaids get the official minimum wage – but I am not sure. Most women are thankful to get at least a job to support their families.

In the middle of 1985 I left Mlimani Park because of personal problems and the management's unfair treatment. My boyfriend got involved in a fight and the management wanted me take the responsibility. I refused to take the responsibility or even to apologize. They gave me an ultimatum, to apologize and continue working or else get sacked. I chose the later. I told them I was responsible for my actions and I could not take responsibility for another person's actions. They found out that in actual fact my boyfriend was not to blame. They wanted me to go back and work for them but I never went back even though they apologized.

Making ends meet – Petty business as a Survival Strategy

Two months later they called me back to work but I was too proud to go back, and by that time I had established a small "mradi" (petty trade) of selling scarce commodities such as sugar, wheat flour, rice, beans, ciggarretes etc. So I had a regular income. This was the time when there was a lot of food shortages and everybody went into petty trade and they were doing so well. The duties of petty business were so demanding, and I concentrated fully on the project (mradi). My boyfriend was very supportive and with his pick-up it was easy to move about with heavy sacks of food. But the queues at the National Milling Corporation were so long and I spent a full day there trying to procure commodities. If you did not feel like waiting you could buy items from other buyers who after buying them from the National Milling Corporation immediately sold them at hiked prices outside the gate. So sometimes rather than wait, one gambled and bought from the "Walanguzi" (middlemen) in the hope that you would also hike the prices and make up the difference. A lot of us opted for that instead of the long queues and bureaucratic procedures of securing "vibali" (permits).

My children alo assisted in selling. So while I was away on a buying trip the children sold the commodities to willing customers. They did this before and after school. They have always been helpful! and as soon as I came back I took over and they ran small errands for me. This is how we have co-existed.

These days I also sell fish. I buy fish early in the morning, and during week-ends my daughters get the fish for me. I prepare them in the morning and the children sell them in the evening while I am working at a bar in Sinza. We buy at least four or five kilogrammes everyday at 80/- per kilo. I spend about 320-400/- everyday and re-sell the fish at 30/- 40/- for a big piece and 10/- 20/- for medium size pieces and earn between 800/- – 900/- daily. Sometimes we sell all the fish but there are times when it takes two days. I make a profit of about 500/- a day. If I kept all the money in a bank I think it would be a lot of money, about 10,000/- a month, but the cost of living is too high and we use the money up we as earn it for our daily needs such as food, housing, clothes, water and electricity as well as pocket money for the children. I send some money home to my mother and my son who is completing class seven soon. My mother needs the money for food and to pay for hired labour to cultivate her shamba.

I also sell "mkaa" – charcoal and this is another good source of our income. The majority of people in our neighbourhood use charcoal for cooking, so there is a ready market and high demand for "mkaa". I sell about a bag of charcoal every day. It comes to about 150/- but I make sure I keep 100/- aside and we use the rest of the sales. This is how we survive and manage to make ends meet.

Motherhood and the problems of raising children

All along my aim has been to make a better life for my children. I consider education to be very important. Most of the money I earn is kept aside for the education of my children, their food and clothing.

My first daughter has just completed Form IV (1986) at one of the Private Secondary Schools in Lushoto. When she completed Standard Seven in 1981, she was not selected to join secondary education. My mother wrote to me about this and by then my father was out of detention in Dar es Salaam. I discussed the issue with him and applied for a school for her. She was accepted. I sent the money and the news to my mother and someone travelled with my daughter from Ruvuma to Dar es Salaam. We had made all the preparations, and I was glad she was going to a boarding school. She arrived. She was a big girl and pretty. It was nice to see her in person although we had kept a close relationship through correspondence.

She came home for holidays and either stayed with us or with my father. My father also helped me pay the school fees during the first year. I paid the rest. My second daughter is now in Form 2 in a day school here in Dar es Salaam and I am paying her fees. The third is doing standard Seven now. I am determined to see all of them through into secondary school education. I believe in education although I never went to secondary school myself. I know education is important and I know with education they stand a better chance. "Mimi sikusoma na ninapenda sana wanangu wasome na nitawasomesha". (I am not educated but I am determined to send them to school. And I will do it!)

I do not have much money but I save every penny. I cannot afford to pay school fees in a lump sum, so I approached the school authorities and explained to them my predicament. So far they have been very supportive and understanding so I pay in little instalments, and it has worked out well.

The girls are growing up. I worry about them. For those who have reached the age of puberty I try to explain to them a few facts of life. It is not easy to teach your children about family life education, but I try. I would not like them to go through what I went through because of my ignorance and youth. Children need to be protected and guided. I have a feeling that today's youths are well exposed to various literature on the subject; but a word from a parent is necessary. Take my own case, if any of my daughters got pregnant now or misbehaved, I know people would say they expected it especially with a mother of my historical background. So you see the social stigma stays with you. When people say such things I wonder if ever they feel that I too as a woman and mother have the same anxieties; and that I wish nothing but the best for my children. I am prepared to sacrifice everything so that my children have everything necessary in life. That is why I work so hard. I would like them to be dependent on themselves when they grow up that is why I am investing in their education and they are aware of this. If they fail, it will not be because I never tried. I try to impress upon them how important it is to work hard. I push and I encourage them all the time. If one of them misses school I talk to them and ask them if they have any problem. Sometimes I get angry and report them to their grandfather. He helps me to discipline them. It is painful for me if they are disobedient. Children sometimes do not appreciate the efforts of their parents, but I know when you are young it does not occur to you that you are hurting your parents.

My father has been supportive all the time. He appreciates what I am doing for the children and he tries to make the children understand. Sometimes he takes them for a weekend and during the school holidays the younger children sometimes stay with him. He spoils them with gifts and he loves them. He buys them clothes or shoes and when they come back he gives them money which we all use. I know that this is his indirect way of helping me out, and I do appreciate it very much. My daughter now works for him as a clerk in his small business. I know she would like to work elsewhere but it is not easy to find a job in these parastatals unless you have connections. After Form IV she was selected to go for a teacher training course but she refused. I don't know why girls think office work is better.

My youngest child is now eight years old. I am not planning to have another one. I think I can afford to maintain five. You see I became pregnant again in 1979 and decided to have the baby. We had good relationship with my boyfriend and he has always been supportive but neither of us wanted to get married any way, as I said he was already married. No, I had not planned for it and I didn't want to have an abortion. I am against it and in any case it is too expensive! and risky, especially if you are single and you have children. Back street abortions can cost your life and then who would look after your children? Considering my case I am the mother, the father and everything else! What is one more mouth to feed? You can always accomodate one rather than risk dying. You take what God gives you. I think God has forgiven me. My health is good but sometimes I get stomach pains. I once saw a doctor and he thought I should go for D & C but I have not gone – I am afraid I might get pregnant "kama wakinisafisha!" (If they do a Dilation and curretage they say you become more fertile if you do that).

Life as a single parent has it's ups and downs, just like married life. I have had a number of relationships. Some of them have been very helpful. For the last five years one man has been very supportive both to me and my children. He treated them like his own and they have a lot of respect for him. He was very supportive in disciplining the children. Economically it is difficult for single parents with low income to cope with child rearing even if the mother is devoted to the children. Chilren need more than just devotion and love.

On the other hand married life has its own ups and downs too. The woman may not have much say in decision making especially where finances are concerned. I know of couples whose husbands spend all the money on drinks and the wife is left to fend for herself, the chilren and the husband. You see, that is why all over Dar es Salaam women are busy engaging themselves in a small "mradi" for sustaining their families.

I am trying to make children understand and struggle to work hard. My children know about their father and the fact that he does not support them. I cannot take any legal action against him for child maintenance because he is too far and they know. This is important to me and they are supportive too. I think I should be grateful for their support and assistance.

My future Plans or Dreams?

My first ambition is to educate my children. I would also like to own a house and establish a sound business. I would like to own and run a beer-store. It is lucrative especially if you have the knacks for business. I would also roast meat, chicken and sell food and cigarettes. My father is willing to give me initial capital to start the business. I could start it on my own if I had my own house. Right now I rent a room in a house and you thus cannot run such business. It is very difficult to find rooms in Dar es Salaam. Of late they have become too expensive, you can even pay up to 900/- per single room! I could do other business I know, but I have long experience in barwork and I think I could run it successfully.

I am saving some money, perhaps one day I will build my own house even if not for business. I need a house for my children. I am hopeful that my daughter, when she gets a better job, she will help me educate one of the children. The last one will be educated by his father. He has said so and he often sends financial support for the children's upkeep.

Some Comments from the Co-Author

Like Anna, every parent places much importance on education as it is the key with which one can open up the way to a better life! So no matter how poor a woman or a couple is they strive to provide an education for their children even if they themselves did not get it. Education is highly valued. Education is not only seen in the context of enlightenment and future employment opportunities. It is also an investment for ones old age. People expect their children to look after them when they are old and they can best do this if they have a good job with a regular income. Parents also expect that those who get the education will reciprocate and help to educate their younger brothers and sisters.

Some of the problems that emerge from Anna's life history are not only personal experience but they have to be seen within a wider context. The Employment Ordinance provision S.25A & B entitles all women employees to 84 days paid maternity leave every three years. We see however in the case of women employed in bars that they can get maternity leave but they do not benefit from paid leave. There are no defined terms and conditions of service, there is no contract and therefore the employer is under no obligation to honour their benefits. This is surely tantamount to high level exploitation of women's cheap labour and the employers know this and use it to their own benefit. Women go into the trade because they have no other alternative. There is no social security to cater for unemployed men and women or even for single parents. The state does provide for free education, so at least each child benefits from seven years of compulsory primary education under the 1979 Universal Primary Education (UPE) scheme.

Sexual harrasment on the job is common in many institutions but worse for bar girls. They are open to all kinds of abuses from day to day and there is no law which clearly protects women from this abuse. The social stigma attached to the job itself is enough to stop the women from persuing justice legally as Anna clearly points out; although one can take legal steps against such abuses. It is time consuming because of curruptive tactics applied by those with the technical know how, who can pay their way out. So a woman finds her own defence and protective survival strategies.

Groups like the Women's Research and Documentation Project

(WRDP) could assist fellow sisters by providing information on legal aid and counselling clinics which are available from the Legal Aid Committee of the University – Faculty of Law. Information on credit facilities available to women of low income should also be made public so that women could take up loans and strengthen their own petty trading ventures. But we know there are a lot of bottlenecks associated with the securing of credit, such as the need to have collateral or security against which one can secure these loans. As a result the assistance which in theory is aimed at assisting poor women does not reach them, instead it is the middle and upper class women who benefit. Something should be done to ensure that poor women benefit from the assistance set aside for them.

The question of assisting barmaids with credit facilities so that they could make use of their experiences of working in bars and beer stores to open up their own bars and stores in order to become self-reliant should be taken very seriously. Anna boasted of having enough experience but she lacked capital to enable her establish her own viable business.

The rural urban dichotomy which makes it necessary for both men and women to migrate to the urban areas where the "pastures are greener" than the rural areas should be narrowed down. Attempts to improve social services in the rural areas are an encouraging development-it is slow but visible. More should be done in the agricultural sector, for example an improvement in appropriate farm technology, improved infrastructure such as roads to enable the transportation of farm produce. It also means an improvement in management and running of marketing cooperatives, so that peasants are paid on the spot for their produce. If people can earn money visibly many youths may be attracted to remain in the rural areas, and the experiences of their parents are enough to attract them to stay.

The question of developing rural technology as an aspect of not only simplifying work but also liberating women in the rural sector should also be taken into consideration. Perhaps with developed rural technology Anna's dual migration: urban to rural and then rural to urban would not have taken place.

Teenage pregnancies are common, so are expulsions from school. I personally think that these girls are innocent and society should not punish them further for mistakes done in ignorance. Getting a baby and being expelled and ostracized by their families is already more than enough.

The state should look into other ways of helping the youth. The introduction of family life education in the curriculum is a positive step which is expected to bear fruits. Allowing girls to come back after delivering to continue with their education and providing social security for both the girls and their children is another useful step to be taken. Older men who make these girls pregnant should be punished for being irresponsible and selfish

On job security for barmaids, according to the law every employer is obliged to pay not less the statutory minimum wage which is currently 3,500/- for urban workers, a category which includes barmaids. The provisions for this comes under the Regulation of Wages and Terms of Employment Ordinance Cap. 300 and orders made under that Legislation.

Under this Employment Ordinance Cap 366, termination of employment of a weekly and monthly contract employee must be at 30 days Notice or 30 days Wages in lieu thereof. The security of Employment Act, 1964 Cap 574 restricts arbitrary dismissal/termination of employees, unless it is for good cause e.g. breach of contract, discipline etc. Otherwise an employee is entitled to challenge wrongful dismissal/termination and sue for damages or compensation. These protective legislative provisions apply to barmaids as well.

With regard to the Provident Fund Schemes, the National Provident Fund Act, 1964 obliges employers who employ at least 5 workers in the establishment to participate in the N.P.F. Scheme accordingly. Civil and Criminal sanctions may be brought against an employer who fails to do so by the N.P.F. directorate.

The fact that barmaids or any other workers do not benefit from this minimum right is compounded by lack of the basic legal consciousness of these rights on their part. There is a need for groups like WRDP in collaboration with legal professionals to conscientize those in need. The establishement of the Women's section in the Tanzania's Trade Union (JUWATA) could certainly do a lot for women workers in terms of providing information on their rights in employment.

There is also need to re-examine the marriage Act so that it can be reviewed in favour of women interests as well as solve some basic marriage problems such as divorce and the harrassment and oppression of wives by their husbands. The divorce of Anna's parents and later on of her own with her husband greatly affected Anna's life and her children.

There is also the need to fight against the attitude that barmaids are either prostitutes or potential prostitutes. For it is alleged that it is on the basis of this attitude that the bar owners either pay barmaids very small salaries and in some cases they do not pay them at all expecting that they survive on tips and friendship with male customers. What is suprising is that when the same job is done by men they are respected like any other worker, and are paid legal wages. Ways, therefore, need to be found to make women service labour in bars as respectable and deserving equal pay as men service labour.

FOOTNOTES

[1]Since the detention of Anna's father and uncle has great impact on her life perhaps there is need to understand the political environment of the 1950s and 1960s particularly in relation to the trade union movement. In the 1950s the trade unions, particularly the Tanganyika Federation of Labour (TFL) worked in great cooperation with TANU in the struggle for independence. After independence struggle between TANU and TFL leadership began to develop leading into the establishment of NUTA as a single trade union under the control of TANU in 1964. In the struggle of 1960s many trade unionists fell victim of the situation, thus detentions. Thus the detention of Anna's father is likely to be a result of that political environment

CHAPTER FOUR

A Migrant Peasant Woman in the City: Her Struggle for Survival

Eva with Anna Nkebukwa

Introduction

Eva as a Research Partner

Eva is now about 60 years old but she is still strong enough to pursue a variety of income-generating activities including agriculture. She is a Nyamwezi and was born in Tabora, in West-Central Tanzania. She has always used her father's name, according to tradition. There were three children in the family, two girls and a boy. Eva's father had only one permanent wife. She says that her mother could not stand a co-wife. Her father married two other women in his old age but both left due to the overall strong position of his first wife. The two other children are now dead, her sister died before marriage and her brother died in March 1986. He committed suicide after his children had died consecutively. This left Eva alone. Her parents also died years ago when she was still young. Eva has been married twice and has three sons, one from the first marriage and two from the second marriage. She has 10 grand children and two great grandchildren.

When I asked her to write her history she retorted; "Hivi unaniona nina akili za kutosha kufanya kazi kama hiyo" This was Eva's immediate response to my suggestion that the two of us should form a team to record her life history. She wondered what made me think she was intelligent enough to do that kind of assignment. Her statement is a neat summary of one of my reasons for choosing a woman with a strong peasant background for this life history study. It is a reason which is also in line with WRDP's main objective in writing women's life histories, which is in short, that the lives of women in Tanzania and their contribution to society have so far been largely neglected, giving prominence to men, especially politicians.

The neglect of women in history has led to their being treated as "invisible", thus leading to concepts like "integrating women in development", which wrongly assumes that women have been standing passively aside watching men struggle to develop the nation. But women's labour has all along been the backbone of that development. Rural women have been at the heart of the economy which depends largely on agriculture Many people who have been by-passing women in history would ask how women could be so important to the nation, especially peasant women. They would also wonder as to what impact would be made by the life of one peasant woman. The main contribution of this history is that it adds a voice to the annals of Tanzania's history. Educated women and wives of elites have had plenty of room to express their views on bride price, marriage, land owner-ship, divorce, polygamy, school-girl pregnancies, biases against girls in the provision of education and similar issues. But the women whose pen has been the hoe, who do not read newspapers, who are never heard on the radio, have remained the silent, and almost invisible majority.

The few Tanzanian women whose history was recorded have had some-thing to do with politics. But even the roles of these women who contributed a lot in Tanzania's nationalist struggle are underplayed. The position of peasant women is worse. Their contributions and that of many other women went unnoticed. I chose to work with a peasant cum-petty trader because I felt this class is still very much missing from the recorded histories of women, and the motives of single, migrant peasant women in town are largely misun-derstood. Peasant women have a lot to share with everybody else in Tan-zania because the majority of Tanzanians come from a peasant background. We are aware of the struggles in the lives of the women peasants in the vil-lages, but these struggles have gone largely unrecorded. That is what I told Eva in response to her doubts as to her ability to cope with the research I responded: "Hii siyo kazi, ni mazungumzo juu ya jitihada zako kuyakabili maisha ya mjini". (This is not work as such but a discussion of your endeavours to survive in town). The life of peasant woman in town is bound to be very different from that of those who were born and grew in town or even in a peri-urban setting. She has different ideas on agriculture, moderni-zation, politics, and other issues.

After seeking clarifications on other aspects of this study, including how she would benefit from it, we finally, settled down to work. The question of how she would benefit from the study was central to her because of the nature of her activities. On several occasions she had to take time-off from her trade or agricultural activities to sit with me for the recording sessions. But in spite of the initial difficulty in convincing her about the importance of this research, especially to her, the fact that she gave me a full account of her activities means that an amicable agreement was reached. But what assisted me more in convincing her to take part in this project is the fact that we have been sort of friends for a long time. If this hadn't been the case, I wouldn't have managed to convince her to interrupt her activities so as to work on this project. She is very strict on a number of subjects; the proper use of time and the keeping of promises being on top of the list, closely followed by cleanliness and preparation of cheap but proper meals. So in short, given the nature of her day to day activities, Eva sacrificed a lot of time to work with me on this life history project.

The burning issues that remained concerning this research, were how much of the discussion would be included in the final document, and whether the respondent should remain anonymous or have her name written on the final document.

Research Methodology

The research method employed in this study, besides library and archival research, was interviewing and observation. The interviews were conducted mainly in our homes. Conversations and observations took place in Eva' home and recording took place at my own home. I was also assisted in this research by my long time acquintance with Eva and some of her family members. I had seen her work and was rather fascinated by her hard work and by the way she handled certain issues which will be discussed later in this chapter. One problem which I came across was that while I found recording to be a very effective interviewing aid, I found transcribing to be time consuming. Another problem which I mentioned in the previous section was the question of time on the part of Eva, but a solution was found. Due to the nature of our activities the main body of interviewing which started in November 1986 was not completed until June 1987 for everyday I met with Eva I learnt or deserved something new about her, her activities or her family.

The questions guiding our conversations were related to the woman's entire life, in her variety of roles as a daughter, a wife, a mother, a peasant, a migrant woman trying to grapple with life in this cauldron of cultures called the city, as a tenant, and similar issues. But the woman is being interviewed not only because of her gender, but also as a Tanzanian trying to grapple with the difficult economic situation either as an individual or in a group. The life history of the woman is thus linked with broader socio-economic issues, moving it from an individual to encompass the system of life. The questions thus include family background, marriage, Arab and Missionary influence on marriage, practices, bride-prices, cultural taboos, formal and informal education of girls, health facilities, reproduction, family planning, women participation in politics, experience as a petty-trader-cum-peasant in town, factors leading to the migration of women to town and similar issues.

Another observation about the research was the problem of how to make the conversation and the entire activity interesting for both of us but especially for my research partner. For me I was learning something new and interesting almost in every conversation. So after the first introductory session, I started telling her stories from my ethnic origin so that some sessions became of a comparative nature and this raised her enthusiasm in the session. Another problem was for me to learn to be extra patient when she was narrating some exciting or very amusing experiences in her life. Patience is very important because as it has been advised by experts on oral history, "the researcher has to learn above all to listen, not to interrupt. This is the absolute key doctrine – listen a bit longer than you think is comfortable. The contract in an interview is that you have come to hear." This becomes more important depending on the socio-economic difference existing between the researcher and the interviewee.

Another problem is how to assess the worth of the evidence given, how to detect an understatement or an exaggeration. This problem was minimised by doing library research on the area of study and by having a general idea of the situation of women in Tanzania. This point serves to emphasize the importance of having a long research period in which the researcher and the research partners get to know one another and assist each other in obtaining the required information.

II. Marriage, Motherhood and Divorce

Eva's first marriage was based on coercion. She did not like the prospective husband after seeing him. When she first saw him he was with his brothers. When she learnt that one of them was interested in marrying her, she says, her first response was "Sitaki, mikubwa yote hiyo." That is, I don't want them, they are too grown-up. Her parents and the boy's friends, relatives and brothers tried to assure her that he was young but to no avail. Whenever the boy's representatives came to visit her home, she would sit at a distance and give them a calculatedly cold reception and be very formal with them. One of her prospective brothers in-law visited her once and was received coldly and never went back. On another day, the visitors came ready with part of the bride-price. Fortunately her sister got hold of this piece of news and informed Eva that "Wameleta posa". She refused to see the visitors and she was so annoyed with her sister whom she suspected of having gone to greet the visitors. She told her sister: "Posa wanakuposa wewe!" that is, may be it is for you that they have brought that bride-price. She refused to see the visitors and her sister got so annoyed at this reaction that she threatened to report it to the parents. Eva told her sister to go right ahead and report. As for her, she reiterated her first reaction by saying

"Mimi sitaki. Mwanamume mkubwa namna ile. Atanioa mimi huyu! Refu mno silitaki!" Briefly meaning that she couldn't imagine herself marrying such a big and tall (giant) person! Even after so many years, the vehemence with which she relates this story serves to indicate the genuinness of her refusal to get married to that particular boy.

On that particular day, the visitors pleaded with her to accept their relative, but to no avail as she reports it: "Wakanibembeleza, lakini mpaka wameondoka, wala hawakuambulia chochote. Sikwenda hata kuwaaga, kuwatoa."

She never even bade them goodbye, but her sister did. To her surprise and chargin, they came back very early the next day. They were living not too far from her own home. She says: "Wanang'ang'ania wewe watu wa nyumbani kwetu wakikupenda!"

Once a girl has been selected, they really stick to her. This time she said tearfully that if she is forced to marry him she would kill herself, as she puts it with all force:

"Mie nitajinyonga mie. Nitakufa kabisa. Tena nasema huku nalia. Naogopa! Siku ya pili wameondoka pia bila kuambulia chochote. Wakaenda kukaa na kufanya kampeni".

They left and went to think of new strategies of convincing her.

They planned to use someone to go and talk to her father. But she said she didn't want anyone to talk to her father about this. If they did or sent someone to do so on their behalf, she would quit home and disappear. But they took a short cut and took a "mkoba wa kuchumbia" to her father. This was a piece of cow hide cut off from the hide used to tie a cow when milking it, some article given to a girl's father to establish the fact that a certain man wanted to marry his daughter. If the father rejected this article then the engagement was off but if he accepted it, then it was on. Unfortunately for Eva, her father accepted the "mkoba". He had so far never harrassed her. He had left her alone in what he saw as her stubbornness. But by accepting the "mkoba" then the deal was on and from then on, the girl was treated to all intents and purposes as someone's bride so she could not go to the dances, especially at night, and other social and cultural restrictions were imposed on her. Her father told her all this after he had accepted the article but she still insisted that she was not interested in the boy mainly because he was too old for her. Her father said that the boy was just "mtoto mwenzie" but she still refused and wondered if he would force her to accept the marriage. She cried a lot but even her mother joined her father in supporting the marriage proposal.

Refusing a husband approved by her parents would have been an embarrassment to her own mother and the entire village. So on the basis of her mother's appeal, the girl gave in to the proposal but even after the marriage, she was crying daily until some traditional medicine was given to her to make her love her husband. To compound the problem, she was married when she was too young, that is, one year before starting her menses. All these put together, it is small wonder that the marriage didn't last long

The reasons why parents force girls into early marriages are acquisition of bride-price and to avoid pregnancy out of wedlock or even loss of virginity both of which would bring shame upon the family. In many traditional practices in Tanzania, the amount of bride-price a parent charges corresponds directly with the age of the girl and her physical state. If she is very young and a virgin she fetches a lot of cows. When I asked Eva why different bride-price amounts were charged for her step-daughters whom she brought up and participated in marrying-off, she said:

Idadi ya ng'ombe unaowatoza inategemea na binti yako mwenyewe – kama ana heshima ... Maanake unavyojikakamua wewe mzazi eti mimi nataka mnipe kiasi kadhaa, unaona kitu chako kimekamilika, lakini kama unaona kitu chako kibovu, huwezi. Unaweza ukatoza hata shilingi 100 au 200, kuliko watoto kubeba mamimba tu kuyaleta ndani.

Here Eva briefly summarises the traditional expectations from a "high quality" would-be bride, who should be young and a virgin, otherwise you can marry her off even for as little as 100/-. She herself fetched 26 cows and 20 goats for her father!

Eva was therefore not forced into marriage because of any physical problems on her part, but because of struggles between herself and her parents on the choice of the would-be husband, and the time factor. Eva says she was a lucky girl in getting early marriage offers, some of which she appreciated, but at the same time, she would have liked to stay free a little longer like some of her friends, as she puts it:

Nilikuwa nataka kwanza niote maziwa nione ujana.
Nilikuwa naona wenzangu wanavyopendeza.

But no one cared about her inner feelings and ambitions. But she admits she had been willing to relinquish her freedom early only for one person. That was a chief! The chief asked for her hand but her mother who had a fairly powerful voice and could influence her own husband, refused the offer saying that marrying a chief would turn her daughter into a prostitute. Eva explains thus:

What happens when a young girl gets married to a chief is

that the chief enjoys being with her during the first few months of marriage. Once she has her first baby he relegates her to second place and marries another one. So the previous girl is left for other men at the Chief's court. This is not good. My mother understood this, that is why she refused the Chief's request. Of course when you are married to a Chief you get a good house, good food and clothing but your husband has no time for you. My mother's decision hurt me but I believe she was right. Moreover when I got married to someone else, I didn't miss the material benefits much. I used to lead a good life with both husbands. Both had a lot of cows and goats, and they weren't stingy. They would slaughter a cow or goat once in a while to make sure we didn't eat greens for too many days. There was plenty of milk and food. So materially I didn't miss much by not marrying a Chief. I only failed to stay long with my husbands only because they were bullies.

Eva had only three sons but not out of choice. She had her first child in the second year of her marriage. She then had a miscarriage of a five-month pregnancy of a baby girl. Eva became seriously sick thereafter and she divorced her husband after four years of marriage. After one year of staying with her parents, she started an affair with her second husband and conceived. He later took her to his home and stayed with her for seven years without being married to her properly. This is to say he delayed paying bride-price for her. But this time her father was not very demanding. He said she could stay with the man and see if they could live together for long. So Eva had her second son but thereafter she stayed for many years without conceiving again. She tried all sorts of traditional cures, to no avail. Her second son grew up, went to school, started working and got married twice, had his first child in his second marriage who was Eva's first grandchild, before Eva conceived again. She had her third son, who is now 20 years old when her first grandchild had just stopped breast feeding. By that time her second son was working in town.

Sooner or later Eva began suffering from paralysis of one hand and so the second son took her for medical check-up and treatment. In the meantime she revealed to her daughter-in-law, that is, her son's second wife a lot of other problems, who advised her to go and see a doctor. The doctor treated her. When she went back home to her husband she conceived again Even though she has three children, she still says that if she had seen the doctor earlier, she would have had more children. Eva later returned to town to deliver her third son in hospital.

After delivering, her son paid her fare back to her husband. In response to my question whether her husband ever went to see her in hospital, she laughed in a disappointed manner saying: "Wanaume wa matala si shida tu"; that is, husbands in a polygamous marriage are problematic. He had his other wife. When Eva was hospitalised her husband didn't allow her co-wife to accompany her as is often the case in such marriages. She stayed behind to serve him. But he used to send food through a friend of his. Eva too had taken plenty of food with her from the village. Her aunt and uncle were also there to help her.

Regarding delivering her baby in hospital, Eva says that even though modern medical services enabled her to conceive again after many years, she still regrets having delivered her son in hospital. She says that unlike during village deliveries where you get a lot of attention and assistance, in the hospital no one cared for her. The following is her story:

> Nilipomzaa hata mtu wa kunikanda maji, mama nilipata shida. Nimezalia hospitali. Nilikuwa na matatizo ya damu. Sasa hapo angepatikana mtu wa kunikanyaga maji. Nimejifungua usiku kama saa tatu, nikalala hivyo hivyo, damu zimejaa pale nilipolala. Maanake mimi nilikuwa na damu nyingi sana, ndiyo maana mwili ukaporomoka haraka sana. Maanake nilipozalia pale wakanitoa manesi nikapewa kitanda cha pili nikaambiwa nenda ukapumzike pale, mtoto akalalishwa kwenye miguu. Nikalala hapa. Asubuhi nimelala mpaka saa mbili sina mtu wa kunikanyaga maji. Nikatoka. Nilikuwa mbali sana na kijijini nilikokuwa nakaa. Aliyeenda kunipikia ni mkwe wangu, naye ni mtoto mdogo.

In a nutshell, she missed a post-delivery hot water compressor service for a whole night as well as proper care.

Another problem that she encountered in hospital and for the first time in her life was that she could not get proper food according to her tradition. In hospital she was not allowed to eat rice. She ate only ugali. In the mornings, the hospital provided milkless tea which she always refused. When I asked her why, she laughed and then asked me: "Hivi wewe unanionaje mimi? Kunywa chai ya hospitali! Unaona mavikombe yenyewe!" She wondered what I thought of her standard, to assume that she would accept tea provided by the hospital in those dirty cups! She also used to refuse the hospital food. Eva says:–

> Sisi kwetu hatuli vibaya, tunakula vizuri kweli. Na kama ni
> mwanausafi ndiyo mimi mwenyewe, umenipata. Siwezi
> kula maugali machafu!

If you are looking for a clean woman, that's me. I can't eat dirty food. That is Eva in a nutshell! She goes to show then, that contrary to earlier popular belief, civilization was not introduced to the African by the colonialists. Some of the practices had always been there but had never been documented.

Divorce

We have seen that when Eva had a miscarriage of her second pregnancy in the first marriage, she became seriously ill. But her husband did'nt care at all. Her problems with him increased. So her parents, took her to their home to nurse her. Her husband never went to see her except once when she was convalescing, but he was told that he could no longer claim his wife as he had neglected her grossly. The man demanded refund of his cattle saying that after all she had given birth to only one child for him so he was entitled to a refund of 23 cows, minus three for the one child. But the parents appealed to the "Baraza" (Local Court) and the case was settled in favour of the brides parents, that is there was to be no refund at all. His negligence of his wife, had been proved beyond reasonable doubt. In retaliation Eva was not allowed to stay with her son. He was taken to stay with his grandmother and uncle. They said they had paid too much dowry and only got one child. So they made sure she didn't keep him. Eva stayed with her parents until she got married for a second time.

But her second husband had another wife when Eva got married to him. He was also extremely jealous. He always got furious if he found his wives talking and laughing together. He said his anger was prompted by suspicion that his wives were discussing other men. But another possible reason could have been his lack of a sense of security. In many polygamous families, men prefer their wives to get close just to maintain a minimum peace in the family. But when they became almost intimate friends, then the husband gets worried and puts a stop to it. The man was also a bully. Eva narrates how he once beat up her son mercilessly until he started nose-bleeding. This prompted him to increase the beatings, claiming that the boy was "pretending to bleed"! She says bitterly:

> The beating took place in the evening, so I couldn't do any-
> thing. I kept quiet until the next morning when I told him
> that if he beats my son again like that I would report him to
> Police, and if my son died he would eat the body. I was very

furious and no longer feared him. After all did he buy me? (He paid normal bride price). I told him that he had many other children but I had only one with him. And he wasn't even interested in helping me to get a cure so that I could have more children.

Incidentally it is the first wife of this very son who later assisted her (Eva) to get treatment so that she could conceive again after so many years.

But having a second son for her husband did not improve their relations. Her husband maintained his cruelty until she was forced to quit, taking with her the younger son who still live with her today. She relates her decision to quit thus:

> Nikaona ujinga. Niliondoka akiwa mchanga. Sibembelezi mwanamume. Mimi mama roho yangu ndogo. Sitaki kunyanyaswa. Hasa nikifikiria, nimezaliwa kuzuri, nije ninyanyaswe na mtu, kanikuta mie mdogo, na yeye mkubwa, kwa nini aninyanyase namna hiyo. Nikaona niondoke tu niende nikakae na ndugu zangu kwa yule mwanangu mkubwa. Mwishowe nikaamua kuja huku Dar.

III. Education and Religion

Eva did not go to school, neither during her childhood nor later. In many ethnic groups in Tanzania, formal education was not for girls. A girl learnt from her mother the skills necessary to make her a good future wife. In fact Eva says that if a girl got married and failed to cook or look after her husband and the house, she was sent back to her mother to be re-trained. When they thought she was ready, they would return her to her husband. If upon her return she was found to be still lacking in the performance of her wifely duties, she was sent back to her parents for good. Her parents had then to refund all the bride-price paid for her. So it was a mother's duty to couch her daughters as thoroughly as possible to avoid this future shame and the economic loss that would result from refunding the bride-price. Thus the mother was used as an instrument in the perpetuation of the oppressive division of labour. She did not query it because, not having been exposed to a different system, for example through formal education, she would not envisage an alternative life style for herself or her daughters.

Thus Eva received very thorough informal education, as a result of which she is a very good cook, house-keeper, pottery maker, beer brewer, cultivator and petty business trader. Regarding trading, she started off by selling "sungwi" when she was still very young. Her mother never allowed her much free time to play with other children. She was always doing something productive. She was also taught meat smoking. The technique is as follows: A wide and deep pit is dug in the ground. Trees are felled and laid across the pit, their leaves are spread on the logs in thick layers. Meat which has been cut lengthwise is washed and salted and is laid neatly on the leaves. Fire is lit inside the pit and the smoke which results cures the meat. One person stays around to regulate the fire so that it does not scorch the meat.

Another food preservation technique is that of drying potatoes. When potatoes are harvested, the good ones especially those known as *makobolwa* are sorted out for preservation. They are dried without peeling them. One just leaves them on the ground and covers them with leaves, for one week. During the second week they are boiled, left to cool, peeled and dried for preservation. This is just one method. Other and less cumbersome techiniques are used in preserving foodstuffs and green vegetables.

Many parents believe that educating girls created a wider possibility for them to become pregnant before marriage. Eva does not have any firm belief in educating girls. In fact when I mentioned the idea of family life education in schools and asked her what she thought about it, at first she said that if "they", (that is, the government) had already decided that it should be done, what would the likes of her say about it. After I had explained to her that the government had not yet started implementing the plan and was still seeking people's views, all she said was that they could go ahead and teach them as long as girls were taught by women only. Eva admires former President Nyerere. She always refered to him as "yule Baba yetu", that father of ours. She praises him for having helped to reduce the oppression of women even at village level. She gives the example of wife-beating saying that during the past a wife could be beaten and had no where to appeal. But after the introduction of TANU and now C.C.M. cells at the grassroots, a wife whose in-laws are hostile to her has a chance of reporting her husband to the party organs if she has enough courage and is not afraid of follow-up beatings. So although Eva is not literate and has never been a member of TANU, C.C.M. nor U.W.T. she is still fully aware of political developments, especially those which affect women. Asked why she has never joined the political party, she responded that her hands are too full with projects for survival. She cannot find the time to participate. She says that her niece was an active member of TANU Youth League and used to spend a lot of her time on those activities. Eva could not afford even a quarter of her time for such activities, especially considering that she was most of the time running her projects on her own and had to be there all the time.

Regarding religion, Eva says she attempted to undergo instructions for baptism during her second marriage. Her second husband had no religion (traditionalist) and when he married Eva he already had another wife. So the three of them decided to go for religious instructions. Eva learned faster and got ahead of the other two, and was thus ready for baptism before them. This annoyed her husband and he prevented her from getting baptised wondering how she could be baptised before him.

When he was finally ready for baptism another problem arose. The Church told him to choose only one wife and get married properly in the Church. They assisted him in decision making by saying that he should marry the first wife and not Eva, who was the second wife. He refused to leave her but later on, after she had left him because of his cruelty, he and his wife got baptised, got married in Church and stayed together until the man died. Eva says her co-wife was a very tolerant woman.

IV. Migration of Women to Town: A general discussion

There are four main reasons why women migrate to town. Indeed there are certainly many others which could be considered, especially today, but Eva's time show that four reasons were primary. These included rejection of family labour; difficult marriages; material incentives in town; and accompanying husbands.

(a) Diminishing Returns From Unpaid Family labour:

One woman once said that all the services she provided to her family are not paid for. She got married while she was still young but as she grows old her responsibilities increase while the returns from her family diminish. The increase in demands does not match with the increase in resources especially if the main source of income is the traditional agricultural production whose returns decrease as land gets over-used and exhausted or even under-cultivated. So a woman may get scared of such demands and decide to opt out of marriage, and go to town, hoping that in town she will be able to earn enough to satisfy her own basic needs and send something home, especially clothes for her children. She may end up living there for good.

(b) Difficult Relationships In Marriage and Disillusionment:

A woman may decide to opt out of marriage due to problems emanating from beatings, lack of the necessary care and other forms of oppression like failure to cope with the extended family, co-wives, and similar problems.

In some ethnic groups or some types of marriages the wife may willingly and gladly assume responsibilities which later outweigh her. For example, soon after her second marriage, Eva was handed over the responsibility of looking after her co-wife's children. The co-wife was divorced soon after the new wife came in, the main accusation against her was that she wasn't bringing up the children properly. Eva gladly accepted this added responsibility and fortunately the children never let her down. She is very happy to talk about the way she brought them up until they got married.

In most cases the divorced wives are not invited to celebrate their children's marriages. All arrangements are made and executed by the stepmother. But on many occassions, step-children have been the cause of disruption of marriages.

The time it takes for disillusionment to set in marriage is often determined by the tradition prevailing in the area. One example is the Haya tribe where the reception and conditions which a bride finds at her new home are rather unrealistic and when they are suddenly removed disillusionment sets in very quickly. Traditionaly when a girl gets married, she stays in the house for a given period. Initially the period was two years but now it has been reduced to even a single day depending on the bride and her husband's official commitments.

In the olden days when the 2 years period of seclusion was the rule, the bride spent her days being bathed and decorated by her in-laws. The husband's task was to bring food, beautiful soap, cream and other materials to aid his mother, aunts and sisters in their task of "beutifying" his wife. There was competition among women in the village to see whose daughter-in-law, or whatever the relatioship was with the bride, would have a lighter complexion and smooth skin and put on weight ahead of all others. Obviously, during this period there were no major quarrels or reprimands addressed to the bride. She was not supposed to work except in some occassions to cook meals for the family.

Christian brides were supposed to go to church every Sunday, but they would be fully covered leaving only a small opening for the eyes to see the way. They were not supposed to talk but only to whisper. If they were caught talking that would mean ashaming their mothers for not having trained them properly.

On a chosen day at the end of the two years or the period allocated for her seclusion, the bride was taken out and handed all the necessary tools for housework. She was taken to the river to fetch water, given a pot to cook, etc. Once more she found herself "free" to bear full responsibilities in the home. It is at this juncture that the true characters of people, starting with the husband and in-laws residing in the same house, started manifesting themselves. Soap, creams and many other things gradually stopped coming in, other problems based on oppression also started. Often, these pressures became so much for the young bride and she finally opted out of marriage and moved to town. As many did not have the requisite skills for employment, they ended up in prostitution. And some remained in town permanently.

Another example of how disillusionment sets in a marriage is from the Nyamwezi. Traditionally, when a girl got married, the man used to move to the girl's home where he was given a house to stay for a period ranging from six months to one year before the couple moved to their own home (semi-matrilineal). Sometimes this period was longer, depending on the immaturity of the bride. During this period he works for his wife's parents. The wife also works as usual. She is not kept in seclusion for long. Naturally, due to the proximity of the wife's parents, he restrains from harrassing the wife.

The groom's mother was also bringing food to the couple, which is quite a rare practice in everyday life. At the end of that stay, the couple are escorted in style by 20 – 30 men and women to their new home. They are given utensils, cows and food. On arrival at the husband's home, more food and cows are given to the couple and they continue celebrating for a few more days. But as soon as they settle down, then the true colours of both begin to show. These can lead to quarrels and divorce.

Eva says repeatedly that the main reason why she decided to go to town was because her second husband failed to respect her, especially after the death of her parents. Her parents died in two consecutive years. The father died first. Her own children were still very young, so they couldn't help her. Her husband had used to fear her parents a lot because they could always fine him for misbehaviour. He also respected them and not the wife, because, as he used to tell her, it is to them that he had paid the bride-price, and not to the woman herself. The woman has no say in the bride-price negotiations, so her duty is to obey her husband, failing which she is mistreated, regardless of whether the failure is real or imagined by the husband. A woman's refusal to be mistreated leads to desertion or divorce in favour of younger and more obedient girls. A newly married bride undergoes special training called "kufunda". This one-sided course on marital life stresses respect and obedience to the husband. It is conducted while the couple is still residing at the bride's parental home. A man continues with his normal life and no one observes him closely. As such he can pretend to be a good "mkwilima" (son-in-law) and reserve his wicked traits for display in his own home, as happened in this case of Eva. But also during his one year or so stay with his in-law, some of his true colours are seen. In fact, in Eva's case, she was advised by some people, including her father, early in her marriage after she had her first child to leave the man due to his cruelty but Eva refused saying that she couldn't leave him, she was prepared to learn to love him and tolerate his behaviour, and secondly, she didn't want to get married to someone else and scatter her children. Her father said he had started being disillussioned by his son-in-law even when the couple was still residing at his home.

(c) Prospects For Quick Acquisition of Materials

Women's migration to town enticed the hope of generating quick riches. This reason applies to both men and women. In Tanzania, the influx of youth to towns in search for jobs is a problem of no small dimensions. The girls from the villages are enticed by promises of paid employment which carries shorter and specific working hours. In town there is also a cut-down on the number and intensity of social and cultural restrictions imposed on girls and women in the rural setting.

The decision to go to town is usually based on stories from the "been-to-'s" who, after staying in town for some time and engaging in non-agricultural activities, return home in a seemingly improved state and with a few modern goods which are not easily available in the village. These stories from such "returnees" do not include the difficulties involved in living in town, for example, the problem of housing, finding a job, transport, food and others. They paint a rosy picture of town life, thus enticing people to flock to town with high expectations.

(d) Accompanying Husbands:

For most rural women, their first ticket to town is on the basis of accompanying their spouses. During the colonial period, due to non-availability of accommodation for entire families, women were not encouraged to follow their spouses in urban areas. However as changes took place especially after 1961 men made independent decisions to take their wives if they wished or to marry and retain their wives in town. Available census statistics (1978; 1988) confirm the composition of the female gender in towns to be dominated by married women. Eva also explains her own driving force to town under this category.

We also note that women need their husbands. It is common practice that the decision to move to town is more often than not made by the man. Quite a good number of women stay in the fields while their husbands stay as pseudo-bachelors in town. Once one begins to examine whose interests both partners are serving, a lot of issues arise and this situation calls for a proper study.

Eva relates that her move to the city was not for her making. She came to the city not particularly for the city's attractions but because she followed her lover whom she had married after leaving her second husband. He asked her to follow him so that they could live together only to find out, upon her arrival in Dar es Salaam, that he had a wife already, who didn't want another woman around. So for the third time, Eva had to walk out of a liason with a man. She found it easy to decide to leave the man but not to go back to her village. She asked him for fare back home but he refused, so she stayed in town and the conditions forced her to stay permanently, against her original intentions. She believed that she could survive in the city and bring up her son on her own. Eva came to Dar es Salaam when her son who is now 20 years old had just started walking. He was about 1½ years old then, which would put the date to 1967. She had no intention of getting married because, she asks "How many times can one woman get married?" And she has kept to her decision.

V. City Life and Activities

When Eva left her second husband, she stayed for a short time with her relatives. During this times she supported herself and her youngest son mainly by agricultural production. She supplemented this with beer brewing, a trade she had learnt from her mother when she was still a young unmarried girl. Her mother had also taught her cookery and pottery, and she insisted on cleanliness. These lessons, with the exception of pottery, proved to be valuable assets to her in the struggle for survival in town.

During her first two marriages Eva concentrated on pottery. She used to earn reasonable income because earthenware are the traditional utensils preferred by many women in her ethnic group and several others in Tanzania. She plans to resume her project when she goes back to Tabora. She tried to do the same in Dar es Salaam but the clay is not so good. So in Dar es Salaam she engaged herself in other projects. Regarding beer brewing, she says that when she got married, her husband prevented her from the trade saying that he didn't want men to touch her (as they do in restaurants and bars). Her second husband said the same. She attributes this to their jealousness. But another reason can be the fear of the husbands over the woman's economic independence which comes more easily with beer-brewing. This point is illustrated by Abrahams (1981) writing on Unyamwezi who says of Vumilia Village which in 1974, had 56 adult women members and only 18 men, and depended largely on beer brewing:

> The combination of relatively independent womanhood
> and beer brewing is not uncommon in itself in this area, but
> it was unusual as the basis of a whole community and it was
> clearly not a type of village which officials wished to see
> developed in large numbers in the area. (p. 84).

Eva would like to engage more in beer-brewing because it generates quick money, but the business being unofficial, she is afraid of the fines imposed on offenders. These can sometimes be exorbitant. Eva was once put in a lock-up for one day for such an offence. She will never forget the harrowing experience and police brutality she endured during that arrest. This is her story: "When I was arrested I had been suffering from diarrhoea for a few days. I told the police about this but they said that was not their problem So they put me in a lock-up, overnight, and I continued like that without any assistance. The following day I pleaded with them to allow me to go to the clinic but they said they would take me to their own hospital but I refused, knowing anyway that this was not true. Finally they allowed me to go to a dispensary, where I was immediately admitted and given drip water. I was also given food. After resting a bit I was discharged and went home. On my way home I was feeling very embarrassed by the foul smell emanating from my clothes. I had cheated the police that I had no relatives. I feared that if my son knew of what had transpired he would have come to the police station and created havoc. Thus I was happy when I met my son when I was already safely away from these brutes.

Beer brewing has got a lot of other disadvantages. Brewing beer without proper storage facilities is problematic in that if the beer is not sold it has to be poured away thus causing a loss. Beer brewing is also difficult if one does not own a house, as the owner of the house may discourage beer brewing and either evict the brewer or stop you from doing it. Alternatively they may hike the rent to such an impossible level that you have no alternative but to stop brewing.

Cooking Food and Bites

When she quit the company of her lover, Eva went to stay with her niece. She immediately employed the cookery skills she had learnt during her girlhood. She prepared 150 rice buns (vitumbua) daily. This sometimes demanded that she stay awake throughout the night (kukesha). She used to sell them at 20 cents each. A kilogramme of sugar was costing 1/-. She found the business very profitable but her niece spoilt it. Eva used to take her rice buns to a nearby shop for sale. Her niece used to go to the shop and obtain cigarettes, the cost of which was deducted from money accruing from rice buns sales. One day Eva took her buns to the shop as usual. Later her niece went and collected two packets of cigarettes, thus leaving very little cash balance. And when Eva collected the balance, she used it to buy food and thus had to close the business. When asked how she got capital to start the business in the first place, she responded: "Mtu kama yuko hai atakosa msingi?", that is, a living person cannot fail to get capital.

Later on, a friend of hers invited her to join her to cook food mainly for casual labourers at building sites at the University of Dar es Salaam. After doing the business for sometime she earned enough money to rent her own room. When I first met her in 1983 she was still providing this vital service.

Throughout the time she was running these projects, Eva had to get up very early in the morning so that by 6.00 a.m. she was already at the site. She used to prepare some of the bites at home and she would prepare some at the site when the first-supply was finished. Eva had no watch so she just estimated the time to start her business. She remembers a day when she woke up a bit too early and had to take shelter on the way to wait until the day was clear.

Eva was very clean and prepared very good food. She had a lot of customers. She relates how one time she was sick and left her male partner and her grand daughter to prepare food for customers. The food was of such poor quality that customers started deserting her. When she got the report that she was losing business, she had to drag herself out of bed and cook so as to restore her credibility. Her customers came back. Her motto is that when people pay their money for a service it should be good.

Regarding her male partner, Eva says he was useful only when all ingredients were there and all was okay. He could then carry water for her and even collect some firewood. But if there was no food he would never bother to go and hunt for it (e.g. beans, sugar etc). Eva had to do this on her own She was the leader. If there was nothing he would stay in bed or just pass his time doing nothing. She says that is why it is important for men to realise that women are important. "A woman cannot always depend on a man. Some times she is the more dynamic of the two as was the case with me and my partner. I taught him a lot of business sense including cleanliness. This is the reality."

Eva says she used to earn a "lot of money" from her projects but she could not build her own house in the city. This is because whenever she saved enough money something croped up which forced her to spend the money. Usually the reason had to do with her son. In 1984 her son was seriously sick and this took all her savings. But she doesn't regret this as her son is well now.

Sometime when she had accumulated plenty of money, thieves robbed her of all her capital.

But Eva has always managed to raise capital to resume her businesses. She does this mainly by working on people's farms. As soon as she has earned enough capital she invests it in her own businesses. She at the same time maintains her shambas. She says that sometimes she tried to get some

78

money from her son and other relatives but "generally, I preter to earn money through my own efforts. I feel happy with such money because, I know I don't owe anybody and I am not obliged to say "Thank you sir to anybody". This is one reason why she failed in her attempts to be employed in peoples homes.

Eva stresses that it is not quite easy for a woman who is on her own to run projects. The food stall (magenge) business popularly known as 'mama nitilie" (or Hilton hotels) is quite tough. You have to look for firewood, and sometimes the ingredients themselves are too expensive. For example, if ordinary meat is sold at 100/- a kilo, eva asks: "How much profit can one make from selling food with such meat? You have to count the costs of firewood, salt, tomatoes, onions, fetching water, and cleaning the pots and other utensils. There is also the hazards of inhaling smoke. The main advantage in cooking is that unlike beer-brewing you feed yourself while also making profit.

There is also the problem of competition. But she carried researches before embarking on a project. She analyses the possible projects and their likely profits, losses, locational problems and who is already running such projects in the relevant areas. She says for example if she wanted to sell charcoal, she would not establish such a business in an area like where she is living now where the existing charcoal seller is already popular. She also sells it at a slightly cheaper price because her husband is a driver and brings in loads of charcoal sacks. So the lady can sell even as many as six sacks in half a day. Obviously she would outdo all other competitors.

Another survey she made was when she wanted to start preparing soup (makongoro). She visited spots where this was being prepared and found it to be good business. But the labour and the amount of fire-wood or charcoal involved was so much that she decided against the business. She found that it was cheaper to prepare (tail) soup (mikia) and did it for some time.

Agricultural Activities

When Eva started living in the city on her own, she managed to get a shamba which she cultivated and harvested two sacks of paddy. Later the owners of the shamba re-claimed it. This upset her because at the time she was earning reasonable income from her other businesses and was planning to hire someone to assist her on the shamba. She had now to look for another shamba which she soon acquired and started growing tomatoes and earned a lot of money but thieves stole a lot of them and she abandoned the business. Now she is growing green vegetables, especially peas. When it is very hot and dry, she engages in irrigation, carrying pails of water from a nearby source. So

79

she always has some vegetables for sell and consumption.

Eva says that living in town could not make her forget the way of life in which she had been brought up, that is agriculture. She said that her family and both her husbands were so hard working that the two famines which she has so far experienced in her life left them unscathed. The first one was called "Kabalagata" and this happened when she was still a girl. Her family had enough in store to survive without undue strain. The second one was called "imagembemweli" during which peasants were seen every where carrying hoes looking for people to whom they could sell their labour. This famine occured when she was already married. Her family survived reasonably well. So agriculture is in her blood, but she admits that it is a very demanding activity. She says "Kulima ni moyo. Nisipofanya nitakosa riziki". Farming is commitment, if I don't do it I will not survive. She has no good word for women in non-formal sectors who shun agriculture just because they are living in town. She says:—

> Wanawake wengine wanashindwa kulima kwa sababu hawafanyi kazi kwa dhamira. Akifanya siku moja, mbili, akipata hela anatimiza mahitaji yake ya wakati huo. Anarudi tu kazini akisha maliza hela.

According to her some women fail to farm because they have no commitment. For her, agriculture should supplement other activities and should not be resorted to only when one is hard up. Concerning the growing of rice which many people find demanding, Eva says "mpunga hauna kazi, kazi ni roho ya mtu." It all depends on your own self-determination. She says even when she has to contract out her labour, people like hiring her because she is hard-working and faithful.

VI. Problems of Migrant Peasant, Unmarried Women in the City

Reflecting on the problems of single, migrant women, Eva remarks that the first major problem they face, as experienced by herself, is the fact that this category of women is not respected, especially by men. It is not easy for them to see how a woman can manage to be on her own in the city without being a full-fledged prostitute. It seems that living in the city is the prerogative of men not women. Eva laughs when she remembers how she "rescued" the man who later became her partner in the food stall business (magenge). He was living in the city doing odd jobs, earning money and drinking it all. At that time she was well-established running her food stall project. She invited him to join her and taught him a lot of things concerning business. He learned fast and was extremely co-operative when sober. Every morning he would go to the business site, fetch firewood and water and start boiling the

80

beans or meat. The woman would remain behind collecting ingredients or putting the house in order.

Later she would join the man at the site and cook rice and other foodstuffs. After the customers had eaten, both of them would clean the pots and keep them somewhere and go back home. Eva worked in harmony with this man for about ten (10) years but slowly the man began to drink and heap abuses on Eva and her son. Eva had enough of it so she expelled him from her house. After loitering in town for some months his relatives at home got news that he was in bad shape and came to collect him. Eva gives this experience as an example of women's ability to survive in town without being prostitutes. Many men who approached her when she was living alone and refused to open her door for them used to abuse her asking what she was doing in town on her own and unemployed if she was not a prostitute. Eva worked hard to prove that a woman can live respectably in the city.

Another problem is that of house rents. When business is not good it becomes difficult for the woman to pay rent. But also the rents have been going up at an unbelievable rate. Before Eva moved to the house where she lives now, she used to stay in another house, paying only 150/- for one bed-room and a sitting room. Suddenly the rent was hiked up to 600/-. Eva had to move out fast. She got another room at 200/-.

VII. Future Plans

Eva plans to go back home as soon as she has earned enough income for her fare and for buying items which will be essential in settling at home. She abhors dependency, otherwise she would have gone home long ago at the urge of her first son who is also in Dar es Salaam. She says:–

> I am intending to go home soon but I don't want to be dependent on someone else while I still have enough strength to work. My second son has a house at home which is now being rented. He wants me to go and stay there to make sure the tenants do not spoil the house. I will go when I am ready.

Typical of Eva's class, most women who are unskilled do not venture for too long in town if the rural areas can still absorb them. After accumulating some money they normally go home where they buy land and houses. In this way they create security for their old age. Equally so many working people sooner or later resort to their peasant backgrounds. However, her stated intention is not likely to be realised in the near future, at least not for as long as one of her sons is still dependent on her for his survival. He has yet no inclination to go back to the village and to a life of which he knows nothing so far.

VIII. Concluding Observations

After reading through the fore-going life history, one can draw up many conclusions. Just a few are attempted here. The study is left open for readers to make their own legal, social economic and other observations.

First, the lives of unmarried women are generally misunderstood by men and sometimes by fellow women. This situation can be rectified by more widespread participation of the women themselves either as recorders of their own histories or as co-operators in the recording process. In this way they explain the mystery which surrounds their lives for the benefit of the society and themselves.

Second, although Eva claims not to be interested in politics, she has actually dealt with politics at one level or another. She has made a number of decisions which have enabled her to retain control over her own affairs. This point is very important for many women and therefore deserves elaboration. First of all, Eva moved from the village and out of marriages in which she was being used as an instrument in the production and reproduction processess, to a situation where she could choose whom to toil for as she herself puts it. It is true that the major moves in her life were assisted by external actors, for example her parents in the first marriage, and religion in the second marriage, and a lover in her move to Dar es Salaam. However, the way she took control of her affairs after finding herself in various situations would not have been possible for someone who was devoid of all politics. Eva's history is thus a history of struggles for survival.

After being "rescued by her parents from her first marriage into which they themselves had forced her, she gets into one in which she had to learn to cope with a co-wife. Despite her parents' monogamous marriage she finds herself into a polygamous situation but manages to cope with it and survives the co-wifely struggles for more than 20 years. Her husband's cruelty and decision to get baptised forced her out of marriage and finally landed in the city where she has fended for herself and her son for almost 20 years now, ten of which she spent with another partner whom she "educated" on how to survive in the city.

Another observation to make about Eva's life concerns her ability to recognise her own potential and her confidence, which have enabled her to survive in the city. All the above data make a good case to argue that many women are out of public formal politics but they are daily engaged in some kind of bargaining, decision-making, resource control and distribution all of which form part of the broader political process.

A final observation to make about Eva's struggles for survival in town concerns the overall outcome of those struggles. What emerges from the history is that Eva has not been able to invest her profits from her various businesses into any permanent business or build a house of her own. Thus looked at from the angle of whether Eva has been "successful" in her life in the city, the answer is no. She gives the reasons when she asserts that, on several occasions when she had accumulated enough funds to invest into something meaningful, something cropped up to set her back, for example, the arrest of her son, her son's serious illness and her partner's drunkenness. After spending her savings on such issues she had to start anew. A second reason which has prevented her from achieving "success" was her lack of business know-how. She had the energy and brains to start petty trades and generate income from them but she had no investment and saving techniques. She was also not aware of the means by which she could obtain credit to expand her business. She is only aware of "upatu", an informal savings technique among women. This is typical of the low income groups particularly women who have a great difficulty to get access to credit facilities to enable them to start or expand their business. It follows logically that the small and petty undertaking could not have enabled her make substantial savings. She has also not lived in an area where women's economic groups have been strong. The fact that she is illiterate has also played a big role in her lack of "success".

But after having said that, one can see that Eva's life has had a different kind of success in the sense that she has managed to provide for herself and her dependants the necessities of life without which they could not have survived for long in town. This sort of "invisible success" has been achieved through sheer self-determination which is commendable. It is however necessary to observe that in the traditions of her class, capital accumulation is not typical. It is only the ability to clothe, feed and provide shelter for one's dependants which is highly respected. The ability to rent and keep a room in town is another credit.

Let me finally say that if legal, social, economic, and political interpretations will differ from one reader to another, such is the challenge Eva throws to us.

Footnotes

Abrahams, R.G. 1967: *The Political Organization of Unyamwezi*, Cambridge, Cambidge University Press.

Abrahams, R.G. 1981: *The Nyamwezi today: A Tanzania People in the 1970's* Cambridge, Cambridge University Press.

Bennet, Norman Robert: 1971 *Mirambo of Tanzania, 1870 – 1884* – New York, Oxford University Press.

Cutrufelli, Maria Rosa 1983: *Women of Africa: Roots of Oppression.* London, Zed Press.

Dugan, William Redman & Civille, John R: 1976: *Tanzania and Nyerere:* a study of Ujamaa and Nationhood. New York, orbis.

Hatch, J.C. 1972 *Tanzania: A Profile.* London, Pall Mail Press.

Listowell, Judith: 1965 *The Making of Tanganyika. London, Chatto & Windus.*

Mascarenhas, Ophelia and Mbilinyi, Marjorie 1983 *Women in Tanzania: An Analytical Bibliography.* Upsala, Scandinavian Institute of African Studeis.

Mbilinyi, Marjorie, J. 1969 *The Education of Girls in Tanzania: A study of Attitude of Tanzania Girls and Their Fathers Towards Education* – Dar es Salaam. Institute of Education, University College.

Obbo, Christine: 1982 *African Women: The Struggle for Economic Independence.* London, Zed Press.

Tanzania, Bureau of Statistics. Population Census 1988. Dar es Salaam 1990.

Yongolo, N.D. 1953 *Maisha na Desturi za Wanyamwezi. London,* Sheldon Press.

CHAPTER FIVE

The Life History of a Housewife: Her Life, Work, Income and Property Ownership

Mama Koku with Magdalene K. Ngaiza

Introduction

This is a life history of the late Mama Koku (49), a mother of six children who died a widow in 1990. She was born in Bukoba, Kagera region in 1938. The story depicts her background; colonial education and attendant values, married life, struggle at family level, work and income in the home and property made in 25 years of marriage and life as a widow. The paper is presented in three parts. Part one contains the introduction; methodological issues and the historical context of the study. Part two is made up of the story as told by mama Koku. Mama Koku sadly passed away in March 1990 before her story would be published. She died of cancer leaving her hopes and expectations alomost achieved. In part three an effort is made to raise analytical issues on the gender problematic. The record of Mama Koku's life is interesting and touching in many ways. She narrated the story at leisure. She was told; the story is yours, the document is yours too, but co-authored. She appreciated the fact that someone could value recording her life.

Immediately after all was said, she felt to have found friends, WRDP, through the co-author. The story, she thought, was too unimpressive to deserve being recorded to the extent that some gaps have been left unfilled. The experiences of pain and anguish she had lived with were to be shedded off and left behind as she told her story. In between the lines we note her own realization of progress made by herself. All the same, we went very far from life history. At some stage we started chasing up the credit institutions which she had not known about. I introduced her to some suggestions. Unfortunately she passed away before securing any credit facility.

I want to thank several people for the inspiration to undertake this study; Marjorie Mbilinyi, Susan Gieger and WRDP Workshop and Seminars for the comments which enriched the present material.

Finally I am obliged to Mama Koku for teaching me a lot of things through her life story. Her daughters too, took a lot of interest in this work.

One of them drafted the first sketch of her mother's story to help recall the life experiences. The sketch provided the backbone of the story. I would like to thank the entire family for their struggles and the openness they showed during the discussions. This work is dedicated to the late Mama Koku's four daughters and a son.

Methodological Issues

The lady was identified by myself after having met her in Dar es Salaam during the period of her struggles in 1976. As neighbours, we had quietly sought to know why she was not leaving her husband who was so cruel? I did not know that one day she would be my choice for such a project. She was chosen because her life history represented several types of women: on the one hand she was a homemaker of the colonial origin. On the other, she was a middle class affiliate by virtue of her late husband's status; the husband was a civil servant. Yet on her own, she would be in a low income group if she was employed and in the absence of employment she was a domestic woman in a small business class. When the project was in progress, she was a widow and a female head of a household.

Data was collected in phases. Stage one involved talking to her about women struggles, including my own. This ensured that she understood the subject and why she was chosen and the relevance of her story. Stage two involved reading the project proposal to her to make her aware that it was going into records. After discussing the proposal she was given time to think about it and to ask what should be included and what to leave out. At stage three we presented a set of open ended questions to her to study and begin to recall events. The questions acted as a guideline. It was instructed that she could leave out any questions she felt were not friendly to her. She could also modify others. If she did not feel comfortable at all she could withdraw her story. Further more, it was explained to her that two presentations would be made, one in English and another in Kiswahili, at different times to enable others appreciate and share the life histories. Also the fact that she would also be included in the list of WRDP network was mentioned to her as well as attending the Kiswahili presentation workshop.

During stage four, the first skeleton of recording her story was done. It was preffered that her daughter do the recording to see if the story could take shape. A total of 37 questions were recorded for the first time. In subsequent stages we enriched the answers by checking various events and historical records. A lot of time was spent on polishing the records. The life history maker was a struggling woman. The struggles kept her busy so much that it was very difficult to get her. Sometimes I myself failed to honour my promise. Meeting mama Koku was very sensational. We could sit for hours reviewing her past experiences with her late husband. The discussions could sometime turn into mournful events.

The story maker therefore preffered her name and voice withdrawn because she said she was not really taking into court a departed relative but sharing life experiences with us if it could help us learn or to formulate other knowledge. So we did not tape anything. She also argued, that such events are not for memory, they should pass. Eventually after the first draft was made it was read to her in Kiswahili for her to vet.

Before recording the story other sources of information were consulted. These included records of the colonial and early post-independence times regarding cultural aspects of the areas she lived in, especially Bukoba and Dar es Salaam, regarding women and property ownership as well as socialization. Useful information was found in court cases and other files on women's activities in town. Other books were also read on the aspect of oral and life histories as well as attending two workshops – organized by the Women Reseach and Documentation Project. Besides the life history which Mama Koku narrated we discussed other information obtained elsewhere. Our discussion reflected some interpretations of her life as related to other women. The record is open for everybody's appreciation and interpretation.

The Research Questions

Very little is written about the struggles of women in the economic and social spheres of the households in Tanzania. The changes which have taken place, to show struggles and concerns of women as well as their political participation, beginning with the colonial period to the present are not clearly documented in various ways.

It is always taken for granted that because many women are not involved in the cash economy, then they are dependants of men. Is it not worthy to study how much handcraft sales and the sale of bites in the homes have assured the household security? Is it a correct economic assumption that men are the major or sole suppliers of household cash like ILO echoed as I quote below:

"Estimates of open unemployment rates in Tanzania... The available information suggest that the main problem related with poverty and basic needs is not open unemployment, but rather the underemployment of the *head of household*. Moreover the issue is rather a problem of scarce opportunities to earn a satisfactory income, i.e. what is generally referred to as "invisible underemployment or the question of people *working long hours for low remuneration*. This problem affects two groups of which the first is by far the largest – the *poorest peasant families and the families of the low level informal sector,* a vast majority of the 800,000 urban non-wage earners." (emphasis added) (ILO, 1982: XXIII–13)

Because economists are always concerned with heads of households (males) and payroll economics, until recently it was difficult to trace the contributions of women. In fact, it is a cultural convenience not to give women a definite economic status. As a result many women are "affiliated" to the males' economic status. Women in the rural areas have also been undervalued deliberately but that has already been brought to light by sufficient literature (Mascarenhas & Mbilinyi 1982). To come back to the urban-based women, there are ambivalent assumptions by both male and insensitive female observers. Leslie for example once observed with support from male informants that the urban woman is an "economic liability" to her husband or companion in contrast to the rural wife "at home" who is an investment and an "economic asset" (Leslie 1957:94).

Indeed, some wives have lamented for their being domesticated in town while they have to demand everything from their husbands. They are not in effective command of what to do with their labour. The lamentation is valid and it is an expression of a concern for their household security. Urban social relations among neighbours are manifested through jelousies. For example, a neighbour gets hurt if her neighbours prepare rice or bananas with meat stew more often than she does. Although petty jelousies are typical of women and men, yet they are a form of expression for a wish to be equal with or better than others in terms of well-being.

The life histories of women do indeed capture the economic productiveness of their potential in towns. Also systematic sampling of groups for women have helped to add concrete data to the economic inputs of women in households in town, besides their domestic roles conceptualized as social reproduction of the working people and schooling population. The life of one woman is here intended to provide minute details of everyday life so as to provide all aspects of her involvement or non-involvement; it gives us the chance to have access to the feelings of a woman about her position as either a liability or asset; it unravels the humiliating situations which sensitize a woman to be economically conscious and the alternatives which are available to resort to. Most important we have a chance to record the contradictions which exist at household level for both rural and urban women. In some rural areas men do not want their wives to engage in production for a variety of reasons which are not documented. In town, some men refuse their wives to go to work or to engage in womens groups' projects while the men can only provide for minimum needs. Further intentions of a life history is to echo the lives of many other women who have gone through similar episodes.

For the economists our study raises a question of concern. The Tanzanian economy is still dominated by peasant, petty commodity production. Given the token income which employed men and women receive, which survival dynamics are people engaged in? Should it be taken for granted that men are engaged in business to top up their incomes while women are in their domestic enclaves? Indeed not, for studies on household response to the effects of structural adjustment are proof to the fact that women are doing a lot (Tibaijuka et al. 1988).

Finally, the life history had another purpose which I intend to make central in this presentation. This is the continuity of women struggles in income generating activities with a view to accumulating and taking off. Some women today are considered as "rebels" because of their efforts to earn enough money for themselves. Our struggles today are seen as far fetched, fashioned against the ideas from the developed world. Educated women are blamed, not for their indulgence in income generating projects, but for articulating the ideology of the female dependency syndrome with the purpose of negating it in order to justify and bargain with government to give women a rightfull share in the sectors of the economy and within the household. Women in the Universities and in the Party are called frustrated or too independent and therefore bad elements in the cultural setting. This accusation is false because Tanzania's economic and social philosophy calls for self-reliance and liberation of women.

It will be realized that today's economic struggles by women are a continuation of the past struggles. The only difference is that in the past the women's activities were taken for granted (disregarded) as feminine activities not worth replacing or effectively supplementing the male's income. It was a by the way. Also their work and lives have been characterized as silent revolts, silent protests or submissiveness because nobody wrote about them or acknowledged the impact of their actions in any way. Therefore the present economic and social struggles have a historical legacy and women should support all efforts for both rural and urban women to engage in productive economics so as to transform their lives and those of their families. It is important that women should demand to have their contributions visible in national statistics in order to break the gender superiority-inferiority complexes and to evolve what we see as the women's economic and social revolution.

In this study we intend to draw some facts and suggestions which will be reflected upon in the theoretical framework later. The facts listed hereunder are not to be proved by the life history presented here, rather, they should guide further research to document what is missing and they should guide economists and historians alike to learn to record and reconstruct their work with adequate tools of analysis and with more objectivity. This may suggest the use of non-conventional data collection methods and to question the cultural ideology than to glorify it. The following seem very appropriate as I read and reflected on Mama Koku's story.

1. That a failure on the part of African economists and economic historians to address and account for the contributions of African women, as important, conscious economic producers and consumers, has resulted in partial understanding of African economies and reflects what has commonly been referred to as androncentricism which forms as conceptual error in reframing African materialist phenomenology.

2. That women have been erroneously called economic liabilities due to ideological and cultural manipulation thus neglecting their economic concerns for their families, a situation which has relegated them to a false, weak economic status.

3. That the statistics and women departments be involved in collecting reliable data on women's employment and incomes derived from various activities both in wage employment and self employment. This data base will help to correct the situation and to defeat cultural manipulation in gender property relations.

4. More life histories should be documented to provide a broad base for drawing various general observations as well as correcting the past history.

5. That the phenomena of women accompanying their husbands during transfers must not be taken for granted. It is a loss of opportunity for some women. The women's bureau and other relevant officers must take care of such women with the view to organizing them for remunerative activities.

These few suggestions are made as a contribution towards a correct understanding and, better still, a reconstruction of the nature of African economies. They should guide the democratic procedures that are required to better the life conditions of households and reduce gender conflict.

The Historical Context

The life history of Mama Koku can be contextualized with the political economy of the urban/rural Bukoba district during the 1930s and thereafter. We shall trace her in areas like Tabora, Kigoma, Masasi, Morogoro, Musoma, Maswa, Mbulu, Moshi, Arusha and Dar es Salaam. She sojourned in all these places between 1955 and March, 1990.

The political economy of Bukoba district where the life history maker comes from is traced by Culwick Arthur (1939) who, despite other faults, ably recognized the problem of women's burden and their lack of access to income and property. The position of men and their idleness, is so properly recorded, especialy during the colonial period when they were traced locked in the sedentary banana/coffee agriculture and unable to do any other productive activity while the women go out in the fields annually to grow legumes, potatoes and cassava. The history maker is certainly influenced by this culture in some way especially in terms of family life and gender relations. Issues become complicated when one places Mama Koku within the Haya cultural labour practice as against the effect of colonial education and the attendant indoctrination of a "high culture".

To help us delineate this parallelism the works of Marjorie Mbilinyi (1985) on "City and countryside" which undertakes the analysis and critical examination of colonial records; as well as that of Geiger, S. (1984) which is addressed to producing a correct nationalist history showing women's participation; and the TNA have been particularly useful. Mbilinyi and Geiger have mainly reworked the records of Leslie, J. (1963) and Molohan (1957) about the conditions of the city of Dar es Salaam and the position of women as well as various strategies employed by the colonial office to control them. The analysis by Mbilinyi (1985) does indicate that women were too far ahead than expected. Women in Dar es Salaam according to both Mbilinyi and Leslie's studies owned houses and shambas. This is further supported by the court cases which confirmed that property ownership for women was a usual thing. According to Geiger (1984) women were also active in political struggles.

These two fields, the economic and political, give a historical legacy to women's activities unlike what we are made to believe that historically women were generally poor and quiet. Life and oral histories would have to be involved to create evidence which is reworked to construct available evidence from court cases and colonial reports.

The customs and traditions of the Bahaya explicitly say that women are dependants and as a result the brideswealth that is paid becomes a symbol of superiority-inferiority in gender family relations. Therefore since women did not own property during the period understudy it was obvious that there was no need for the woman to bother herself with money and properties especially when her husband was alive and working. Women had to assume that the husbands had enough money to support the family. The woman was also not supposed to ask the man how much income he earned or spent. The man was also expected to help, besides his own family, the family of his inlaws and his parents.

Handicrafts by women had always meant passtime or the creation of household articles, like mats, for use and as presents. The Haya woman therefore did not think seriously about money. Things began to change during the coffee boom of 1928. At the same time an emerging new behaviour among black women mistresses of colonial staff and Indian merchants who started wearing silk, perfume and high heeled shoes, influenced the local women. African men with money from the coffee boom clothed their wives alike and those without these fetishes remained with the thirsty for these goods (Culwick 1939). This boom did not last beyond the 1940s but left women now beginning to think of independent pocket money.

All these new developments can be traced systematically within the political economy of Bukoba. Until as late as 1950s the economy was both under the great influence of a feudal mode of production known as "Nyarubanja" system of property ownership based on patrilineal relations. This system came to be consolidated during colonialism in order to ensure cheap production of coffee for export. This further resulted into greater subordination of female labour under nyarubanja system. The colonial ideology had imbued the upper class or petty bourgeoisie with an anti-accumulation consciousness. Chiefs for example did not accumulate capital goods. They were encouraged to produce raw materials and to exchange them for light items. Mama Koku and her husband were victims of this ideology because they came from the dominant class of chiefs and associates.

Conflicting interests resulted into a declining faction of the local political elite (nyarubanja" etc.) and gave rise to the petty and commercial bourgeoisie. One sees Mama Koku's paternal family at local level becoming a declining faction after independence when the chiefs were phased out. Her matrimonial family had the problem of belonging to a petty-bourgeoisie without an accumulation consciousness. All through, Mama Koku's families belonged to declining factions and as a woman things would not have been different in any circumstance.

Colonial education also imbued in women and men what was thought of as high culture. Educated men vied for white collar jobs and domestic education was for employees' wives. The society was misled to accept this indoctrination because it had a false promise for riches. Thus women who married

92

working men in town especially teachers and higher clerical officers were also falling in a poverty trap. They were made to believe that they were part of the ruling class and were thus to acquire good manners and customs such as dressing properly, housekeeping, arithmetic and a neat home matching the tastes of the advanced culture (quoted in S. Geiger from the Unsigned memo entitled "The Urban Way" n.d. TNA 540/A 14). These women would be socialized at Community Centres and learn all the possible skills, excluding their traditional handicrafts which were so popular and rewarding if they had developed external markets for them.

The establishment of the African "women's" welfare section by the Women's Service League was to "civilize" African urban women. Eventually the Tanganyika Council of women was formed in 1950 to bring all the racial sections together to see how to further "civilize" African women. In other words colonial mentality towards women matched the Haya cultural ideology.

While those women from the working families were being "Civilized", their fellow women were being recruited to plantations of coffee, sisal and tea as casual labourers and others were engaged in petty trades thus having access to personal income. What is to be noted here is that the African wives of the working men lost an opportunity. In the first place, when they finished class four (IV) and class eight (8) they had very limited chances for further education when compared to boys. In Bukoba for example while there were eight upper primary schools (classes 5–8) at several catholic and lutheran parishes, there were only two of those for girls in the region. There was no girls' secondary school in the region until 1965. At national level there were equally a few girls secondary schools to go to. By that period, 1930s to early 1960s, class eight was the highest grade women could go. Those were prepared for teaching and nursing professions and a few went into community development (Bibi Maendeleo). Many of them are now retired.

It becomes important to take note of this historical error for domestic wives of all classes in urban settings. In most cases they are migrants. For example while in Bukoba, Mama Koku would be expected to perform her farm duties such as weeding, planting beans and yams and bambara nuts so that when she comes home on leave with her family she should be proud to eat her own food. But if Mama Koku lived with her husband in town as she did, this entailed that her husband had to send money home to take care of the coffee-banana farm. Alternatively the wife would have had to shuttle during agricultural seasons between town and village. Urban non-working wives have continued to live as if that is all they could be. Their potential for self-reliance has recently begun to be exploited but there is no proper trace of the many women who are not yet able to find their proper position in urban settings. It is through traces of life histories and economic activities of women that mobilization of their energies can be successfully done. It will be empty rhetoric to talk of women's access to income without analysing the circumstances in which they live with a view to changing that reality and to opening a way for their liberation.

In the TNA records mentioned earlier on, it has been found out that in court cases (1940s – 1950s) where women fought against male kins for property rights, the courts did not lower the claims of women. Of course there were other struggles between women and the colonial regime with the latter seeking to take over women's businesses (Mbilinyi Marjorie, 1984) and this was fought by the indigenous population in defence of women. It will be appreciated that in order to trace the nature of changing life and work for women in the cities it is necessary to trace their origins and the purposes which cause their migration to towns and the fate which befall them. Some women are single while others are married but success had mostly been difficult to come by without great sacrifices.

PART II

The Life History of Mama Koku

I was born on 5th May, 1938 at Kagondo hospital in Kianja division. I am the first born of the family of Mr. & Mrs. Kazi from Kitendagulo village Itahwa division. We are only three children, two girls and one boy. I lived with my parents all the time except when I was at the boarding school. In 1946 I went to school, grade one near our home until 1949. Thereafter, I joined an upper boarding school at Kashozi, for class five to eight. I completed the primary school grades in 1953 and I had no further chance to continue. Therefore, I had to stay in the village with my parents helping them as necessary.

The village of Kitendagulo was relatively rich and not very far from Bukoba town (5 km.). Our family was also relatively richer than others. We had six acres of land with bananas and coffee trees as well as three cows.

In the family, we did not have much work really. We had enough bananas and so agricultural work outside our farm was not much. Also we had paid labourers. I can hardly remember fetching water from the river while I was in upper school. I remember that I never had problems with food, clothing, school fees and needs.

As a girl in the home, I was a bit coyish. Many times I refused to go with other girls to places as we were near the urban area. I did not think it was necessary to roam streets. My auntie would come home to reproach me and to tell my mother that I was unbelievably anti-social. This did not change me because I had made up my mind that it was lazy talk and walk. So, I would walk home straight from Church. There was no strict control from my parents because Sundays were left free for all. Normally girls would meet their boyfriends near their homes or while coming from Church services. These times were the only chances for meeting because other week days were reserved for farms and other work.

My parents were also from relatively rich families. My father for example was a son of a chief while my mother was a daughter of a well-known man, a former employee of the District Commissioner. My mother was among the first graduates of Kashozi Upper boarding Primary School, which I joined later. She had completed class eight and became very keen on girls' education. Herself and her sister, who later became a teacher, completed school and insisted that their children should go to school. Even the Dutch headmistress of the school was happy to receive children of her former students. She loved us as her grandchildren.

However things changed when another headmistress took over She did not like the girls from rich or chiefly families. In fact she encouraged those who were poor and those who seemed to be very Christian to do better and to qualify for further training and other jobs even though they were not necessarily brilliant. A number of girls met this unfortunate treatment. But my mother said I should be satisfied with the education I had. She said going overlake (across Lake Victoria) may bring you the misfortune of getting pregnant. It was shameful to get pregnant before marriage. My mother told me that other women were illiterate and she was tired of reading letters or writing for them. My mother would then sing a song for us in appreciation of having her children going to school amidst village rediicule that girls were useless to educate because they should learn to do home chores and get married, This is the song which I think all school children were later taught:

Asiyependa shule ni mjinga kabisa
Barua ikija, huitembeza pote ...

If one wanted to go for further training one had to be nominated by the school or to have a working relative overlake, which I did not have. We did not have many relatives.

During that time, I was considered a highly educated girl. I was equally expected to behave differently from unschooled girls. Everybody also expected me to be employed as a teacher or a nurse or to continue with training. If I married, then my destiny was to marry an educated man who was certainly employed with prospects of being rich. None of the educated girls thought of marrying a village boy whom we called "ensimbulano" or who had not gone to school. We were really building castles in the air. I stayed with my parents for one year after the upper school. The following year I got a prospective husband and we got married a year later, in 1955. Like all girls I was excited to get married especially to an employed man.

The Traditional Set Up

In the traditional Haya society women are automatically dependants of men by virtue of working on non-cash jobs and they are subservient to their whims. However, on the other hand, a woman is a property while a man represents power and protection. It was never envisaged that a woman owned property before first marriage unless she inherited two or three coffee trees from her late father or so.

There are no short cuts to explain this situation other than the fact that property belongs to the clan so that if a woman owns property she may transfer it to another clan which is her marital connection. Property in those days was considerd to be land, a house, domestic animals and other household tools such as a bicycle, and farm tools. Property was a function of hardwork. Men inherited land and were expected to add more to that or to improve it. Women did not inherit, but worked much harder and they were not expected to ðwn any property. In the event of broken marriages a woman was expected to just pack her clothing and leave. She was not even allowed to sell her produce or even transfer it. Coming to think of it today, it was hell. Nobody ever put herself/himself in the shoes of a divorced woman. Nobody, even today shares her feelings, pains and even to fight back with her. Many times, even her sisters and mother in law are against her. What I am telling you is true. I remember my sister in law. She is now divorced from my brother. I struggled to enable her get access to her children. That has earned me an expensive price, to lose my friendship with my brother! That's it my daughter, we no longer talk! Last time, we met in town and brushed shoulders! But thanks to my late mother, she had warned me. She saw my ailing marriage while my sister and brother were propertied. This is what she said to me:

> "... be careful, I will not live
> long, but I can see that your
> father cares for property from
> his other children. When I am
> dead, they may discriminate
> you. Only try your best..."

I tried then to take care of my father with the little I had. I would send sugar and even go to see him in Bukoba. Upon his death, he pronounced his will; it was not in writing. He said:

> "... I leave my house and part
> of my farm to the girls
> including their step mother
> and I leave part of the plot
> to the boy..."

This did not please my brother at all. But theoretically, as girls, we had won the day. A share in the family property, including a house for girls when the boy is there was very unusual. If our brother wants trouble, he may disturb this arrangements through customary law of which I know very little But this is the present situation.

Married Life History

Mine is a long story. I am really not anxious to repeat it because I am glad it is over. The only thing I am happy about are my children and that upon death my husband reconciled with me. He said at his last hour:

> "... if I were to come back
> I would apologize to my wife
> and treat her kindly, I wouldn't
> do what I did no her..."
> (here we cried together)

I started married life early in 1955 at the age of 17 years. I was really excited to marry a man of my expectations who at that time was a teacher. It meant travelling to various places, it meant living a life different from the village girls and other women.

Our married life was bright from the start. At wed day as it is tradition, I got a lot of presents from my relatives and mother's friends. The presents are normally household items for the kitchen. So I got many of these items. I got clothes as well as money. I did not have in my mind the wish for more property than those items. I considered myself set to join my husband and start a new life although I did not know how.

My husband was a teacher in Tabora so from Bukoba our first station was Tabora. That was my first time to meet other ethnic groups. I did not mix much besides knowing other teachers' wives. In 1957–1958 we were in Kasulu and in 1959/61 we were in Kibondo (Kigoma region). These two places were very backward compared to all the places I had seen. There wasn't much to talk about. From there we moved to Newala in 1962 where my husband became a District Officer and that was the beginning and the end of his administrative career. In the same year he decided to do law studies, so we moved to Morogoro where he studied law at Mzumbe to become a magistrate.

In 1964 he became a magistrate and we moved to Masasi in Southern Tanganyika. As a magistrate he had to move after every six months to avoid people befriending him and offering him bribes. In 1965 we moved to Musoma and later in the year we moved to Maswa. In Musoma we stayed near the lake away from other people. There were four houses only.

In 1966 we moved to Mbulu where we stayed for almost a year before moving to Arusha in 1967. Before a year elapsed we moved to Moshi. Accommodation set up was segregated so it was very difficult to meet with people. I would only go out with my husband and children with our car. We stayed in Moshi for two years because there was now a policy for magistrates to move after two years and not in every six months. Finally in 1969 we moved to Dar es Salaam. Unfortunately we did not live in harmony in Dar es Salaam until when he died in 1980. The causes of family disharmony were sawn while we were still in Moshi when he got another woman. So as we finished our trips, our peace ended as well.

You can see for yourself that my life was my husband's working life. I am sure that is not the same for all women who are married to working men. In 14 years we covered almost the whole country. I got tired of packing and unpacking. I also wondered why we had so many transfers. I sometimes thought he was a stubborn man. I really became fed up. My dilemma was twofold. One was that, we did not have a home of our own or a farm where I would go back to. Secondly, I had a duty to be with my husband. It was upon him to decide whether I should be in the village or with him. So we lived together until when he died in 1980.

Economic Activities

I learnt to do embroidery when I was in upper primary school. In the home I did quite a lot of embroidery and sold it. The money I got helped in the upkeep of the family. In fact during the colonial period African women were being encouraged to learn sewing, knitting and embroidery work. The wives of the colonial staff taught these skills. African women on the other hand were engaged in agriculture, beer brewing, making scones and *chapatis* for sale. They also did handicrafts, and other decorations.

When I moved to Tabora I joined women groups which were sewing and doing embroidery work. We taught each other all sorts of styles and learnt from white women too. Finally we sold our products and divided the proceeds, about 300 shs. among ourselves.

Husbands were not against women going to these clubs to learn "civilized" skills. It was politics in which wives of workers were not allowed to participate since our husbands were allowed too. Women encouraged each other to join groups and learn skills as a way of uplifting themselves. In many of the stations we moved to, I taught girls to sew: for example in Kigoma - at Mwibuye Middle School; in Newala while my husband was a district officer I taught women about sewing and child care as well as environmental sanitation. All in all, in all the stations we lived, I did not interact with women adequately to my household demands. I also noted that while women in Newala were very poor, women in Maswa and Moshi were very active in groups and made money. After the Colonial period, women welfare centres became inactive.

During the period between 1955-1968 working people were regarded as lucky and rich especially if they had a car. We fell in the same trap. We had nothing else besides our car and household items. My husband expected to inherit property (land) from his father, which he did. But for me, I was always to depend on what he was doing. When I moved to Dar es Salaam in 1969 things really changed. And this is what I call the second phase of my married life which not only showed me the other side of the coin, but taught me what it meant to be a dependent wife.

I found women were economically better off. All my neighbours were either working or having projects here and there. The women were not complaining of want of basic needs while I was. At this time, my options were very few. In the first place, I would not secure a respectable job now, something I would have got in the 1950s and early 1960s. Even if I wanted to, my husband was not willing to let me do so. What surprised me most was the fact that he was not able to support us comfortably and neither to establish a project for me. I started thinking very seriously about my role in the family. I thought of all women in the villages and women in the towns who were doing petty trade. Soon I realized that I was stranded partly because of my husband's status. But it was all up to me either to enjoy his status or to support myself and my children. I immediately started a project of making baskets.

The money I got from the sale of baskets was used for home upkeep. We bought extra food which my husband did not provide. I could not go beyond this. In 1979 my husband went on a trip and left exactly ten (10) shillings for his six children for two weeks. It then dawned on me that he was speaking a language which I had not understood all this time. In fact it all appeared devilish. You sit down and imagine a man giving you ten shillings for six children! Earlier on, he had ordered me to remove from his grounds the few chicken I was rearing. When he was away, I ran around to look for a possible project which would give us more money. A neighbour gave me a helping hand. She said: do not wait, if need be I will give your husband a piece of mind.

It was like a miracle when I talked to him. Perhaps he felt guilty while he was away. I applied for a loan of 1,000/- from him, and permission to rear chicken in his grounds. He did not fight me. Instead he said, give me three days. After those days he gave me an advance of 1,000/- not as a loan but as starting capital. He said:

"... this is not a loan, go and
try, if you succeed alright,
if you do not that is up to you..."

This was good news to friends and relatives alike. They all promised to help me in one way or another. For example my brother offered to buy the fencing wire, and my sister and friends gave me a little money each. Soon everything was in full swing. We started with 100 chicken and realized a profit of 4000/-. It encouraged me so much. I was ever thinking that he would one day stop my project. Luckily he did not. However, when he went on leave in the village he told his relatives that I loved my children and that I was thinking of building for them and not building at my paternal home! This gave me an idea that my husband and I had really become two, not one. My relatives were not happy about the way he treated us. They always insisted that I leave him. I refused this advice. I paid a price of losing friendship with my only sister on that issue. I guess then that he thought I was waiting to snatch his money before I left so that I could build a home at my father's ground.

Many times, I had advised him on the need to build a home before he retired. This discussion always earned me trouble with serious beating and complete silence in the home sometimes over weeks. Then the time came when the weaker became stronger. My husband fell sick and he was not recovering. The more the sick he was the more unfriendly and aggressive he became to me even while on his hospital bed. One day he took 2,500/- and gave it to me with the following instructions.

"... take this money and help
your children and your project
so that you may build for the
children because I was irresponsible
and now my health is ailing..."

At that time our family life was extremely bad such that I feared it would affect the children's thinking and future. I am now trying to change or at least influence them positively towards family life and the economic role of each spouse. My economic position was now changing but it needed reinforcement. My real luck at this difficult time was that he had seen to it that his children had properly attended school and even went into secondary school. Three of them had finished form IV. One of them, a boy, was in high school. He is the one I personally felt that his father did not give him due attention at that time because he was not happy with his studies. The children got his personal tuition during their studies and they were clever. This is one of the things that he did very well. Even before his death he taught the last born until one month before he died. You can see that he gave a foundation to their present lives.

As soon as he relized that I was becoming economically sound, and that when he came home we would give him food which he never bought, it annoyed him! For him this was a success story of his enemy number one. Unfortunately, he did not see this as a success of his children. As a response to this, or to recover his contributions, he handed over to me all the electricity and water bills he had not settled for several months which amounted to 3,500/-. I went to pay the bills triumphantly. I was also proud to feed my children. Two of my daughters had also finished school and started working in 1976 and 1979 respectively. He had assigned them to provide for tea and laundry in the home respectively without regard to their incomes or future lives.

In 1980 the father of my children died, sick and tired of seeing us. God knows it all. As I said, he repented his sins and pleased me. I attended him till the last hour to fulfil the demands of matrimony. May God rest him in peace. After all these events, there was no insurance or pension benefits left on his account as it had been spent elsewhere. The escort we had given him during his working career was just a waste of time. A real waste my sister. One does not realize this until it happens. We learn by mistakes but it is painfull. Two of my children had not finished school as well when he died but we pulled through. In such a case whom does one take to court? No one. We learn to begin doing things in a different way though too late.

Supporting my Family

I considered my self a retired worker and insisted that the nation should recognize that. Behind my late husband who earnestly served the nation for 27 years, was a woman who deserved a pension. It was like a joke but I appealed to all those who had the goodwill and the understanding. One of them being President Nyerere. I only needed recognition on behalf of other women toiling in the domestic enclaves. Other men joked me around. But I tell you again, the President absorbed every word I told him. I told him that I needed a plot to construct my house and that I needed permission to retain the government house until I finished building. He granted me all these and promised to see me to the end of my struggles as far as building was concerned. But he added: 'never commit the blunder of selling the house:' He then allowed a 100,000 TAS cheque for me! This was a bigger pension than my late husband's 53,000/-. So when one says that Mwalimu Nyerere understands and cares about women's problem it is true. Women should use this concern and support to air our main problems.

The chicken project was and still is our saviour. One of my daughters was in a private secondary school so we had to pay for her form IV expenses. Another daughter was to join a government secondary school later. We also paid for all the expenses from the project. She has now finished and joined the National Service. Hopefully she will join the University. The building project is still continuing. You know one can't build fast unless one is a business woman. Our chicken project, as I told you before, is besset by financial problems which then affect my building speed. As a result my daughter who is a secretary has to help. I am glad you have told me about credit arrangements by the Women's Corporation. But as I requested you, please help me to get to the right person because to be true to you, I do not trust that women of my class can get so much help without problems. Besides, I am tired and sick of building for long. The prices are going up and one loses the energy. After building, I will plan what else to be done because as long as the chicken project survives my survival is guaranteed.

Patching up With Lost Friends

I was telling you that I lost the friendship of my only brother and sister. I am their elder sister and the least educated. They are rich. I am not. During my early troubles, they first sympathized and then got fed up. Surely, there is a limit to what one can do in a given circumstance, but with these two friends we differed on what was to be done. I should have gone back to the village to support the aging parents and these rich ones would have given me financial support. But as I said earlier, this was not my line of thinking. My brother had divorced his first wife with whom we were friends and I could understand her feelings about her children who were left behind and were being mistreated by their step mother. So I had to help them in the little possible way I could. After all they are my children also. But my brother saw me as enemy number two because I supported his former wife, who was his enemy number one. Then as for my sister, she had once married a rich man and divorced him but she was not denied seeing her children and she had a job. Using her own experience she saw divorce as an easy matter.

I am not sure what would have become of me if I had left my husband. I argued with my conscience like this: that this man will have won if I gave him the chance to bring a wife in this home. So, much as I am not the winner either, my children should not suffer alone. I must awaken and find some better ways of living.

Now that I have almost made ends meet, and as the eldest of the three, perhaps I should seek reunion because in Africa no one stays alone, outside the clan. But after three years of silence, nobody is interested in me. I feel like acting proudly as well, to sit down and forget them. I am sure I will find many other friends. As for my husband's clansmen, I have not much to share with them. I lived away most of the time and my husband rarely went home. Now that he is no more I do not want to pretend to go to his piece of land. That land now belongs to my son for whom I have the greatest responsibility to see to it that he recovers properly and begins to live like others. He had been badly affected. I also have to see my daughters through. I hope though that I will give them good lessons to become independent women and loving mothers if they get children.

Lessons Learned

When I revisit my life I do not altogether regret. In the village some women who get fed up with mistreatment and lack of economic support run to towns to do petty trade and prostitution. Projects which are affordable in town like my chicken project or building a home are not possible in the village. It was a good thing that I chose to persevere with my children in town. I cannot predict the results if I had done otherwise. Right now, I have enough experience and confidence to maintain my family alone.

I now think that women should be economic leaders in the family because they can own property and bring wealth in many ways for the benefit of the family. The time element is also important on changes taking place. I am of the opinion that mothers should educate their daughters not to enter marriages empty handed. They should have projects somewhere before they get married so that they can face other challenges courageously. Projects could be started as small activities like sewing, animal farming, baking and other trades. Later on they should enter into investments. I hope my life history will give light to many other women who are either stranded like I was or intended to enter marriages empty handed. Thank you my daughter.

PART III

On Theoretical Framework

Gender: An African Problematic

Theoretically, we find that the question of African women is explained within the theories of underdevelopment, class and strata, patriarch and neo-colonialism. We go through all those theories when we read the story of Mama Koku. During the last two decades, feminists have also argued for the use of gender as an analytical category which does not treat women as independent actors but as influenced persons who undeniably and like all species, live in interaction with others. The arising nature of relations which exist between the male and female genders in production and reproduction should be analysed within the gender analytical framework as an issue. The outcome is that regardless of the colonial oppression and underdevelopment, regardless of class and strata, gender applies in all circumstances.

The life historian was concerned about the interpretation of her labour input and material formation in the life of the household. What was the value of her labour power and how can one account for it? From that account of her life the dilemma of most African women is also posed and a challenge has to be faced by economists and economic historians to explain the African economic phenomena in its proper context.

In otherwords, a gap still exists which should be filled by explaining the African materialist phenomenology. A systematic account of household systems and how property is created and by whom is still urgently required. Social relations of production and ownership of the means of production are always criticized when discussing the exploitation of the toiling masses by capitalism. It is also echoed when developed countries are reminded of how they exploit developing countries but not how those developing countries exploit women. The question which life histories raise, particularly in this chapter is the process of material formation which we call materialist phenomenology in Africa. If the process of material creation is the same with historical materialism why then doesn't African states especially those of the socialist type, create special socialism for women in their countries? In other words, an analysis which not only gives women place, but also a take-off point is urgently required.

The life historian is advancing her cause. She is not telling her story for its own sake, she is convinced that somehow something should be done about it. The climax of her struggles are relevant to material formation and control not only within the middle strata in which she was affiliated but also to the peasant women, domestic servants and even women affiliated to the high class. Apparently, the fate of these women become similar. A woman labours in the domestic enclave in town while undertaking small projects to support the family. Ironically this income is disregarded. The wage of a domestic servant is calculated under the minimum pay criteria. High class women are instrumental in guarding their husband's properties and may never be directly involved in its formation. All these women's lives are characterized by not realizing or having claim to anything which represents their expended labour. In African countries the critical point to support the above asertion is that when a man dies his relatives invade the house claiming to take everything (property). A lot of unrecorded incidents of this nature are well known and manipulated by the cultural practices – under the logic that even the woman herself is "property" to be acquired by one of the male relatives, therefore how can property (woman) acquire property? i.e. land, cattle, other items.

Another dimension arises and this has to do with family, gender and property relations. During the working life of men and women in a household, property is never divided to identify the owners of each item. It it taken for granted by outsiders that the man must be the owner. When the wife dies, her relatives do not come to claim her properties assuming that she had nothing to do with property or that it would be unbecoming to do so. It is posited finally that women's history both political, economic and cultural should provide a challenge to dominant history to unravel the cultural manipulations. This historical approach must give strength to the demands being made by women in all spheres. Access to credit and resources as well as real democracy for women may help to cause change in life improvement and must therefore be strengthened. Third world nations with particular reference to Tanzania are reviewing the strengths and weaknesses of their economies. It is mere logic perhaps that Economic Recovery Programmes especially structural adjustments should consider the release of women's potential in supporting the economic recovery of the household as a basic unit of production. It should be emphasized that more life histories should be recorded depicting the economic lives of women in all spheres in order to be able to write a correct historical materialist phenomenology and to change it in the favour of all those who toil. Such an approach should avoid stereotypes by using practice to inform theory and reshape theory by re-examining practice at various conjectures. A question which still buffles the world is: How do African households survive? If they survive because of women's labour then we have to put those words more clearly to liberate those who toil and to improve their conditions (See also Mies 1986). The process of re-situating a correct African Materialist Phenomena should also engage gender analysis in order to arrive at correct conclusions.

The story also raises another question of resisting divorce or separation by women. The household seems a fragile than a solid entity. Women are permanently potential refugees throughout their lives unless their husbands die first. Mama Koku refused to leave her marital home like many other women at the risk of being battered and dehumanized. The broarder question then which this issue raises is the right of the individual on a day to day basis. African societies close or resolve these problems with divorce. One would like to suggest here that women should be reconsidered in the national welfare laws and marriage contracts. Women, it would seem logical, should be the ones to retain the matrimonial homes when marriages can no longer hold on grounds of wife and children battering. Our experiences have recorded enough of battered wives seeking accommodation at the aunties, uncles, friends and neighbours. It is an inconvenience which another gender needs to experience or to learn to solve.

The life of a woman is full of many issues one may wish to discuss. But this has been left for everyone to do so in order to generate many independent views. We are aware also that in households there are many other important issues and trivial which give life to a marriage, but all we are seeing here in this story is the powerlessness of a partner in a so called contract and we wish this contract, the marriage law to be reconsidered.

References

AAWORD: Seminar on Research on African Women: What type of methodology? December 5th–9th, 1983, Dakar.

Ba Mariam 1982: *So long a letter,* London, Virago Press.

Babu, A.M.: 1981 *African Socialism or Socialist Africa?* Dar es Salaam, T.P.H

Bader, Zinnat K. 1975. "Women, private property and production in Bukoba District." Unpublished M.A. dissertation, University of Dar es Salaam.

Campbell, Horace: "The Impact of Walter Rodney and Progressive Scholars on the Dar es Salaam School." Paper presented at History Research Seminar (Series) 20th March, 1986. History Dept. University of Dar es Salaam.

Culwick, Arthur, T.: "The land tenure in the Bukoba District" in: Culwick, A.T. The population problem in the Bukoba District, Bukoba, 1938 (Cory file 239)

Dumont, Rene, 1966: *False start in Africa,* London *Sphere* Book.

Freire, Paulo: 1977: *Pedagogy of the Oppressed.* New York, Penguin Books,

Geiger, S.: "Life history research", Dar es Salaam, University WRDP Paper No, 1, 1985.

Geiger, Susan.:Women in nationalist struggle: Dar es Salaam's TANU Activities – a preliminary research report presented to the History Dept. Seminar November 22nd, 1984. University of Dar es Salaam.

International Labour Organization: Basic Needs in Danger: A basic needs oriented development strategy for Tanzania Addis Ababa, ILO – Jobs and Skills Programme for Africa, 1982, p. xxiii – 13.

Jipemoyo 1/1977 edited by Marja-Liisa Swantz and Helena Jerman. Dar es Salaam,

Tanzania. Ministry of National Culture and Youth. Dept. of Research and Planning.

Leslie, J.A.K. 1957: *A Survey of Dar es Salaam,* London, 1963.

Marx, Karl: Karl, Marx, Social Economist, edited by William R. Waters *Review of SOcial Economy.* Vol. XXXVII, December 1979. (Special issue). New York. Association for Social Economics, (various articles).

Mascarenhas, O. & Mbilinyi M. 1983: *Women in Tanzania: An analytical bibliography.* Uppsala: Scandinavian Institute of African Studies,

Mbilinyi, Marjorie "City' and Countryside' in Colonial Tanganyika" Paper presented to WRDP seminar, October, 1985. University of Dar es Salaam.

Mies, Maria 1986: *Patriarchy and Accumulation on a word scale; Women in the International division of labour,* London, Zed Books Ltd.,

Mustafa, Kemal: Notes towards the construction of a materialist phenomenology for socialist Development Research on the Jipemoyo Project. In *Jipemoyo: Development and Culture Research 1/1977. op. cit.* p. 33-54.

Smith, Barbara (ed.) 1983: Home Girls: a Black Feminist Anthology. New York, Kitchen table. Women of Color Press Inc.

Stead, Filomena C. "Research Methodology and investigative framework for Social change: The case of African Women" In AAWORD 1983, *op. cit.* p. 12-21.

Tibaijuka, A. 1988: The Impact of Structural Adjustment Programmes on Women; the case of Tanzania. A report for CIDA. Dar es Salaam.

Tanganyika Annual Summaries of the Department of Education 1925-1964. Dar es Salaam.

Voice of America: Interview with eight American women of achievement: Grace Hopper, Betty Friedman, Maya Angelou and others by Chantal Mompoullan of the Africa Field Service 1983-84. Produced for the UN-Decade of Women, 1985 Voice of America.

Waane, S. "Material Culture". Paper presented at a Workshop on Culture and Development" organized by the Ministry of Community Development and Youth. March 1985. Dar es Salaam.

Workshop on the Aspects of Social History held at Ruskin College, Oxford U.K. 27th July – 7th August, 1985 – a report by Anne Nkebukwa.

Archival Materials

Bukoba District Book (MF 56 – 58)
Dar es Salaam District Book Vol. 1-II (MF 30)
Haya tribe (MF 56)
Zaramo (MF 56)

Court Cases

13/14	Clementine Timothio	vs	Juma bin Simba
14/44	Fatuma Pazi	vs	John Rupia
12/44	Salim Kiranga	vs	Fatuma Nyembo

561/10/51	Said Salim	vs	Salima Mohamed (1941)
561/5/47	Madina Hatibu	vs	Fatma Saruru (1941)
561/10/50	Athman Pembe	vs	Asha Binti Kondo (1941)
561/DNE/4/44			

re: DNEB. 1800/1974 Mgeni binti Hamisi vs Mwajuma binti Kheri (1941)

| 561/5/45 | Muhamad Juma | vs | Mtumwa Muhamed (1941) |
| 561/B. 1298/44 | Mashavu binti Salim | vs | Representative of Miss Mashavu. |

TNA File Nos For Further Reading

67.	CD/CR/ML/55	1965–68	Mass Education Among Women
76.	CD/CR/KCD/31	1962–65	Kisarawe District Comm. Dev.
78.	CR/CR/KKW	1965–67	Community Dev. Kisarawe
99.	CD/CR/WA/75	1961–69	Women Activities
105.	CD/DD/40	1965–68	Kariakoo Zone
106.	CD/DD/41	"	Kinondoni Zone
107.	CD/DD/46	"	Kigamboni Zone
166.	CD/MCC/60	1965–69	Msimbazi Community Centre
244.	CDD/23	1964–68	U.W.T.
346.	DD6	"	Women's group
377.	EPLUC/404	1951–51	Land settlement
379.	HC/5	1954–59	Housing Committee
460.	T.3/5031	1954–58	Trade + Industry – Kigamboni Market
552.	3/1	1954–56	Native affairs – Distressed & Native Laws
573.	3/37/11	1956–58	Native affairs – Property
575.	3/37	1950–51	Native affairs – Personal Matters
580.	3/38/A	1956	Native Court Cases
608.	3/85	1950–52	Bahaya Union – UDSM Branch
904.	18/3	1947–48	Pop. census – Native – non-native

All files above year 1945 were still closed against public consumption. These could have more information.

CHAPTER SIX

Grassroot Struggles for Women's Advancement: the Story of Rebeka Kalindile

Rebeka Kalindile and Marjorie Mbilinyi with Tusajigwe Sambulika

Introduction

This history is about my life (Rebeka Kalindile's) and that of my familiy, friends and neighbours in Rungwe where I was born and have lived for most of my life. Rungwe is located in the mountains overlooking Lake Nyasa in what was once called the Southern Highlands Province. Masoko, where I was born, is the heartland of the Nyakyusa people. It's just down the road, only a few miles from Katusyo.

When I was born in 1914, Rungwe was still suffering from the scourges of the First World War which was fought on our soil by African troops on behalf of the British and the Germans. The Germans maintained local rule by means of an army base in Masoko (my home place) along with their (*akida*) government officers after the military conquest of local rulers in the 1880s and 1890s. Many of the stories which I learned from old men in my family were about the battles fought with the Germans in the 1880s by those waNyakyusa 'Princes' who resisted the occupation.

German missionaries and settler farmers took away much of the most fertile land to grow coffee and do mixed farming by then, and were allowed by the British to return to their farms and plantations after the war. Land began to get scarce for us waNyakyusa. People also had to farm more in order to meet money expenses which included head taxes levied against all men who had reached fifteen years of age, licences and fines and the new manufactured goods like cloth and kerosene. Cash money was needed to purchase nearly everything – though we still bartered among ourselves for vegetables, maize and other basics.

At the time of my puberty rights (unyago), money had already become an essential part of our existence. New crops like coffee were being grown because there was a local market structure ready to buy them for export to Europe. Our relatives went to work on the sisal plantations in Tanga and the Lupa goldfields in Chunya during the 1920' and 1930, and our sons and nephews worked as miners on the Copperbelt in Zambia in the 1950s. All of us spent some time, especially when young, weeding or harvesting or working in the factory of the coffee and later the tea plantations bordering our village. Many boys paid for their school fees by plucking tea during holidays and weekends, and many women began to earn enough to buy themselves khanga (cloth) wraps.

The Moravian church was a very significant part of local history, and remains a central aspect of our society. The European missionaries were located in Rungwe Mission, many miles to the south, and at Rutengano and Kyimbila which were closer. Our local church was part of Kyimbila congregation which connected several villages together; our women's groups carried out many activities together, including the competition in arts and crafts described in this chapter. We had our own catechist school which was named 'Kitusyo School' by our pastor, Rev. Mwankemwa. Our village now gets its name from this old school, which formerly provided one or two years of reading, writing and arithmetic. The school has since become part of the government school system and reaches Standard 7.

When we were little, most of us learned how to read and write at the church schools (often called 'bush' schools in the literature) and by reading the church catechism and hymnal. Very few boys got the chance to go on with their schooling, and no girls in my generation. Most women didn't even know how to read or speak in Kiswahili.

I came here to live, with my husband's people when I was still only a little girl – my mother carried me on her back, like my fellow co-wife who was married at the same time. *I* was the *senior* wife; another, third wife, joined us later, who was the same age as our own children. She now lives in Mbeya where one of her sons built her a house. My fellow wife and I remained here in Katusyo, living in our late husband's compound – though he died several years ago and the farms are now owned by our sons. Tusajigwe Sambulika, my eldest and sole living daughter, owns nothing and never will, because she is a woman.

I am a fulltime peasant farmer, though nowadays I can't work any longer on the farm – just too weak and frail with my coughing and old age. I have done many other things as well – most of the babies delivered in this village were delivered by me while I was practising as the local village midwife. I used to be a leading organiser of women's groups in Katusyo, and travelled all over our district and even down to Kyela as part of our church activities. I taught women not only in Katusyo, but also in a neighbouring village, not only about handicrafts and modern housekeeping, but also about being a good Christian wife and maintaining a stable family. Learning how to be a good Christian wife was not easy in polygamous households, but helped us to keep our men.

Much of what I know was learned from my own experience. Traditional midwifery began with bearing my own children – I hid in the bush and delivered some of my own alone, with no assistance. None of the babies delivered by me had 'accidents' at childbirth, which makes me very proud – they all survived the first moments at least. As for me, there were a total of nine children, but four of them died during the first year or two of life, and one when she was already grown up. This is still very painful for me. I remember each one of them, the day they were born, the day they died, their ages, how they looked.

Story-telling is another of my basic skills and hobbies. Being known as one of the most competent story–teller around gives me great pleasure. I had to learn to pay attention, to make use of my natural curiosity in order to find out things, and to remember facts about events which often happened long before I was grown up. This skill in story-telling became important in the production of this work.

It's important to include a description of Marjorie Mbilinyi in this introduction. As the producer of this text, she has had a major influence on its contents: challenging me with questions, asking for more details, encouraging me to tell more of my stories. Mbilinyi was born in New York, USA, in 1943 (around the time of my youngest daughter, the one I lost. – Marjorie seems to have come to take her place, and maybe it's mutual, since she lost her mother when she was 16 years old). She came to Tanzania to get married to her fiancee in 1967, and became a citizen of Tanzania and bore her first child in that year. Her husband is a mNgoni from Songea, a mtani or joking relation because we waNyakyusa, fought wars with waNgoni in the old days. Mbilinyi gave birth to only four children, but three have survived compared to my four out of nine. Her youngest, and the only boy, died just after reaching a year of age; this is a painful subject for Marjorie as for me, but the death of children is still too common in our country, which is why we agreed to include the stories of these deaths in our writing.

Young women these days don't want to bear many children the way we did, even our sons don't want it. Too expensive, and more of them survive these days.

Besides being a wife and a mother, Mbilinyi teaches at the University of Dar es Salaam. She's been doing research and writing about issues concerning women for many years now, along with education and agriculture reform.

My eldest daughter, Tusajigwe Sambulika, who was born in 1932, has also influenced the writing of this text. Sambulika helped, not so much with translations, but rather to elaborate or explain some of my points which depended on familiarity with our Nyakyusa culture and history. She also participated in our debates which are recorded verbatim.

My daughter has lived in Dar es Salaam, Moshi, Mbeya town, Sumbawanga, even the Copperbelt in Zambia and in Lusaka, before returning to live in Tukuyu and more recently with me, here in Katusyo. She is presently separated from her last husband, and has her youngest daughter with her. Out of six children, five have survived – the others are either grown up and working and/or married or enrolled in post-primary education. Sambulika does all the farming for two of us, making use of land that her younger brothers have shared with her. She also plaits mats to sell locally, and was formerly an active member of one of the most successful women's cooperatives in Tukuyu town. Right now she's been staying with me to help nurse me through my bad spells of coughing.

We'll go into more details about the way we wrote this text in the last section. However, let me emphasise that most of our conversations were held in Kiswahili. I taught myself Kiswahili when I was still a relatively young woman, while visiting my oldest son's family in Tanga, by talking to people and by reading the Kiswahili Bible along with our Kinyakyusa catechism.

My Childhood

My parents recounted that I was just learning to sit on my own when the First World War came to Rungwe. We saw the Germans withdraw with our very own eyes from their base camp in Masoko. Formerly many soldiers stayed there. Later, the Germans and the British came to an agreement among themselves in Europe and the former were allowed to return, but only as subjects of the British.

We are told stories about the hardships during that war, especially for men. The youngest, strongest men were forced to carry head-loads of arms, ammunition and other things during the German's retreat. Many never returned – we heard that some died of fever, others of hunger, and still others were shot during the battle. We lost many young men as a result of the European's war.

There were no cars in those days. There was one German, I'll tell you, 'Mwaisumo', who tortured many people. He forced men to carry him from Busokelo, around Manow Mission, all the way to Mwakaleli, more than twenty Kilometres away. He refused to walk on his own two feet and insisted on being carried on a stretcher up and down the mountains. His fierceness and cruelty was widely known. If he met a person on the way, he would command his servants to put him down immediately, and he always would shout, "Don't let me fall down!" Nevertheless, Mwaisumo was a missionary; he was supposed to preach the word of God.

We never had European missionaries around our village; they were based in Rutengano. Our own teacher of catechism was a Malawian trained by European missionaries at the Lutheran Mission in Manow. The earliest Christians were mostly products of Manow.

My father

My father's maternal uncle (*mjomba*) was still a chief when I was born. If a cow wandered into our area, my father – being a rather rambunctuous youth – would grab the cow and take him to his uncle, the 'sultan'. Many had to be returned to the original owners, but some were retained by my father, and that's how he acquired lots of cattle. He never knew his own father, who died long ago; his uncle was responsible for him.

My father was a traditional herbalist; he knew about all sorts of medicines, partly because his uncle was always accompanied by a traditional healer ('mganga'). He was also an artisan and made wire bracelets and waistline bands. We knew all about the process by helping him to weld the metal. He himself wore six around his waist, others wore ten. Remember, in those days people dressed differently, they didn't wear the European clothes which people wear nowadays.

Every year he slaughtered a cow which was distributed to all of the family members. Long after we were married, we would all come home for the slaughter. A small calf would be slaughtered, roasted and consumed on the spot while waiting for the cow to be butchered, skinned and divided into portions. All five of us daughters received portions to take home with us to our husbands, including big hunks of meat from the legs. He'd keep adding more meat: "Put these in your basket! Return to your husbands ('mabwana')!" By then, I already had more than three children; my three eldest living children have all eaten meat provided by my father.

School and Baptism

My father was a pagan; he had four wives, though some left because of his ill-treatment and brutality. He used to beat them with a stick, but he was always gentle with me.

It seems to me now that I always yearned to be baptised from the time I was born. Our Malawian catechist teachers from Manow who came to replace the German missionaries for a short while after the war were very impressive. We had African missionaries then. They opened up their own schools and taught people how to read along with praying.

In those days, women were very inferior, much more so than today. Even in language, they were kept down. For example, they never learned German, only men did. The only men who learned German, however, were the domestic servants who worked as cooks in their homes. It wasn't the same then as it was later, under the British, who allowed English to spread around more widely.

One of the things that attracted me to Christianity was the European clothing – we all desired it. We wore barkcloth then, and our mothers carried us around in wraps made of soft leather which looked very attractive. At the time of my marriage (as a child), all I wore was the barkcloth of the banana tree, that's what we had in those days. To become Christian was to wear 'clothes'. "If I get married by a Christian I'll be able to wear clothes!" We used to say:

> Our fellow sisters had been married according to pagan ways and were not allowed to pray in the Chrisitan way. We were different! We were educated in school!

My mother was an extremely fine person. Way back then when teachers roamed around looking for pupils to go school, most parents hid their children in the lofts of their houses. My mother didn't hide me. Instead, she gave me permission to go – "Take this one!". She recognised that I was desperate to get an education. The teacher warned me, "There is a great deal of work to do," but I assured him "I want to study."

In general that's how I was (and am), very hard working. The only thing I was frightened of was getting caned. I was beaten only once at school. Other pupils often absconded from school or they stayed home, but I went to school every day. I didn't want to miss a single day! The minute the gong sounded, the ring we used to use as a bell – 'krrulupulupulupu – I would run to get there on time. I loved school. I studied enthusiastically at Mpata and had progressed very far because of my quickness to learn by the time our teacher moved. We were taught their language, English. They would say:

"Ahhh if you please sir [pronounced sah]. If you please sir."
"Yeeeeeeeeeeeeeessssssh" [they Kinyakyusa sssh intonation]
If you please sir."
'Yesh."

The meaning of all this was completely unknown to us – we repeated the words like parrots.

Mathematics was the real challenge! He gave us mental calculations to solve and I was first every time. He'd tell us,

114

All right. We are going to have how many things if I pick up a chicken at Manow, a cow at Kiigura, another chicken at Maskulu, and a chicken has two legs and one head, and a cow has four legs and one head and one tail? How many parts will there be?

I always was the one to get it! We would answer in English, we didn't know Kiswahili then. We used to say "twenty, thirty, fifty, hundred, thousand – one thousand fifty-four."

Our teacher was very pleased. If he said that was correct, well, I just went on talking and talking, and the boys went on making mistakes. The teacher would give me the cane and tell me, "Beat those fellows! They can't do it!" And I would beat them – something which makes me laugh now when I remember.

Baptism

I was baptized in 1930 when I was 16 years old, on October 5th. My father was extremely pleased – he respected me a great deal because of becoming a Christian. His fierceness has already been mentioned – my father was a hard man. If he was fighting with his wife and he saw me, he would shut up. Otherwise, should they continue to fight, I would speak out, "Be quiet," and the quarrel would stop. Father would say, "My child doesn't allow me to fight, she says that God will be angry with me." If his wife (my mother) heard all this, she'd rush to him complaining, "The girl has been disrespectful. Do you see this child!" but father would reply, "Rubbish. Shut up Mama Kalindile Leave her alone, let her continue."

If Mother still didn't listen and Father got angry, I would tell him, "Ohhh Father, Father you're being a fool." mother would get so angry, she'd tell me, "You're just taking your father's side." All of this because she said that I was interfering when I told Father to stop fighting. The problem was that when I did speak, Farther was able to stop, whereas mother was still boiling with rage. She was quarrelsome. If I criticised her for going wrong, she would get furious and denounce me to Father, but he refused to listen to her. She really wanted to silence me. When he was gone, she'd come and tell me, "Be quiet my child." She would scold me! All my mothers, the co-wives thought he was a fool because of the way he tolerated my views. What especially got Mother angry was his failure to take her side when she told on me.

Puberty

Long ago we went to live with our husbands while still small children. Our mothers-in-law took care of us, and we helped them with cooking, toting water farming, and all the other chores women do. We slept with our husbands, and they were responsible for us as husbands are, but we remained virgins until our puberty rites.

After reaching puberty, we returned to our own homes in preparation for initiation ceremonies and the proper wedding. This was especially significant and elaborate in the case of the senior wife, such as myself. Going through the puberty rites was extremely important to me – that was the only way to ensure that I would be the senior wife of the household. The key to everything was to "wash" with my husband.

There were many activities associated with puberty, which involved both households, that of my parents and of my in-laws. Usually menstruation began when you were already at the home of your husband and his family. You would go tell a neighbour, "Ehhh, I'm sick." She would ask you, "What is it, my child?" and you replied, "Blood is coming out." She told your mother-in-law, who came rushing over to take charge.

The women made a medicine from the leaves of special tree, *ndumila*. It's called *ndumila* to signify that "she has been spoiled, she has crossed the boundary now between childhood and adulthood. She won't suceed to get men without taking this medicine." It's really like welcoming you to adulthood.

The roots of the tree are pounded and the powder placed between some of its leaves and given to a young girl to chew. The resulting mixture is combined with water and drunk by the *mwali* (young woman entering puberty). One woman held me and fed me like a baby. Afterwards, they dressed me in the special bark cloth, *mabi,* which is worn whenever a woman menstruates.

The *mabi* is made from a large tree which has been cultivated specially for this purpose. Its branches are cut as it grows, which helps to make the desirable texture and consistency of the bark. Later, the bark is cut off tree with a knife and the outer hard covering separated from the softer, white layer inside. This is boiled in the kitchen until ready, and then removed from the fire to cool down slowly, at room temprature. A cow's horn is used to pound the bark like a hammer. The horn is really beautiful; its insides have been hollowed out and scrapped clean and designs engraved on the outside. They pound that bark until it becomes extremely soft. Then they prepare an ointment made out of raw castor oil seeds which they have ground and mixed with another ingredient until it becomes red. After the ointment is rushed into the dark, the bark is laid carefully on the ground and then folded up in a special way. A certain expertise is involved in this process of folding – not everyone can do it. Afterwards, they sew the belt with an umbrella needle. (a nedle made from one of the spokes of an umbrella)

The mabi is worn everyday during menstrution. It has to be regularly cleaned and treated with the castor oil ointments in order to maintain its consistency and cleanliness, and is very attractive to wear.

My father in-law looked for a grown-up woman to take me to my father's place. On arrival, she snowed me off and said, "This child has made a mistake." My father replied. "What mistake has she made?" "*Akulile ubusungu*" [She has begun to menstruate"] My father responded with joy. "Thank you! Thank you!"

My escort returned to the village of my husband and I stayed behind at my father's place. In the evening, my mother went to get all the young neighbour girls in the village to come home so that we could 'eat' together. In fact, they stayed with me for a full month – we ate together, slept together. My mother had alot of work to do, cooking for all of us. We were not supposed to bathe, to make *ugali* [stiff porridge, eaten as the starch component of a meal with stew, curdled milk or relish], to pound maize, even to hold a knife! We just sat, a real holiday. At any one time, we had up to thirty young girls staying in this one room together. Some could come and go, but two had to stay the whole time, sitting behind me. It was taboo for them to leave.

After a month, Father sent someone to tell my father-in-law that "your woman" has begun menstruating. He replied that they were coming but then he had to look for the go-between to come to us, bearing a gift of a chicken. When he arrived at our place, he also presented some money, it could be twenty cents, even a shilling. He expressed my in-laws' appreciation and gratitude for having taken care of me and requested my return so "we could wash our hands" together. "The husband says that his wife has not come, that it isn't his fault. He wants her to return to his compound."

All of the young girls in the village who had already entered puberty were called to escort me to my husband's place. we arrived in a big group of girls plus two grown women neighbours, and found another group waiting for us, consisting of all my husband's relatives and neighbours in the village.

Before departure, the women had anointed my entire body with special oil made out of *zetuni*. This oil is extremely fine, and makes your skin very soft – we call it *nyemba*. All of us were anointed with it. I also wore the same *mabi* cloth which was put on me that first day of menstruation and carried a new one in my hand made out of a blue, green and red belt. If you young women had seen us you would have been amazed – we looked beutiful!

Last year the mission asked me to help organise a special exhibition about the waNyakyusa. We made the belts for display. In reality, ours was the last age group to wear them.

117

My husband and I were placed in front of everyone, standing up. A cup had been filled with water and a medicine powder made from a special tree was placed in each of our hands. They slowly poured water from the cup onto my husband's hands while he rinsed away the powder, and this 'dirty' water trickled down from his hands to wash away the powder on my own waiting below. Water was poured a second time over his hands into mine.

While my husband and I were washing our hands together this way, my mother in law was washing her hands with my father-in-law. Later, when I returned home to my parents' place, I washed hands with Maria, my sister, who played the role of my mother because she had already washed her hands with my older sister. You can't do it twice. The next step was that some of my husband's medicine was put into my hands, I was given water, and they told us to go and rest. They undressed me, taking the old mabi away which I wore from my first day of menstruation, bathed me and put the new mabi on me.

The meaning of the whole medicine-and-washing process is to come to an understanding. The understanding which was of most significance to me revolved around seniority position in the extended family. By being accepted to wash hands with my husband, my position as senior wife among all wives was assured. This also ensured that my eldest son would become the senior heir at the time of my husband's death, with full authority over the family property and over the family's welfare.

Moreover, assuming that I would bear children, my first born son would be entitled to wash his hands with wife, the same as us. In that way, his children would be assured their senior position in the family, following that of his father, my husband, and even more important, my position as senior wife. However, his wife would have to fulfill the prerequisities of becoming a senior wife, which had nothing to do with order of marriage. It didn't matter how many wives a man might have, the senior wife was the first one he married who was a virgin at the time of puberty rights and the washing ceremony, and who had been initiated according to the traditional ceremonies described above. In addition, of course, she had participated in the washing ceremony with her husband.

Christians could not participate in these ceremonies after baptism. The church didn't allow it. That is why I deliberately timed my baptism to come after these ceremonies had been completed.

After the ceremony is finally over, we all returned home, to my father's place, including my husband and mother-in-law and found my relatives and neighbours waiting, especially the women. The women on my side were the first to start inquiring about my status as a virgin, asking "Is this child already grown up?" To be grown up meant that she had already 'known' a man. i.e.

had sexual intercource. By this time, my mother-in-law would already have checked out the situation from her son, my husband, probably during the first day of my menstruation period. She'd ask him, "Is this your wife?" "No," "You left her alone? "I left her alone." If so, she knew that it was all right to have my virginity examined. If he had sexual relations with me, he would have replied, "Yes, Mother, she is my wife." Then, they would have told the group of women when they returned me home, "This is the wife of somebody."

In our case, the women took me aside away from the others and asked me, "Are you still a child? Let's examine you." And they did.

If the women pronounce *"mchikutu"* meaning "an adult, a grown up," then we know that the girl did not take care of herself. "Heh, *ubura mchikutu"*. If a virgin, we say that she is still "mtoto mchanga", an infant, since an infant doesn't eat anything. Men will refuse to have sex with this small child because she doesn't know anything. Unless she is 'grown up', no longer a virgin, in which case they will say that this one has already learned everything.

If they discover her to be *mchikutu* but the husband insists that he hasn't had sex with her they take her *mabi* and lay it like a line on the floor. They tell the man to jump over it. If he is telling the truth, he will cross over it – there is nothing to fear. It is taboo to jump over it if he is telling a lie, that would be disastrous for him and his family; they would be cured. Next, the girl is told to jump over it. Should she start to refuse, they say, "So, you are the guilty one!"

Personally, I think that this process of examining for virginity is significant and I am in favour of keeping it. If a man starts having relations with a woman and takes her home without having her examined, she will assure him that she is his property, that he was the first and therefore possesses her in all senses. But how? A marriage is not perpetually happy and agreeable. Every now and then the husband will ask himself, and her, "Are these children really mine? Was I really the first one, the first man?" They will fight every day until the woman ends up saying,

> "If you want to be married to me, come get me. I am second-hand goods. Take this piece of paper and this pen and this envelope. Write a letter to my father and demand your rights."

This simply meant that he didn't have to pay the extra payment of appreciation for having married a virgin, the *"ndama ya shukrani"*. In many cases, the marriage continues – all the man is concerned about is property! He doesn't want to pay that extra calf for virginity unless it is justly deserved.

My father had to undergo substantive preparations for the next step in these events. He had to prepare great amounts of food and numerous calabashes of milk for the feast which is held to celebrate. We call it the *kusumbulila* feast (i.e. the examination feast). People used to stay as long as three weeks, eating, drinking curdled milk, everyone joyous.

After the preparations were complete, he sent a messenger to my husband inviting him to come to our place for the feast. My mother-in-law accompanied my husband, bearing a bunch of cooking bananas and a calabash full of curdled milk and presented them to my father. There was *ngoma* (traditional dance), using fiddles called *ipango* – only the men danced. Afterwards, my husband and his mates entered the house where I was sitting with my group of female friends. The whole floor was covered with banana leaves which reached up to our knees, there were so many. These men came in, stamping on the leaves inside, dancing. And outside, our fathers were doing the same thing, stamping and dancing. Afterwards, my husband and his group returned to their home.

Around this time, instruction on marriage and sex was given to me by our women. First they anointed me with oil. Then the lessons began: "A woman is happy." "She collects water."

They tell you how to please a man and keep him happy: "Do this and this and that," They teach you all the secret things which we all know, since we are women. They explained this way, "If *bwana* [master, husband] tells you this, don't be stubborn and refuse him." "If *bwana* does this to you, you must respond like this. If he is in front, respond in an appropriate way."

If you had misbehaved in any way or had some bad traits, they would warn you about them, even beat you: "You are an arrogant child with us!" "If you continue to be bad, they will divorce you. You didn't take any maize over there. They have no need of you." If they tell you to run, you run, because you have been arrogant and they are punishing you.

Nyakyusa puberty and marriage rites do not go into explicit details about how to please a man sexually like the education which our Islamic sisters receive. They simply insist that we should not be "arrogant", that we should submit to our husbands' demands and desires. Nor is there any practice of female circumcision, not even male circumscision, and there never has been such a practice. Those of us from long ago have never known such a thing. Only waNyakyusa Muslim men have done it. I have heard that the Kuria in Mara Region circumcise their women, but we don't. We did have two unique practices, however, for women. One was to use knives and stones to sharpen out teeth. The other was to tatoo special designs on our stomachs at the time of puberty. For example, Tusajigwe has the design of a bird's footprints.

After about two days back home, my mother-in-law returned, bringing bananas and a chicken, and fussed that it was time for me to return: "The millet beer (ulezi) has fermented. Let her come and drink." This signified our marriage ceremony, *unyago wa harusi*. "Her husband wants her to come and shave her head."

A group of ten girls escorted me back to sleep at my husband's place. Others have gone with twenty, even thirty. We slept the night and next day, the ceremony began with millet beer. My husband and I had our hair shaved off, and then they anointed our bodies with a special cream. "You don't sleep alone with that ointment on your body, it's for sleeping with a man. I slept that day with my husband and had sex for the first time.

After our hair was shaved and bodies anointed, we were taken down to the riverside where they dressed us both in banana leaves. Otherwise we were naked, of course, as was customary in those days, especially for women. They pushed me towards him, telling me: "You and your husband – fight in the river!" and then they left us alone. We bathed together in the river, and "fought" physically, but it was just a game. People stayed to watch and everyone, including us, roared with laughter. Afterwards they called us to come out of water, but we could not put a foot on the ground. Each of us was carried on someone's back, a woman carried me and a man carried my husband, with the whole crowd dancing around us and singing a song – *nyisa mama*. We were taken this way to his place to be dressed. The ceremony has been altered and shortened since then. For example, people are no longer carried from the river. They place the hands of the woman and the man together, instead.

When we got home, we were given a special meal called *kifuge*, made out of pigeon peas, bananas and beans which are cooked together like ugali. We ate while seated together, from the same dish. The trunk of a banana tree had been placed on the ground, stripped of its banana leaves, and they sat each of us down on that log. We ate together, which I want to emphasise.

When we had finished, they brought a young boy whose head had also been shaved. He stood nearby, holding a wooden spoon called *burandika* and called out, *nyoiiii nyoiiii"* and then he ran away. According to custom, a chase began to catch him as he wove in and out of different homesteads in the village. Finally he was captured and brought back to us, and someone cried out, "Gather round. Gather round. This man has caught the young boy!"

Then we were taken to my mother's place, where we slept together for the first time. We didn't stay at his place the first time, but instead were given the house of a neighbouring man living near my mother. Everyone waited to hear the news: "Was she still a virgin? Did they have satisfactory intercourse!" "Women came to our mat bed. This would be the signal that the girl had been a virgin. Of course, sometimes a mother may help the girl, bring in some chicken blood to smear on the sheet and display to everyone outside. Sometimes a man can't perform adequately; if he fails completely, the woman may refuse to remain with him and people will accept her decision.

After we had lain together, they brought in a leather cloth which was used by me and my girl escorts to cover our heads. If you had been a good girl and were still a virgin, people praised you. They entered the house, greeted us, gave us money and then were able to lift the cloth aside and look at us with admiration. My husband had to give money to me as appreciation. My own mother gave me whatever she had, saying "Thank you, thank you child." Later, we went outside and the people who had gathered around all admired us. We walked in a kind of procession through the village with the cloth covering our heads. All along the way, people we met gave us money before lifting aside the cloth.

Girls usually stayed from one to three months at their father's place at this time, ostensibly waiting for the *ndama ya shukurani* (calf of thanks). If a girl was still a virgin, the husband had to bring her mother a calf in appreciation. How long you stay home partly depends on how much your father likes you. If he likes you, two months, but if he lacks enough food to feed you and your retinue only a month.

When the calf is brought to your mother, your father calls all the neighbouring women and men together and the calf is slaughtered and consumed then and there in celebration. However, if you weren't a virgin, no calf is brought – the calf establishes our position as heirs. However, these customs have stopped. The mission refused to allow it to contninue. Instead, wedding ceremonies take place in church. There is no more washing together, even the pagans have stopped, they no longer know the old ceremonies any more.

My older sister washed with her husband and went to wash at our father's place as well. She washed with me in place of my mother, and I inherited my younger sister, washing with her. But ours was the last generation to practise traditional puberty and marriage rituals.

Bearing Children: Joy and Sorrow

As the time of delivery approached, especially the first time, a woman returned to her mother. A special small hut was built where childbearing took place. The husband would come to visit at the mother's place and to find out how the delivery went, but it was taboo for him to enter the hut. In fact, he was not supposed to see you at all, if necessary you had to hide yourself until after seven days or so when the umbilical cord fell off. Then the woman's hair was shaved and it was possible for the husband to come and greet her, along with other relatives.

I had real difficulties during my first delivery, being too young and small. Before the second delivery I took herbal medicine which my husband got from the banks of river Mwakisambwe. We put this medicine into a bottle and drank it every day in the morning. If all was going well, beginning in the eighth month the medicine was slightly warmed up and in the ninth month it was heated till it was hot. This medicine ensured that when labour began, the child would be born without difficulty. That medicine really helped to hasten the speed of deliveries. If I said, "I'm going to pick up something outside" as if I were going to the toilet, in reality I was going to give birth very soon.

Labour pains caught me around 5 pm in the evening the second time. At 7 pm I went to hide among the banana trees without telling anybody. After my experiences during the first delivery, I had decided to bear my child alone. This was because of my mother's behaviour. She was basically a coward. Normally our custom was to call one other person to sit by your feet and watch everything. There's a lot of noise then, isn't there? How will you feel about this person, sitting there?

Well, my mother panicked when I went into labour the first time and she called all her friends, "Come along!" They all came into the hut to watch me. I had to give birth in front of many people. This enraged me, which was why I went to hide by the fig tree during my second delivery.

At first my labour wasn't extremely painful, I began to examine myself and my progress. Now looking back, I find this extremely humorous. I told myself, "Ahhh the baby is near. "I could feel the water break but wasn't afraid, even though I was completely alone. At 7:30 pm the water began to come out. I began to cry out, aiiiiiiiiiii" and began to vomit. "Aiiiiiii" – they heard me. "Heh, my goodness, she's in here. Let's go. Let's go." and they brought me to a banana tree trunk. My mother cried out, "Look at my daughter, just look at her."

I got angry as the number of women assembled there increased. "Aka!" The baby began to come out. I cried out, "eh eyyeh ughhhh." It's a frightening experience. One woman told them to leave after I began to pull back and the baby couldn't come out. Another one joined us and held me from behind as I squatted down by the tree. I pushed and pushed. Another woman interfered, thinking it was too early. It is taboo for us to start pushing before the cervix is opened enough. This woman was holding me down around the cer-

123

vix as if to keep track of the opening and to slow me down. Another woman told her, "You, don't hold her there." My mother added, Eh! Go away! Leave my daughter alone! Eh! Eh! Leave her!" Then the woman realised her mistake and said, "Oh! Please let me leave my daughter alone. You hold on to her yourself." Then I started pushing – "eghhhghhhghhhuug-hhhhhhhh" – just one time! and the baby was out, lying on the ground, eyes in the dirt! perfectly healthy! That was Tusajigwe.

Mother said, "Ehh, filthy." She was frightened of filth.

The second task was to get the placenta out. During this delivery, only part of it came out; nearly half stayed inside my womb. This was extremely dangerous. The women began to comment about it, "Dont you see that the placenta hasn't come out yet." I stayed silent for a while and then asked for a razor. I told myself, "This cloth, this 'bag' has no purpose," and I cut it up inside with the razor until it nearly all came out. Just a bit of the placenta remained. However, a great deal of blood was blocked up inside by that bit of placenta. It pressed down but couldn't get out and just stayed there. I told myself, why should it. Considering myself extremely clever, I decided that it would drop out by the next day. I fixed my clothes and bathed.

Well, I was left with a fever inside and became extremely ill. My stomach was in severe pain. We call it *kaandu*. It hurt me so much that I couldn't eat. I slept that night. The second day I went alone to the fig tree again and tried to shake it out. I reached my hand inside my womb, grabbed that bit of placenta and shook it from side to side. But it would't come out. The third day I wouldn't budge. This time, I tried to hold it differently and to push it as well as pull it, then I held on tight and pulled with all my strength – – hmminmmmmmmmmmm hghmmmmmmmmmmmmmmmm ! It came out. I threw it away. Blood blood blood in the middle it was all curdled up. That part was shaped round like a mango, and just as big. Extremely dangerous. I threw it down and split it open. It was so big. When I split it, it burst with a sound like "twaaa!".

I left the fig tree and went to tell my mother that everything had come out. God helped me. I was 18 years of age – and stubborn.

Mother was so happy – *"Ndaga! Ndaga!"* [Thank you! Thank you! Thank you!] clapping her hands all the while. (We waNyakyusa do that, we clap the palms of our hands together softly when thanking someone, or greeting someone who has come from afar. It is also done when we are wailing in mourning or when someone expresses sympathy with our bereavenent).

For two or three days I was all right, and then bleeding began again. I lost a great deal of blood, enough to fill one basket after another. Curdled blood. Father decided to carry me on his back all the way to my husband's place. He said, "I'm tired now – – the responsibility is too much. Let me take her back to her husband's place. By this time Father had begun to give up and thought I needed more specialised care. I told him, "Ahhhh, my eyes cannot see, Father." I was like a blind person. There was total darkness. But after a while I got better, without going to the hospital.

The other deliveries were easier. I'd sleep a deep sleep and dream. "All that was left was the labour." I'd wake up feeling ill and sweating, and walk around a bit, having diarrhoea. Three times I have diarrhoea and that's it, I go into labour. For example, for the third child I went out, saying I'm going outside to the toilet. There and then I could feel the labour. *Bwana* was totally unaware of what was going on. He just kept sleeping. I pushed - iiiiiiiihhhh – the baby was ready, he was born just there, outside the house. I couldn't walk. My friend was snoring in his sleep. I had to wake him up, "Don't you hear? A baby is crying!"

Actually my mother got me into trouble by insisting that I should have many children." She would say, "Heh my daughter, give birth to many children. Healthy children. You children kept dying on me." She said this because she herself had only five children, and three died, leaving only two, my elder sister and me. A younger brother died after he'd already become grown up and had married, but left no children behind. My mother didn't bear many children, only five.

So I had nine children. Five died. Four healthy children survived Imagine, if I had only five children, I'd have become like her, I'd have been left the same way. You understand.

I'll name all of my children, including those who died, although if I talk much about them, my heart sinks with grief for them. Some Christians sing a song saying that there is happiness when a baby dies – it goes to heaven – but I'm not one of them. To tell the truth it is very difficult.

My first child, deceased, was named Nsekela. She was born in June, 1931 – a girl. She died after only three months. Tusajigwe followed, she was born on December 6th, 1931. Hezron followed, he was born in 1934. Mbonile was born on November 11th, 1939. Ngabagila, meaning "I can't" was born next. I called her that because I'm not able to bear female children successfully – they all die. She was born on December 6th, 1941 and died while still a baby. Another girl, Nyambilila, was born on March 15, 1944. She died of hookworms *(safura)* when she was 19 years old, after many years of illness. "That's why she didn't leave me even one grandchild. Normally when we reach 16 years or so, we start having children. Nyambilila was skilled artisan, she could do all sorts of things with her hands. All she had to do was look at a dress and she'd have it all sewn up. She was a singer, too, one of the best. She also knew how to assess people. She'd look a visitor over and say, "This one? Uh huh." [negative].

When she died, I refused to cry. I had cried for all my other children, all those four who had died in their infancy. I told myself, "He is even taking this big one'!" I would not cry. I went to church to pray. I began singing at the funeral and leading the others. Some people got frightened: "Is she crazy?" But others silenced them, "She's not crazy. Her daughter has died."

Marjorie reminds me of Nyambilila. I keep saying, "She has come to replace my Nyambilila." They were born around the same time, 1944 and 1943. Perhaps she is my lost daughter, born to me without any labour pains.

Brown was born on April 7th, 1947. Austina, a boy, was born on June 2nd, 1950, and died after a year. He was already walking. Saita a girl, was born on December 6th, 1952. She had a beautiful face. People were shocked when she died, she was a year and one month. God welcomed my girls to his place. Pehaps there's a sickness in me, which kills girls. I don't know. This is what I believe: children used to die much more then than they do now. They don't die nowadays like they used to. In the past they died. When you give birth to a baby, you have no high hopes that your baby will live. How can you be sure? However, I used to know my children. I'd have a bad dream, around the eighth month of pregnancy. If I dreamt that I had given birth to a baby who was covered in excrement, when I gave birth, I found my baby covered in excrement and I gave up hope. If my babies were healthy I didn't have dreams.

To believe ahead of time that your baby will die is good. At least I got accustomed to the idea a little. If in my eighth or ninth month of pregnancy, I had bad dreams, I told myself, "Hmmm, if I have a baby it will die." This happened for each of the four who died as infants. We mourn. Untold numbers of our babies die. For example, in some cases a woman gives birth to ten children and not one remains. The man leaves me alone because all the children have died. Should God choose, not one remains. It is very sad. It is not true that one is healed by forgetting. I say this because I had had hopes for each and every one of them.

Adult Educator

Here I'd like to describe my activities as a teacher in Katumba Village. Katumba is not far from our village, you can see it across the valley if you stand in the right places. The leader of our women's group, the late Elizabeth Ipungu, took me there the first time.

In the past we didn't just pray together when we went on evangelical visits, we also taught the women. We would tell them, "do this or that", "behave well at home", "don't fight with your husband." I would instruct women this way:

"If your man speaks harshly, don't answer back. Stay quiet. When you see him acting normal again, ask him, "How have I wronged you?" The man may reply, "Heh! People are saying this or that about you," Maybe accusing you of having boyfriends. "Ahh no, my man, I don't do this or that."

It turns out to be a good thing to be a Christian. If your man refuses to give you money, don't complain to anybody. Instead ask God, kneel down and beg him. "My God, why does my husband go on like this, what's bothering him?" Don't say to Him, "Bad God", instead say, "What have I done wrong? What sin have I committed, God? My man, my companion and I do not agree with each other. What have I done wrong?" The sin must be mine, because I have been denied.

Don't ask secretly as some do when it's time to pray, "God, you've given me a bad man!" If you think that way, you will fight. Don't you talk like that.

I remember that around the time I began working in Katumba, there was a big central meeting of the women in our church congregation based at Kyimbila. They said that all the women's groups in the village churches would make things for display. There would be a competition: "Every group will work, and we will visit each, and later select the best." Two people were selected from each village to meet in Kyimbila for the final exhibition and competition.

I was one of the church leaders selected to be a judge in the competition. We went around, visiting every single village. We travelled everywhere. Whenever we arrived at a village, Ipungu would take out her book and read a lesson, preaching something relevant to our work. Then we would examine the things which a given group had displayed for us, with special focus on craftsmanship and originality. The majority of activities engaged in were handwork of some kind, like embroidery. Leadership mattered. If a group had chosen a leader who was not competent in organizing or lacked the necessary artisanship, it was revealed in these exhibits. People were very critical: "Eh! What is this? Friends, what have you been doing?" Originality and excellence also aroused comment, usually positive: "My, this is different. We don't do things like that, how do you do it?"

We leaders moved all around the locale of our congregation, from one village to another, meeting with women's groups, and finally arrived at my 'own' village, Katumba. Beforehand, my sisters there had moaned and groaned, expecting total failure. I chastised them, "Go ahead and try!" and even made up a song, "If you moan, you can't get better."

Producers, what are you complaining about? 'To moan is not work'. You must work. Too much moaning and you won't recover. Work! Stand up for yourself!

Finally, I won them over to at least make an effort. They had to be encouraged to develop the skills they already had, using the resources within their reach:

My sisters, don't covet embroidered clothes so much, when you don't wear them or use them yourselves. We are poor. We don't have anything. If they say, "Let's have tea and go", you want to take tea, but we don't have it. We are poor. Tea we don't have. Who has sugar these days for the tea?

Weaving *miriri* mats, *vilago,* is work that we know. Weave *vilago* mats. Don't wish for clothes, clothes are for the rich over there. Their clothes are fancy, we wear the same everyday. Will we buy clothes just to show off on this one day?

We will display our culture. We will exhibit our *kiNyakyusa of Masoko.*

Although they agreed with me, dutifully – "Yes, Mama," it didn't mean a thing. They were totally dispirited. The next time we met I brought my own knife along. Determined that this endeavour should succeed, I ran from my village to theirs. As soon as I had arrived and before others had shown up, I began cutting some of the dried banana leaves called *fungubo,* off the trees. In fact, I went from one house to another, showing each member of the group the *fungubo* and how to identify the right leaves on the tree.

It was like working with a bunch of children; they had to be nursed all the way.

Let's go cut *fungubo.* Let's weave *vilago* mats, We will not buy clothing, we will make our own things. Don't desire clothing, don't desire cloth, oh no! Let's weave *vilago*

Let's do our craftsmanship which belongs to our culture. We are people of Masoko. This is our wealth – we have no other.

So I cut and I cut *fungubo,* and began to weave the *vilago* mats. Surprisingly enough, so many young women had not been taught these skills, and that was long ago, in the late 1950s. It was necessary to demonstrate the steps by doing it myself. This got them interested and eventually, enthusiastic. I wove an original design which I patterned after the wild bird, *kangara,* which we call the *kiwale.* Using three different colours, I wove something very beautiful. This won them over. They were impressed. "All right, we're ready to weave mats, after all, this is something we already know how to do, anyway." One said, "Ahhh Mama, we don't want to hear about getting cloth anymore." I told them, "*Ndaga. Ndaga.* Thank you very much. I am extremely happy," and bowed ceremoniously. We were all delighted. Those times were good.

On the day of the exhibition for the visiting leaders, we prepared everything beforehand. I had instructed the group not to bring out their products first thing. They should be hidden so as to increase the surprise effect later. Instead, we should have prayers conducted first. Then when they asked to see our handwork, one person should enter the house where we stored the things and show them a few things only, at first.

My fellow leaders had very low expectations for Katumba, and when they arrived, they were openly sarcastic, saying "We have come to see the work of our sisters of Katumba." They laughed at us because they considered Katumba people to be poor, undeveloped and lacking sense. Well, the big women came and we prayed, as planned, and then they gave the blessing. All of the visiting leaders sat together on one side, our Katumba group sat together on another side. I preached at this gathering, and could hear them beginning to mumble among themselves, taking pity on the group, convinced we had nothing to show them: "Our friends don't know enough yet ..."

> Dear sisters, as you know, we have been visiting all of our fellow women in the different church groups. In each case, all of your sisters have worked hard. We have discovered beautiful embroidered clothing and cloth.
> When we leave, they tell us, 'We are continuing our work!' They are not satisfied yet with their accomplishments.
> Now, Katumba, bring us your work. Let us see it.

We did. We brought out our display of things. The women had pots they had made from clay, beaded decorations we call 'roosters', and – yes, there were a few embroidered pillow cases and cloth. One cloth in particular was extremely beautiful, very well done. All sorts of things had been woven or decorated, including spears – *megege,* even *ngwego* – all different kinds of spears. I also brought a *kitana,* the bamboo container we use for milk, on the outside of which I had fashioned an original pattern.

They were truly amazed. We were ecstatic but tried not to show it too much. Ipungu exclaimed, "Goodness, what have you been doing! How have you accomplished all this?" In fact, she began to choose things she wanted for herself, as well as for the big exhibition at Kyimbila. Like my mat:

"Ahh," she said, "I am taking this *kilago*. This *kilago* has a story to it." We told them, "we're still working, You haven't seen it all. There is more to come. We have more to do.'

Debates

The three of us, Mbilinyi, Sambulika and myself, often got into heated discussions about a variety of things, which centred around the theme of slavery and equality – i.e. the relations between women and men! (We will reproduce these debates verbatim). One was about bridewealth.

Bridewealth

Mbilinyi: Some people say that we ought to get rid of bridewealth – that bridewealth imprisons women.

Others think differently. To me, it looks as if bridewealth has been a real load to carry for many women in Katusyo.

Sambulika: The truth is that bridewealth is marriage here in Katusyo. That is how it is for us. If a person tries to evade paying bridewealth, we disapprove. But if a person marries by paying bridewealth, we say, "Good. We have married our wife!"

That's why a person won't agree to go live with a man without bridewealth. In Rungwe, even if we don't want to register our marriage at district headquarters, that's fine, so long as he brings the bridewealth home, so long as he has it ready.

Even if it's true that bridewealth imprisons us women, it is the only way to get respect. When a person is married by bridewealth, people say, "That's his real wife."

Kalindile: I would be ashamed. If my daughter Sambulika went to stay with some one who didn't pay the cows, I wouldn't go and visit them. I'd say, "Who have you been staying with? Not a husband!"

I couldn't accept it. They don't want many cows. Even if they gave two, that's enough. For us, for me, for my father it was six. Others, eight. The chiefs told my husband's people, "Loooo! You are paying a lot!"

If someone marries royalty, they have to take cattle every year.

They don't pay all the cattle at once. At first, the husband gives three. I, the woman, goes to him. If he gets problems, he returns them. It's like a loan. He'll finish later, after I

130

	start bearing children. He pays bit by bit. Even if he should marry three times to three different women, even if he ends up marrying someone young enough to be the age of my own child, he'll still be paying off my bridewealth, too.
Mbilinyi:	What if we could develop a different kind of custom, one that didn't imprison women, but achieved the same objectives?
Sambulika:	Bridewealth!
Mbilinyi:	We could have a different way to show respect, without using cattle which imprisons women.
Sambulika:	It's true that many couples simply live together. But people say, "If the man lives with her like that, she won't stay home."
Kalindile:	Living together without even one cow being paid? Ha!
Mbilinyi:	But surely these are other ways to express and receive appreciation?
Sambulika:	No! Here, we could, after raising our child – but others …
Kalindile:	Some don't pay the cows.
Sambulika:	Young people misbehave badly! They just go off to live with a man, and he doesn't even give a 50 cent coin to their families!
Kalindile:	I look at it this way. To live together without bridewealth makes a person a prostitute.
Sambulika:	Meaning that in the old days, the children who were born of such relationships did not belong to the man and his clan. If he didn't pay the bridewealth, he didn't even get his name attached to them.
Kalindile:	Later on, he comes to claim them, saying, "My children". "Heh! Give me my children!" You reply, "Does a dog have a husband? She bears children, even a chicken bears children." She bears children randomly, without any plan.
Mbilinyi:	What if you lived with the man for ten years?
Kalindile:	Ten years? Still, who conceived the child? Is there only one 'thing'?

Why Me?

It struck me in 1987, when we were going through the transcripts, that it was kind of amazing, our finding each other this way, and my being involved as the life historian whose work and life became the basis of the work. "Why me?" The way I explained it to myself, and later told Mbilinyi, was my interest in local history and my commitment. Describing how I approached our work in 1985, I told Mbilinyi.

> Sometimes I didn't sleep, and stayed awake instead thinking abou my life and what I would tell you about it. It's also true that I know a lot. Many other women don't know that much. People say that I'm very intelligent.

Many people have asked us how we began to work together on this project, to write a life history based on my own experiences. It was not accidental, in that Mbilinyi was introduced to me by one of our children, Mwaiseje Polisya, who was a former student of hers at the University. He is the first son of our third co-wife, the one who was married when she was the same age as Sambulika, my own daughter.

Mbilinyi sought Polisya's advice when she was preparing her research proposal in 1984, to come to Rungwe to study local history with people in the area. She needed to choose a village which would become a central locale for her work, and she needed to consider an appropriate way of identifying women with whom to write histories! Later, we both realised how much work was involved, even in making one.

Polisya suggested that she come to live and work at Katusyo Village, and said that he knew 'just the per: n' for the life history – me. According to him, I was an "old-timer" with roc in the area, and was both knowledgeable and enthusiastic about local cu..ure and history. My critical attitude towards society and especially gender relations which oppressed women meant that Mbilinyi and I would share similar positions on many issues, and it would enhance the work itself. The very first day we met, I began to tell her about the conditions of women in polygamous marriage, using our next-door neighbour's 'city' of multiple wives as an example: "We Rungwe women are slaves!" This outlook – that women were and are slaves to men in Rungwe – summarised my general outlook on gender and became the central core of this text.

However, Polisya did not go into details like this during that first 'briefing' – he just asked me to teach Mbilinyi some local history.

Another consideration Polisya later noted was that I was one of the more culturally enlightened people of my generation, male or female, but especially among women. This was partly because of my having attended the local 'bush school' run by one of the local African Moravian churches. This made me literate in kiNyakyusa, and enabled me later to teach myslef to read kiswahili by comparing our kiNyakyusa hymnal with the Kiswahili Bible. My love of reading anything that became available augmented this process of self-education, as did my travels to distant locations like Tanga Dar es Salaam and, closer to home, Mbeya town. My activities in the church deepened this process of cultural enlightenment. As Polisya noted, "Kalindile was not afraid of anything!"

Struck like me by the challenge of our task and the accomplishments thus far, in February 1987 Mbilinyi asked Polisya why he had encouraged us to work together. He emphasised intelligence and level of intensity: "Kalindile is intense about everything – everything is important to her." Personally I think this is also true of Mbilinyi, and helped to explain the leaps we took in our imaginations as well as the capacity we had to produce new knowledge together, as well as the sparks that often flew between us. We didn't always agree with each other, and our discussions were often extremely heated debates.

Polisya felt that I was 'ahead of my time". If I had been a young woman today, I would have gone on to University. He told Mbilinyi that I would have been "very daring and courageous", and she replied, "but Kalindile is daring and courageous within her own context and location, historically in a temporal and geographic sense."

One day they simply showed up, Polisya, Mbilinyi and a friend of Polisya's. Mbilinyi was introduced to me as Polisya's "Professor", and Polisya explained that she needed to identify knowledgeable elderly women who could teach her local history. Nothing was said about a life history. I agreed that the project sounded interesting – one thing more enjoyable than anything to me is talking about local history, the customs of the waNyakyusa – and was willing to give it a try. Then Polisya went to make arrangements with another half-brother of his, the son of my second co-wife, who lived right across the road from my house. We're all in the same compound, but have separate houses, separate farms. This brother/son is very active in the church, is in fact one of the local church elders. He also agreed that the project sounded useful and welcomed Mbilinyi to come and live at his house.

That was in the summer of 1985, and Mbilinyi ended up living with us for two months. She's been back several times since, first in February 1987 for about ten days, to correct the transcripts of our talks together, and again in August 1987, for about three weeks to edit the first draft of our text together, only part of which is reproduced here. In 1988 she came for a brief visit, strictly 'family', no work. And in 1989, we had more time to discuss issues raised in our text together when she came for three months, in conjunction with another project on women in plantantions and peasant farms (down in Bujela Village, though she lived with us, as before).

My Objectives

Why did I persist in working on this text, in spite of the work involved and sometime anguish? My major aim was to use the narrative as a witness to the sufferings and tribulations faced by Rungwe women and the ways that they have struggled for life and dignity. Another aim was to educate people, beginning with the younger generations of uNyakyusa, about Nyakyusa culture, history and society.

Three central themes became evident in the narrative: 1) my personal struggles to survive and to change society; 2) efforts by women to advance themselves; and 3) the lives and achievements of women in Rungwe, using myself as an example. Women have accomplished a great deal, in spite of the hard work, discrimination and outright violence which they faced. They have been much more than wives and mothers: mid-wives, historians, adult-educators, religious leaders, grassroots organisers, and story-tellers. Underlying all of these is the central question of gender relations in marriage, the family and society in general. Colonialism, racial segregation, class – all of these phenomenon are real and provide the background context to my stories. But they are not my central focus. We knew about colonialism and racism, how could we not know? But I wanted to use this text to tell stories not their stories.

According to Mbilinyi, this makes my approach similar to that of Mamie Garvin Fields, an African-American woman who wrote about her life in Southern United States in the early 1900s, not long after the abolition of slavery. According to her co-author and grand-daughter, Karen Fields (1985: xix-xx):

> ... my grandmother dealt in actual people and places, in the choices that she or her neighbour confronted, in what a man or woman did given a particular circumstance... She was not trying to convey 'how black people fared in Charleston over the first half of the century', but 'how we led our lives, how we led good lives.

The controversial views of Zora Neala Hurston are also relevant (cited in Walker 1983: 115):

> I am not tragically coloured. There is no great sorrow dammed up in my soul, nor lurking behind my eyes. I do not mind at all. I do not belong to the sobbing school of Negrohood who hold that nature somehow has given them a lowdown dirty deal and whose feelings are all hurt about it ... No, I do not weep at the world – I am too busy sharpening my oyster knife.

We might have changed this for me to read, "I am not tragically an African woman," in that we didn't sit like passive victims and weep about our fate. Instead, we devised strategies of survival and *ujanja* [cleverness] – to fool men into thinking they were in control, when sometimes they weren't, or that they were adored when sometimes it was the opposite. I used our sessions in church groups to instruct women on how to get around male rule and avoid male violence. Moreover, there is much to be joyous of, especially in our culture, so often embodied in women's activities and crafts, and in our families and friends.

But rage? yes, I felt – and still feel – rage at the way women are treated in my society. And I think it is unfortunate that I was made a woman. Once Mbilinyi asked me, "If you were going to summarise all that you think about women or women's position, what would you say?", I replied, "I wish I was a man."

Mbilinyi's Objectives

Mbilinyi wanted to use my life history as a means to illuminate the history of the people of Rungwe and Tanzania from a woman's point of view. Of special concern were the multiple ways in which women responded to changes which occured during colonialism, and the impact of their responses on the policies of employers and the colonial state. The aim was to show that women were not 'passive victims' – that they had accommodated themselves to new developments, learned how to cope with adversity and, in many cases, had developed new forms of resistances against male oppression. These resistances sometimes took advantage of spaces created by new institutions like local African churches, European missions, schools and the state-supervised 'native' courts. Women's responses were likely to be contradictory, in that they faced triple oppression: colonialism, racism and 'patriarchism', all of which were embodied in the kind of capitalism which emerged in Tanzania and other southern African nations dependent on migrant labour and European settler enterprise.

According to Mbilinyi, women had been left out of Tanzanian history in multiple ways. For example, very few women were 'professional' historians or had had their stories published. The University's History Department had failed to produce even one Tanzanian female historian at the doctorate level and had a poor employment record: not one Tanzanian woman had ever been hired as a member of staff. Most historians ignored women entirely: they did not consider them appropriate subjects of history and did not include them in oral and archival procedures of data collection. Finally, gender relations and their impact on class and other social relations were usually ignored or misunderstood, even when women were included as 'informants' or objects of analysis.

This had resulted in a distorted view of the world which 'left out' half the population – women, and was also responsible for many errors in basic analysis. For example, in the past people assumed that women had not been active in the colonial 'labour force', because relatively few women workers were counted by colonial labour officers when compiling their labour census. These statistics focused on more regularly employed women and men who had been hired on contract terms as migrant workers, and usually missed those hired on a casual and seasonal basis. In many areas, the majority of wage workers were casual, seasonal workers and they were women, including farm workers on coffee estates and largescale mixed farms.

By focusing on women workers, it has been discovered that the casual labour system was as significant in the colonial days as into migrant labour system, in terms of numbers of people absorbed into the labour force. Many more villagers were part-time workers than was recognised before; whole communities of women and children were semi-proletarianised, whether they lived 'at home' in their villages or in plantation labour camps. Households in many areas like Rungwe depended on the income derived from three different labour regimes: migrant labour, casual labour and peasant labour. Looked at from the point of view of the workers themselves and their households, there is a need to examine how these labour regimes interacted. This will require careful study of the entire system of patriarchal farming and customary marriage in the smallholder peasant sector and its role in reproducing cheap labour for employers and in maintaining local government under the system of indirect rule.

Another set of goals Mbilinyi told me she had was to produce new knowledge on the basis of our capacity to critique our knowledge of the past and the present together, and to present it in narrative form, which would attract more people to read what we had learned. She - and I - wanted to tell a good story, one that attracted people while at the same time challenging their ideas about themselves and the world. People needed to recognise how the world we now lived in was partly shaped by the way that people behaved in the past, so that they could develop hope in their capacity to change the present world for the future. This is especially important today, as Tanzania and Africa become poorer and more dependent on donor nations, and governments become more authoritarian in order to meet the demands of the donors for economic reform and keep themselves in power.

Hopefully, readers will be moved by this narrative to ask themsleves questions about their own histories and the lives they lead now. Our debates may stimulate others to join in, on issues of bridewealth, marriage and justice. And we also hope that readers will take pride in themselves after reading this account of someone who is an ordinary, elderly, village woman. According to Mbilinyi, she sought in this narrative to express the power and authority, the knowledge and artistry, the courage and humour of me and my stories. Kalindile – the Kalindile of this narrative – can become a model for others to emulate, a model of courage, self-pride and resistance. Not because this 'Kalindile' is perfect, but because she is human, based on a real person with all her foibles and weaknesses and doubts. We have tried to expose these as well. No one is perfect, but everyone can make a difference in this world.

The Social Significance of One Person's Life History

There are many connections between the story of my life, which is the life of a simple village woman, and this wider picture. For example, my husband worked on the mission's coffee estate near Katusyo, and eventually became a 'gang' leader in charge of supervising a group of harvesters. My co-wife and I used to work under him, picking coffee: we'd take turns, one week she would work while I stayed home to do the farming on the household plots and the other household chores like cooking and child-care, and the next week we'd switch places. At the end of the month, we we'd split the pay and buy cloth for ourselves.

We had to keep the household farms going, including the food farms which we controlled and the coffe and food plots owned by our husband. At the same time, we couldn't earn much cash on the family farms; the wages from the coffee estate were needed to pay for things like children's clothing, our clothes and school uniforms.

While growing up, our boys worked part-time on the new, tea plantations which were established on the old cofee estates in the 1940s and 1950s. They earned their own school costs that way. After they were grown, one of my sons migrated down to the Copperbelt where he worked as a miner and in petty trade for several years. My sister's sons also worked as miners down there, and one has settled permanently in Zambia. Even my daughter, Sambulika, lived for several years in Sumbawanga and then in Lusaka.

Our farms produced these young people who went to work on the big mines of the South or in the petty trades and other activities of the informal sector which developed to maintain the migrant labour force. At the same time, our farms were not lucrative enough to provide them with the kind of income and standard of living which they wanted. Going South was one way to get it.

My history concentrates on activities in our local Moravian church, including women's groups and bush school. The missions, churches and schools were highly significant in colonial history: they helped to sustain colonial rule, by providing a new set of values compatible with capitalist work ethics and submission to the new rules. At the same time, they could also become subversive, especially in the case of women, by teaching them new ideas about freedom, love, marriage, parenthood, and skills and knowledge which could be used to put these ideas into action.

The British depended on the system of indirect rule, using local chiefs as their local administrators and what they called 'customary' laws and practices to maintain social order. Many of these laws were oppressive, and women resisted them by running away to the Copperbelt and other places. Or they became Christian, which allowed them to refuse, for example, to be inherited by their husband's brothers or uncles when he died.

My stories of women's church activities and organisations illustrate the contradictions within these institutions, and the way women manipulated them for their own benefit. They also illuminate their impact on the development of gender consciousness. My lessons to women about being a good Christian wife were two-sided: new rights went along with the new obligations. Women had the right to expect new forms of respect and financial support from their husbands be they Christian or not. They could go to Church elders for counseling and support in case of mistreatment, such as wife-beating, and the Church could intervene, for example, in cases of forced marriage of young girls of widow-inheritance. Church-going men were also taught how to be good Christian husbands! They really could be diffrent: they listened to their wives more, gave them more freedom in controlling money, and best of all, they remained monogamous. Polygamy is a terrible thing. Many of us wanted to be Christian to escape it.

Our women's groups taught both leaders and ordinary members about organising, the conduct of meetings, the manufacture of certain kinds of products, methods of earning cash income, the administration of funds; and mass mobilisation. We got the opportunity to travel not only to other villages, but also to neighbouring districts and urban centres. Interacting with women from different clans and tribes, we developed a wider view of the world. Observations of how women, and men related to each other elsewhere could also make us realise that things did not have to remain the same, that other ways were possible, for our children if not for ourselves.

Another focus of my stories is on the oppressive nature of 'customary' marriage systems, and way that colonial chiefs helped to support them, usually to the detriment of women. Whereas the colonialists used to label these systems 'traditional' and said that they were beneficial for Africans, I have tried to show how harmful they were for African women. Whether or not they were traditional, they were not beneficial in many respects and caused women both physical and mental harm. This made some of us worried when the nationalists in our area began calling for independence so as to remove all the Europeans and bring back 'black' rule like it used to be. We did not want the old, male rule which allowed husbands to beat their wives and even murder them. In the past, men weren't afraid of doing these things, all they had to do was pay a fine. It was only after the Europeans brought us protection that our men began to fear being hung for killing their wives.

Methods Used to Produce the Narrative

As noted already, we began in 1985. Mbilinyi lived with us for two months, which gave us many opportunities to walk, especially in the evening after she'd completed interviews with other people. Many of our talks were impromptu, but about 17 sessions were recorded on tape in 1985, and several more in 1987 and 1989.

Sambulika participated in most of the 1985 sessions, especially at the beginning when we didn't know Mbilinyi well and were't sure of what she was doing. In 1987 and 1989 Sambulika was usually too busy to join in, and by that time our ability to communicate together had improved.

Early on in our 1985 sessions, Sambulika became personally interested in the project, and concentrated on helping to explain ideas or reference which were unfamiliar to Mbilinyi. I often referred to local culture or events which an outsider could not possibly understand. Sambulika rarely interrupted my presentations, though she often would signal to Mbilinyi when such a reference had occured: "Don't worry, I'll explain later" or "You don't understand this (though you think you do). I'll elaborate afterwards."

When I was tired or excited I sometimes broke into kiNyakyusa, often without any consciousness of having done so. Sambulika had to translate these passages later into kiSwahili. And there were some words which I did not know in Kiswahili. Sometimes she and I had different opinions about things, however. I once told Mbilinyi, "I don't trust all of her stories, "I'd wait till she'd finished, and then go on with my own tale.

We did nearly all our work in my kitchen-house where most of my time is spent these days. This allowed me, and Sambulika when she was with us, to keep on cooking, weaving mats, receiving visitors or to rest when bothered by poor health. I have a bad cough condition and Sambulika has asthma, and we sometimes had bad spells. Most of our sessions were in the late afternoon and went on till after nightfall, when there were fewer visitors and we could relax over tea or a meal of ugali or roasted banana.

Occasionally visitors were present. Sometimes they came, chatted and left. Other times they listened, especially when I was telling some of the old stories from the past or describing aspects of nyaKyusa culture. There are so many things that younger people no longer know. Our discussions occasionally provoked others to ask questions for further information or elaboration, and in one or two instances, an elderly male friend of mine joined in to help teach Mbilinyi some of our local history.

Sometimes the themes of our sessions were initiated by questions which Mbilinyi raised, and sometimes I chose what to talk about. Even when she asked us to discuss a certain topic, I was able to guide the discussion along certain lines, and could reject issues or ideas that seemed irrelevant or wrong, or none of Mbilinyi's business. Sometimes we turned the tape recorder off, so as not to record certain conversations which were too sensitive for others to hear or know about.

Format

There are three different kinds of texts in this narrative, which reflected the different styles used to produce the information. One kind are stories which I had complete control over, from beginning to end, and often initiated myself. Mbilinyi might have raised questions, but only for points of clarification or elaboration. These included the stories my fathers told me which we reproduced, and some of the accounts I gave about my life, including the one reproduced here about my education work in Katumba Village. Another kind of a text was produced on the basis of interview which Mbilinyi conducted with me, such as the descriptions of my early schooling and baptism. These two were not completely separated; often the interviews stimulated me to remember certain events in detail. I'd plan the content of what I wanted to say, sometimes staying awake all night to think about it. This is what happened in the case of my stories about midwifery, which are not included here, and about puberty and marriage rights, which are.

The third kind of text was the presentation of our debates, nearly verbatim, with only the editing out of unnecessary repetition. These debates were usually stimulated by questions posed by Mbilinyi, though they happened in all cases late in the evening, when we were relaxed, and were mostly a follow-up to earlier discussions.

The decision to present debates like this, in the form of dialogue, was made when it bacame apparent that the two of us had very different views about certain issues. Mbilinyi got very upset mid-way through our work in 1985, because she could not see how we could reconcile what were sometimes opposing positions on major issues. This led her to question the entire process of producing a narrative, and the ownership relations involved. Who owns this text, for example? The person whose life is being written about (me), or the life historian? The person who is responsible for most of the steps in the production process itself, including the design of the research projects, the writing of a proposal, the recording, and in many cases, the transcribing, writing, and editing (the producer, i.e. Mbilinyi)?

The question was even more complex in a participatory framework, where the producer takes an active part in producing the knowledge, with the life historian. In our case, from the begining, Mbilinyi did not remain silent nor did she agree with everything I said. That was the point of adopting a critical and participatory approach, one that enabled her to voice her own point of view while acknowledging mine.

Disturbed by her recognition that many issues had been left unresolved. unable to grasp the nuances of several passages, and sensing my unease with certain aspects of our work without being able to identify the problem, Mbilinyi finally realised that it would not be correct for her to produce the final text alone. She would have to find a way to return so that we could edit the transcripts and the final manuscript together. This would give me more control over the final text, enable me to edit any material which might be controversial, especially locally, and allow us to jointly decide on major issues concerning both format and content.

On my side, I had been greatly disturbed by Mbilinyi's interpretation of my church work as "teaching women to be slaves", and her evident inability to hear what I was trying to say. She thought I had been upset by her views on equality and theology, including her critique of the patriarchal ideologies reproduced in the Bible, but the real crisis for me centred around our interpretation of my work as an organiser and educator.

Most of the text is presented in the first person, I form. The content here reflects my own account and the ideas which were formulated during our work together. The text is the product of all of our talks, our discussions, the stories I thought up on my own, her responses to them, and the way these have been organised together and edited (and translated in the case of the English version). Mwaiseje Polisya also assisted in editing the manuscript, by copy-editing the Kiswahili version in their entirety

The final construction of the text did not follow the pattern of our sessions, instead it was organised around themes which we agreed about during our first transcription session. Rather than presenting one point of view in cases of major differences, we agreed to present both sides. The debates are self-explanatory, in showing each of our views. This avoided the silencing of one or the other, and gave the reader more insight into the debate itself. Moreover, these parts of the text illustrated the process used to produce the whole narrative and the active role of each one of us.

Mbilinyi transcribed our sessions after leaving and then returned so that we could correct the transcriptions together in early 1987. Later, she produced the first version of the text in manuscript form, and brought that back to me in 1987 for us to edit together. Since then, we have been expanding on certain themes and topics already found in the text.

I have tried to shape the stories told here, the way I normally structure the stories I tell. This means paying attention to the audience, and choosing stories which are good to listen to. They should be interesting and instructive at the same time. The personal stories have been told in a way which I hope moves the reader to empathise with the plight of Rungwe women and get angry enough to try and change things. The way a story is structured is as important as what it says. So is the tone of voice used by the story-teller and the way she dramatises every word and every action. Unfortunately the reader cannot see and hear the stories being told, but hopefully a sense of the emphasis and emotion is communicated.

The existence of taped recordings which we could refer to has been a continual resource – we only wished we had video recordings as well, to capture more of the feeling, action and intent. The recording process worked in our favour, and was not intrusive or a barrier to communication. However, I often had to remind Mbilinyi to put the machine on, or to check that the batteries were still functioning properly, because of the poor quality available at that time.

The taped recordings served several purposes, the most important of which was that they provided a precise record of what had been said. Mbilinyi ocassionaly misunderstood my meaning during our first sessions, and only realised what was going on when she worked on the transcripts. Moreover, it meant that she could concentrate on following the line of our discussions, because she was freed from the need to record every word in her notebook. Instead, she used hand-written notes to jot down questions for further discussion, which arose from our talks, and to sketch an outline of the flow of ideas. The tapes also allowed her to have a record of the changing tone, the silences, the pauses, the exclamations and the songs as well as the kiNyakyusa passages.

I'm glad that all of these aspects were realised by the tapes, because it made sure that a true interpretation was presented. At the same time, I enjoyed listening to our tapes being played back. I am a story-teller, and my stories are meant to be heard more than read. I couldn't help laughing to myself when we played back the humorous passages (Mbilinyi always returned with the full set), and I would often play them back alone.

Mbilinyi didn't go through the same participatory process of transcribing and editing for the other interviews she conducted in Rungwe in 1985, and told me later that this was a problem. Most research is not conducted in this way; interviews are held, questionnaires are filled out, and the researchers (or their assistants) are free to interpret what was said and the meaning without any cross-checking procedures. Problems of interpretation and meaning existed in the case of large-scale surveys as much as in the case of in-depth life histories like this one. It is obvious in this case that two entirely different texts could have been produced, on the basis of a first version, which lacked my input after the initial creation stage, and a second, jointly edited one. Not only would the first one have been erroneous in many respects, it would also have been a mis-representation of my personal views on matters of great importance to me.

The Crisis in Our Work Relations

I nearly withdrew from the project in 1985, because of Mbilinyi's dismissal of my work with women as being ultimately a means of reproducing oppressive relations: "teaching women to be slaves", or what has been described as domestication of women. She told me then that she considered my instructions to women 'to turn the other cheek' when their husbands got angry or cruel, not to fight back, and instead to look for ways of pacifying them, to be typical examples of domestication. She asked me whether or not I agreed with her, and I was so stung by her criticism that I could only repeat her words, after a long moment of silence – "teaching them to be slaves". She took this to mean acquiescence with point of view.

I challenged her by asking her to present alternative actions possible in the face of marital problems, and especially male violence. Mbilinyi was stuck for an answer, and finally said that women should "fight back" – without saying how, and with what means? – and that they could go to court.
Here is a transcript of my 1987 statement:

> ... You said that I spoiled the young women. You criticised me. I'm speaking the truth... I heard you. You said I taught them to be slaves.
>
> I'm saying, 'don't be slaves!'. Do you understand me now?
>
> What will you do if he beats you? If Mbilinyi beats you? Are you strong enough to fight back? ...
>
> You told me, "Why not take him to court?"
>
> Is the court a woman??? Will you bother to accuse him to his fellow

male?

Mbilinyi doesn't deal with the concrete problem of the here and now – that women are faced with male violence now, they need a solution now. My solution was to be clever [*mjanja*], to fool the man. I didn't mean that women should really become obsequious towards men, only that they should pretend to be so, in order to please the man until he calmed down. Men are so unintelligent, all it takes is a few nice words, some apparently-compliant behaviour, for them to be won over. We have to manipulate their egos in order to rule them, and rule them we do.

Mbilinyi's interpretation nullified everything I had been doing, and in a sense, invalidated my entire life's work. This narrative project is like an autobiography which gave meaning to my life as well as projecting a story for others to read. A false portayal of this nature invalidated my existence. In 1985, when the crisis occured, there had been no plan for me to participate in the editing of the final manuscript – so it was even more of a crisis for me. Fortunately Mbilinyi returned and gave me the opportunity to correct this and other errors.

Alarm has been expressed to Mbilinyi, mainly by Western scholars, about her critical approach, her willingness to express a different opinion and to ocassionaly criticise some aspect of my account. Those holding this position did not believe that it was possible for me to maintain my own positions and to argue back. According to them, I had to be intimidated by her because she was a professor and because she was a European in origin.

Of course, Mbilinyi is a Professor, moreover her husband is a 'big man' in the government, and yes, she is a European. All of this mattered more at the beginning of our relationship, before we knew each other better. However, Mbilinyi lived with us, ate with us, as well as sharing her ideas with me and Sambulika in an honest and open fashion, just as she does with her other colleagues at the University. Why can't a peasant debate with a Professor about issues concerning her own life, about which she knows much more than the Professor? From the beginning, Mbilinyi told me that she had come to learn from me, that my job was to teach her. Perhaps some do not believe that I have anything to teach? or that I know what I am talking about? This seems disempowering to me, the failure to acknoledge me and my knowledge, the tendency to patronise, to' perceive people like me as lacking enough self-respect and integrity to maintain our own position unless persuaded otherwise. I could be persuaded to adopt a different point of view as a result of a logical argument, not for any other reason. But in this, as in other cases, I wasn't. Instead, I got Mbilinyi to alter her views about women's use of churches as space for organising other women. She no longer dismisses this as simply a case of domestication.

In another context, she explained her new position as follows:

> I have learned that analyses of women's accommodations, resistances and struggles must study the material circumstances within which actions and ideas emerge, and the way these circumstances are perceived by the actors themselves. The limitations that exist in specific circumstances must be acknowledged, as well as the way in which certain actions help to broaden the space available and increase female autonomy, or otherwise.
>
> Kalindile taught me that reality and history are more complex than we often realise, and that we needed to understand and respect the contradictory ways in which women have had to cope with oppression, even as we criticise them. This is essential if we are going to be successful in generating new and more effective strategies and tactics for the future.

When we edited this part of the manuscript together in August 1987, Mbilinyi asked me whether I thought it had been a mistake for her to have expressed her own views as much as she had. I told her then, your approach is correct. I don't want someone who just listens to me, without providing any real response.

I told her that I had never been frightened or intimidated by her. Before giving Mbilinyi my perception of the 1985 crisis, I had prefaced my comments as follows,

> One thing before you talk any more with your mother, your mother is telling you that she is only speaking the truth. What she opposes, she opposes to you directly, without fear. She doesn't know anything about fear.
>
> If you are angry with someone without explaining why, you are not able to teach that person.

We each taught the other; we were often angry with each other. But if Mbilinyi had never told me her views on domestication, I would not have been in a position to correct her, at least with respect to my own work. Either here or in another context, she would have presented on over-simplified and incorrect interpretation of my work. In this case, silence would have acted as a barrier to the education process which was incorporated into our life history making.

Footnotes

1. This is based on the preliminary manuscript of a book which the authors have been working on since 1985, to be entitled '*Wish I was a Man: Rebeka Kalindile, Woman of Rungwe, Tanzania*. The original text was produced in

Kiswahili and has been edited and translated into English by Mbilinyi with editorial assistance by Mwaiseje Polisya.

We gratefully acknowledge the funding assistance which this project received from many different donors at different stages of the production process. SIDA, IDRC, Dartington Hall Trust, Fund for Human Need (Methodist Church, London) and the Leonard Cohen Fund jointly supported the first period of study, 'creation' and transcription in 1985. WRDP funded the local expenses involved when the transcripts based on the original taped recordings were corrected and edited together in 1987, and SIDA funded travel and local costs entailed in joint editing of the first draft of the manuscript, also in 1987. An additional opportunity to work on the text was provided as a result of the funding provided to Mbilinyi by the Social Science Research Council (New York City, USA) in 1989 in conjunction with the jointly funded project with Susan Geiger on women in plantation and peasant farming.

Additional support for much of the writing was provided as a result of fellowship grants received by Mbilinyi at the Departments of Women's Studies and of African and African-American Studies at the University of Minnesota/Twin Cities (1986), IDS (Sussex) (1987/88) and the Centre for the Humanities, Oregon State University/Carvallis (1990/91).

WRDP provided moral support needed to get initial funding for the original history project, 'A Local History Project about Women and Colonial Development policies from the Point of View of Rungwe Women (1920–1961)', which included the life history-making with Rebeka Kalindile. It accepted the project proposal for 1985 activities in 1984, endorsed the project as part of WRDP activities and provided a covering letter in support of funding applications.

2. "This text is based on material which was jointly written by Kalindile and Mbilinyi with the assistance of Sambulika. The methods used to produce this work are described in the last section of this chapter. The 'original' text for sections two through six was presented by Kalindile, in the context of our discussions. The text for sections one ('Introduction') and seven ('How We Produced this Text') was originally presented by Mbilinyi, based on our discussions and including verbatim quotations from each author. However, we jointly revised and edited tne original text together, *word for word*, including the story of our methodology in the last section."

3. Rev. Mwankemwa was one of the first African clergy to be fully ordained as a pastor by the European missionaries in Rungwe. He and his colleagues were ordained after many years of service, including the war years when German missionaries were forced by the British to leave the area and the

local clergy worked without European 'supervision'. Rev. Mwankemwa bacame the pastor in charge of Kyimbila Church and all the village churches in its congregation, and was known as a dedicated pastor and strict disciplinarian in the church and the community. He participated in the production of the church and the community. He participated in the production of the local history about 'tradition and gender in colonial Rungwe' which Mbilinyi is currently working on, and was interviewed extensively in 1985, just prior to his death.

4. See footnote 2. This section was originally prepared by Mbilinyi, based on earlier discussion together, and then we revised and edited it together, word for word.

References

1. Fields, Mamie Garvin with Karen Fields 1983 *Lemon Swamp and Other Places* New York, Free Press.
2. Walker, Alice 1983 *In Search of Our Mothers' Daughters* New York, Harvest.

Suggested Readings

On participatory research methodology, Yusuf Kassam and Kemal Mustafa eds *Participatory Research* (New Delhi, Society for Participatory Research in Asia, and Toronto, International Council for Adult Education, 1982; Kemal Mustafa ed *African Perspectives on Participatory Research* (Toronto, Participatory Research Group/ICAE, 1982).

Concerning life histories, see Susan Geiger "Life History: content and Method" *Signs* 11:2 (pp 334–351, 1986); Marjorie Mbilinyi "I'd have been a man': Politics and the Labour Process in Producing Personal Narratives" in Personal Narratives Group eds *Interpreting Women's Lives* (Bloomington,Indiana University Press, 1989); the argument for a critical approach in life histories is presented in Richard Johnson et al eds *Making Histories* (London, Hutchinson, 1982).

An anthropological study of 'traditional' social relations of marriage and the family is found in the work of Monica Wilson, such as *Good Company* (Boston, Beacon Press, 1963). The significance of the Moravian Church in the history of the Southern Highlands is studied in detail in Marcia Wright's *German Mission in Tanganyika 1891 – 1914* (Oxford, Clarendon Press, 1971).

On the political economy of Rungwe past and present, and women's conditions within Rungwe, see Marjorie Mbilinyi "Agribusiness and Casual

Labour in Tanzania" *African Economic History* 15 (1986); "Runaway Wives in Rungwe" International J of Sociology of Law 16:1 (1988) and *Big Slavery* (Dar es Salaam University Press, forthcoming).

On women in Tanzania, see Ophelia Mascarenhas and Marjorie Mbilinyi *Women in Tanzania* (Upsala, Scandinavian Institute of African Studies, 1983) and its Kiswahili and reedited version, *Mapambano ya Wanawake Tanzania* translated by Patricia Mbughuni (Dar es Salaam University Press, forthcoming).

CHAPTER SEVEN

From a Peasant to a Worker in the City of Dar es Salaam: The Case of Mwanaidi Salehe Msuya

Mwanaidi with Asseny Muro

Introduction

Mwanaidi Salehe Msuya was born in 1925 in Ugweno, an area situated on the Northern end of the North Pare Plateau. Ugweno is neighboured on the East by Taita of Kenya and on the West by Kilimanjaro. Ugweno is found between 4,000 and 6,000 feet above sea level and usually receives heavy rainfall.

The earliest people who settled in Ugweno migrated from Taita due to clan conflicts. Kimambo,[1] in his historical account of Pare writes that the Yamdai family from Taita are believed to be the ancestors of the Ugweno clans. In the later period we had people from Uchagga migrating to Ugweno. Ugweno people have their own language mainly resembling the Chagga language. In the Southern part of Ugweno and due to long time interaction with the Wapare, many inhabitants can speak both Kipare and Kigweno.

Mwanaidi's clan – Wasuya was the ruling clan of Ugweno but was preceeded by the Shana clan as the ruling clan. Mwanaidi said that her aunt was married to Mangi Minja, the last Gweno Chief before the coming to an end of the chiefdom system after independence. The Wasuya consist of almost one third of the whole population of Ugweno (other clans – Wafinanga, Wamare and Wanana) The rise of the Wasuya clan took place during the 18th century leading to the Wasuya as a ruling clan in the 19th century

The Wagweno fell under Islamic influence in the early 19th Century. Kimambo in his account wrote that Ugweno formed the oldest inroad into the Pare Mountains. The Waswahili caravans to Ugweno and Kilimanjaro had to pass through the Pare plain. By 1861 the Waswahili and Arab traders had become frequent visitors to the area and they had gone as far as Ugweno. Elephant hunting was the most important attraction to the visitors. During those times ivory supply was readily available in Ugweno and the Waswahili traders established a permanent base in the place. So it is no wonder many people in Ugweno and in some parts in Upare are Moslems.

149

It is against this background that we situate the 62 years old lady, Mwanaidi Msuya, whose life history is of significance not only to the history of Wagweno but also to the whole history of Tanzania. Mwanaidi's Life History, as exemplified in her struggles, has shattered the myth that women cannot stand on their own. Mwanaidi's history impresses upon the women folk the possibility and the necessity for standing on their own feet in a world in which they have been "forced" to believe that they cannot make ends meet without the support of men. The Life History of Mwanaidi Salehe Msuya, now a retired officer and resident of Dar es Salaam City is an important account to have in this initial attempt of documenting women's History.

When Mwanaidi, was approached and the purpose of the study spelt out, she offered to co-operate and was delighted and ready to let her life history be shared by other women. Consequently, throughout the data collection period the researcher enjoyed Mwanaidi's readiness to talk to her. Sometimes the researcher would walk into her house at times when she was busy with other tasks, however, they always found time to talk to each other.

Although Mwanaidi and the researcher drew up a tentative schedule of their meetings. Sometimes this did not always work as planned because of other commitments. However, the researcher is highly grateful for Mwanaidi's effort in making this work a success. Without her readiness to contribute and have her life experience shared by the womenfolk it would not have been possible to come up with this chapter. Right from the beginning the researcher was very impressed by Mwanaidi's narration and her ability to articulate issues. All the same, her experience being so extensive, the researcher chose to cover four aspects of her life namely:– growing up in a village as a girl; marriage and divorce; employment in Dar es Salaam City, retirement and a land-lady. These four aspects were discussed in detail with Mwanaidi. Much as the selection of those aspects helped to direct the discussion, the issues chosen rationalized the intention to build Mwanaidi's historical personality in order to highlight her struggles in life.

Growing up in the Village as a Girl

Mwanaidi was the first born in her family and this being the case she took up a lot of responsibilities at a very early age, for example looking after young siblings, fetching water, collecting firewood etc. Mwanaidi's responsibilities increased after her mother had been divorced leaving her and a brother behind at very young age (five and two-and-half years respectively). Mwanaidi had to take care of her young brother and other responsibilities, which under a step mother were even worse. In Ugweno, no wife was allowed to leave with her children when divorced. Children were considered the property of the husband and in the event of divorce he withheld the children.

Mwanaidi's mother divorced Mzee Salehe because she could not tolerate his harsh treatment. The co-wife, Binti Juma was the type who would always report her co-wife negatively to the husband. Even with the understanding that she was leaving behind her children, Mwanaidi's mother said, "enough is enough".

The implications of growing up under a step-mother are known. Mwanaidi narrated that the step-mother with whom they lived, was not good. She used to tell them that their mother was dead. As Mwanaidi grew up, and started realizing issues, she started searching for the truth about her mother. One day she met and recognised her mother at the market place and insisted to be shown where she was residing. Mwanaidi was very delighted that she had traced her mother and that she could now visit her. When she went back home she disclosed the good news to her brother and they resolved to talk it to their father with the intention of receiving permission to go and visit their mother as they wished.

Their father granted the permission on condition that they would not spend a night at their mother's place. When Mwanaidi went to visit her mother and decided to spend days there her father would go personally to collect her. In such instances, he scolded and warned her not to repeat the "offence."

Mwanaidi's mother later on got-married and bore four children with the husband.

Mwanaidi fulfilled the main responsibilities assigned to her according to the traditional division of labour. At home she would help with collecting firewood, cooking, pounding maize, collecting fodder for cattle etc. Her brother would take goats for pasture and often went to Koran School. At that time pots were used for cooking, collecting and keeping water. Women in Ugweno community were not making pots. They used to buy them from the Pare women who were traditionally pot makers. Later on the Ugweno women adopted the pottery art.

Most of the time Mwanaidi was at home doing some work. She grew up with other girls of the same age such as her uncle's daughters (on father's side). Her best and very close girlfriend was Zainabu Kimborido. Zainabu was born more or less the same time as Mwanaidi and the two sucked milk from the latter's mother because the former's mother's breasts were not giving milk. The practice of a young baby sucking milk from another mother is common in many communities in Tanzania.[2]

Mwanaidi explains that there was a lot of fun in growing up in the village with other young girls. According to Mwanaidi, the village *ngomas* (dances) were the most interesting part of the fun. Young boys and girls would attend *ngomas* arranged for different social occasions such as during initiation ceremonies, weddings etc. Young people were encouraged to take part in the ngomas as part of socialization, and with the intention of passing on to the young generation the *ngoma* culture. Mwanaidi observe that some girls found their suitors in such *ngomas*. Asked to cite any ngoma song, Mwanaidi called upon her nieces (her brother's daughters– aged 3, 7 and 13 years old) and asked them to sing and dance a *ngoma* infront of the researcher. These young girls although living in Dar es Salaam, knew some of the Ugweno *ngoma* culture their aunt has attempted to pass on to them.

As a process of socialization and initiation, Mwanaidi underwent circumcision at the age of about eight years. She had not even started school. Mwanaidi was taken to a nearby bush where she found several elder women. Normally one was taken to the bush by surprise; for according to the tradition the concerned is not told before hand. Upon reaching the bush the old women would immediately start working on the girl. Mwanaidi remembers how on entering the bush she was held by several old women and seated on a mortar. The woman who normally conducts the operation was told by the others to bring the "cockroach". This in a way was used as a trick to cheat the girl. Mwanaidi said in the case of a boy they would ask for a "bee". (Meaning the small very sharp knife used for the operation).

Mwanaidi was attentively looking at the woman asked to bring the cockroach and instead of seeing the insect she saw the woman draw out a small knife. This scared Mwanaidi who started shouting and resisting. It was now that she came to her senses that they were going to perform something fishy on her. Mwanaidi said that she really gave the women tough time and the cries she was making made her father intervene. He came close to the bush and shouted to Mwanaidi to keep silent or else he would go to beat her. Mwanaidi had always been scared of her father and she had to calm down for the operation. Two more girls underwent the operation on the same day and they were to stay at one place for two months to heal. They were cautioned never to tell other girls of the operation.

Asked why the girls would be circumcised Mwanaidi does not know the meaning behind. She observes that it is done in order to fulfil a traditional norm. She revealed to the researcher that she has even let her nieces undergo the same operation. She normally takes them to Ugweno for this event. As for the likely health risks emanating from this crude operation, Mwanaidi said that she does not remember a single case of a girl whose health was at risk due to circumcision. She said that traditional medicines used to heal the wound always worked.

Mwanaidi was also involved in farming. As a young girl she was allocated a plot matching her age. The size of the plot was increased as she grew up and as she gained farming skills. Up to the time she married she had a two acre farm. The main intention of allocating a farm to growing up girls like Mwanaidi was to promote her farming skill, a skill which was regarded as very essential for a future mother who at one time would use it to sustain her family. Mwanaidi planted bananas, beans, sugar canes and vegetables in her farm. She did this farming work over and above assisting her step-mother with the family farmwork in the plains – *"nyika"*.

Women of Ugweno used to travel long distances to the "nyika" (nicknamed *Kambi ya Simba)* to grow rice and maize. These crops would not grow well in the highlands where the weather was cold. These areas were claimed and cleared by male members of various families and then women would go to dig and grow crops.

Mwanaidi started school at the age of 11 years and she went as far as class three (standard three). She discontinued schooling because she fell sick. However she had acquired the basic skills of reading and writing. Her brother attended Koran School where he received Islamic knowledge. Mwanaidi did not attend Koran School.

There are several lessons we can draw from Mwanaidi's experience. First, when she was growing up her family and community at large prepared her for the roles she was going to play when married. This preparation was in the form of informal practical education, given mainly by the female relatives, (mother, aunt etc). Second, Mwanaidi's struggle for survival started at a very early age of her life because their mother left them while still very young and they were subjected to step-mother relationship which in most cases is harsh and unjust.

Preparing for Marriage.

Mwanaidi married Abdallah Kililai in 1944, at the age of 19. Abdallah Kililai was a Chaga by origin. His father had moved and settled in Ugweno. So Abdallah was born and had grown in the same village as Mwanaidi. When Still a young-man, Abdallah learnt tailoring and thereafter secured employment at Mwanaidi's father's tailoring shop. Abdallah and Mwanaidi first fell in love with each other before disclosing their relationship to their parents. They used to exchange love letters. Later on they thought they should communicate their intention to their parents. Abdallah conveyed to his father his interests in marrying Mwanaidi Salehe. This information was received positively. Parents of both sides knew and thought their children's marriage would cement their friendship.

In preparation for the marriage, Mwanaidi was put through a lot of

153

teachings. The first caution was to avoid other men who showed interest to court her. The whole village would of course know that Mwanaidi was already bound to a suitor so villager's eyes would also be on her. Mwanaidi had not yet started her menstrual cycle when the courtship started. During those days girls would be bound to fiances at a very young age and would be put under vigorous teachings. There were also conditions to be met before deciding on marriage. These were: the girl had to be circumcized and had had her menstrual cycle started. Before these the suitor could not start marriage negotiations involving mainly the paying of bride-price.

The process of paying bride-price to Mwanaidi's parents started only after the boy, and the girl had given consent and confirmation that they would marry. In Ugweno, the bride-price consisted of local beer, goats and cattle. In Mwanaidi's case, tea was prepared instead of local beer due to Islamic obligations. Remarking on her father's stand on bride-price, Mwanaidi said that her father received the bride-price, not because he wanted to sell her out but rather in order to comply with the cultural norms prevailing at that time. The order followed in presenting the bride-price was as follows:– It started with calling together female relatives from Mwanaidi's side and from Abdallah's side in order for them to familiarize and get to know each other. Tea and food was served. Another sitting called upon male relatives of the two families. These first two meetings are known as relationship stabilization sittings. At the end of these meetings the boy's side was asked to pay the bride-price. This was in kind and cash.

As to the bride-price, Mwanaidi said it was paid in the following manner. Four cattle – initially two cattle (one cow and one bull) were delivered to the girl's father. The remaining two would be paid after the bride delivered a baby. Then followed the payment of six goats. These were converted to cash and thus Mwanaidi's father received Tz. shilling 72/- (12 shillings for each goat). Two more goats were to be given to Mwanaidi's mother if the daughter was found a virgin during the wedding night. The significance of this condition is derived from the cultural norm that it is the mother who is supposed to mould her daughter's behaviour and that the mother is rewarded for fulfilling this and meeting society requirements. The last goat was to be paid to safeguard all the wealth paid – meaning at this stage no other man could be allowed to court the girl. This goat was given a special name in Kigweno – *Mburu yafingirwa*.

The delivering of the bride wealth was done in a special sitting and presentation was done by the *Mshenga*[4] accompanied by other relatives from the suitor's side. Permission for taking the bride was sought in a special sitting, bringing together parents from both sides. This sitting was called after the bride and the groom had agreed on the day they wanted their wedding to take place. Mwanaidi said that the presents given to the girl by her suitor were not counted in the bride wealth.

It was interesting to learn from Mwanaidi that before marrying she was obliged to collect and accumulate firewood for her mother (in her case, her step-mother). Mwanaidi fulfilled this duty through assistance from her suitor and her girlfriends of the same village. Abdallah would often collect other boys, go to the forest and cut down logs of wood. They also sliced the logs to ease carrying. Mwanaidi and other girls would go to collect the firewood and bring it home. This work went on till a fairly big pile was collected. This tradition was intended to make the mother not feel the burden of collecting firewood immediately after her daughter had left. Moreover, this task signified also the importance of firewood to a woman's life.

The period of preparing for marriage for Mwanaidi was quite hectic – she was put under pre-marriage teachings and started her menstrual period. The teachings oriented her to the facts of becoming a wife and a mother. Mwanaidi's experience reveals that girls' marriage arrangements were made by parents when they were very young. Although in some cases (e.g. during festivals) girls met and fell in love with boys, parents were very instrumental in "fixing their children's marriages". In those cases where the teenagers chose their partners themselves, still they themselves sought first their parents' consent before marriage preparations started. The bride-price paid during Mwanaidi's days had started being commercialised due to the fact that goats were converted to cash and this cash was received by her father. Fathers still received the lion's share of the bride wealth paid. This in a way is a contradiction when considering the amount of labour a mother puts in to raise up a daughter. One should not also forget the education and training she had to inculcate to her daughter in order for her to be marriage-worthy. "Furthermore, one should not underrate the effort made by the mother in "protecting" her daughter's virginity".

In spite of all that, the portion of the bride wealth supposed to be received by the girl's mother was given on condition that her daughter would be a virgin. It is also significant to note that the bride was made to fulfill some of her responsibilities like collecting and accumulating firewood for her mother before getting married. In this way, it was believed that the mother would have felt immediately the burden she was leaving on to her as a result of her departure. In a way then, marriage created shortage of labour in the bride's family.

Marriage and Divorce

After paying the bride wealth, Abdallah and Mwanaidi compromised on the day of their wedding. Unfortunately however, before the wedding day arrived, Mwanaidi eloped because she could no longer tolerate the ill-treatment she was receiving from her step-mother. She fled to Abdallah's house. Nevertheless, the elopment occured at the time when all the necessary marriage arrangements had been fulfilled. The *Mshenga* was thus sent to Mwanaidi's parents the following day to report on the secret marriage. On the third day, a Moslem Sheikh was called to officiate the marriage between Mwanaidi and Abdallah. Mwanaidi's wedding was conducted according to Moslem procedures. Mwanaidi was dressed in Moslem style, covering her whole body with a black veil (Baibui). Abdallah bought all the wedding clothes.

Although Mwanaidi had already moved to Abdallah's house, she was brought back to her father's house from where she was taken officially as a bride. Mwanaidi reports with pride that Abdallah found her a virgin. Consequently, "my mother was given her two goat's. She was therefore respected by her in-laws for remaining a virgin until she got married.

Mwanaidi was well received by her in-laws. As Abdallah was the last born to his family, tradition dictated that they should live in their parents' compound (Abdallah's parents). Abdallah's father had passed away when he married and so the newly wed couple had to live with the groom's mother. In Ugweno tradition the male last born inherited his father's farm and house and as a result of this he takes care of his parents.

Mwanaidi was now expected to put into practice whatever knowledge and skills she had acquired as a girl. Few days after her wedding she was entrusted with the main instruments which she would use to fulfill her responsibilities. She was given a blacksmith hoe which she would use for farming; a sickle *(mundo)* for cutting grass for cattle; clay pots (4), wooden spoons, beans and bananas. She was also given cows (4) which were still however in the possession of her mother-in-law. The food items like beans were supposed to last her up to the time she would harvest hers. She was to use the farm which was occupied by her mother-in-law to grow food.

Mwanaidi was well prepared to take up these and other responsibilities. Self-reliance was in-planted in her and she managed things in her husband's absence. After they had lived in the compound of the mother-in-law for two years, Mwanaidi advised her husband to find a separate plot where they would build their own house. Abdallah took the advice. He took a pot of local beer to a certain oldman far away from his mother to ask for a farm. He was allocated a two acres farm by the old man. Mwanaidi said that during those days, a young couple could get a farm through inheritance, or from a male relative or family friends. It was a custom that local beer accompanied a request for a plot of land. Nevertheless, when Mwanaidi married, land scarcity had started being felt as a problem in Ugweno.

Mwanaidi and her husband started working on their newly acquired land by growing coffee and bananas. They also started building a house. Before long they moved to their new residence. They took their old mother with them. Mwanaidi says she got along quite well with her mother-in-law. She always felt as if she was with her own mother.

Mwanaidi was a farmer; she set this record from the beginning. Neighbours and relatives noticed her hardwork from the time she joined them. Consequently, the couple scored rapid progress. On the other hand, Abdallah continued to work in his father-in-law's tailoring shop. He mainly used to return home over the week-ends. Mwanaidi was therefore a *de-facto* head of the household. She was managing the home and the farm because the husband was a fulltime employee. Abdallah was very proud of his wife, whom he commended for hardwork. The mother-in-law was also impressed by Mwanaidi's behaviour and conduct. She was rest assured that she had got herself a daughter. Mwanaidi used to care for her mother-in-law and assisted her in maintaining her farm (their previous shamba). Moreover, Mwanaidi sometimes hired additional plots for growing food crops such as beans and maize.

Similarly, Mwanaidi coped well with other neighbouring women. (Msimamo ukiolewa, uwe na nia na moyo wa kusaidiana na wanawake wenzako unaowakuta). She talked of how women used to co-operate in those days. Women would assist one another in digging, cutting banana barks for roofing, carrying water during house construction etc. During co-operative labour each would bring her own food. Co-operative labour consolidated women's efforts; thus easing some of their work. It was also during co-operative work that women exchanged views and advised one another on how to live and resolve difficulties in life.

Mwanaidi used to get some financial support from her husband but in most cases Mwanaidi was growing all that they required for food. Sometimes she would sell surplus food crops and buy herself some clothes. The husband often bought her pairs of Khanga (piece of cloth to wrap around the body).

Mwanaidi's family progress was however interrupted by her failure to bear children for her husband. After five years of marriage, Mwanaidi had not conceived. Meanwhile, she had gone to see traditional herbalists and medicine-men but in vain. As years passed much concern was raised not so, by the husband but by relatives on the husband side. Mwanaidi took the initiative of advising her husband to look for another wife. Both of them did not however, know where the problem lay as they had not been checked in any modern hospital. Marrying a second wife would help to establish who between Abdallah and Mwanaidi had a problem. Initially, Abdallah opposed the idea. However, when pressure from his relatives and from his wife increased he requested the wife to identify the lady she wanted to be her co-wife.

Mwanaidi co-operated and participated in looking for the co-wife. She selected one, Zaina Juma, who was her cousin. Mwanaidi chose a relative, believing that she could get on well with a co-wife to whom she was related. The second wife was married through the same traditional procedures of paying bridewealth. Mwanaidi said the co-wife was older than herself.

Mwanaidi's parents were not supposed to return any of the bride-price paid for their daughter. However, they were not going to receive the remaining two cows till that time their daughter delivered a child.

The co-wife, Zaina delivered a baby in her first year of marriage. This proved to Mwanaidi that her husband had no problem; the problem lay on her side. She had to accept the truth, and since the husband still wanted her to stay, she was to cope with the situation. She loved and took care of the baby.

Towards the end of the second year of staying with Zaina, conflicts started. The co-wife was sometimes reporting to the husband unfounded complaints concerning Mwanaidi, in return, Abdallah would reprimand her. Sometimes, Mwanaidi heard from her in-laws (Abdallah's brothers) irritating remarks such as; "Let her (Mwanaidi) dig like a donkey, our children will eat". In other words she was working for nothing. Her toiling was to benefit the husband and the co-wife's children. However, traditionally a woman would work hard on the farm to secure food for her children and to safeguard the *shamba* (farm) which would be passed on to her sons through inheritance. Nevertheless, Abdallah tried his level best to treat the two wives fairly. He did not just harass Mwanaidi because she had not bore him children. Neither did he inflict beating on Mwanaidi for all the years they lived together.

However, the environment was no longer condusive for Mwanaidi to continue with the marriage. Mwanaidi disclosed to her husband her intention to leave but he resisted. Mwanaidi eventually left and went back to her parents. The parents were not pleased with the step which Mwanaidi had taken. They could not see what wrong the husband had done to her. They persuaded her to go back to the husband. The main implication of her divorce was that her father would return the bride-price.

Mwanaidi had to officiate her divorce in order for her father to return the bridewealth. Her case was filed in the primary court in Ugweno. The reason she advanced for the divorce was that she was tired of her husband and that she could no longer tolerate the marriage. Even after Mwanaidi had made up her mind to leave the husband the Chief who at that time was presiding in the court recommended further negotiations with a view to reconciling the couple. The first day Mwanaidi's case was mentioned in the court, Mwanaidi was asked to go and live with her *Mshenga*. At the *Mshenga's* house, Mwanaidi was talked into and solicited to go back to her husband However, her stand was firm; she was going to divorce Abdallah.

When the case was called for hearing the second time, it was found that Mwanaidi had not changed her mind. The Chief clarified to the court audience why Mwanaidi wanted to divorce the husband. He stated that Mwanaidi was leaving the husband because she had not been able to deliver a child. This interpretation was true because the husband had not been reported to have ill-treated Mwanaidi.

The third time they came to the court, divorce was granted. Those present in the court was Mwanaidi's father and several other relatives from her father's side. Abdallah was also there accompanied by his *mshenga* and other relatives. The Moslem Sheikh was also there. The Chief was ready to grant the divorce. He however cautioned Mwanaidi's father that he would have to return the bride-wealth he had taken. Mwanaidi's father was ready to do as ordered by the court. Two certificates of divorce were prepared; one for Mwanaidi, and another for Abdallah. On the certificates were written these words *"Kuoana kwa wema na kuachana kwa Wema"*. As explained by Mwanaidi the statement meant the couple had divorced not on very serious grounds.

Mwanaidi's father returned the bridewealth he had received except the last goat which would be paid by the man who would re-marry her; The two goats given to Mwanaidi's mother were not returned. Abdallah did not continue with employment at Mwanaidi's place after the divorce.

This stage and experience of Mwanaidi's married life presents to us several lessons. Mwanaidi's preparations for marriage were hectic and arduous. Even then she did not manage to reach the peak of the preparations. Hardship and ill-treatment from her step-mother forced Mwanaidi to elope. However, Mwanaidi was well baked for that marriage. She was hard working, obedient and humble to her in-laws but this was not enough. Her failure fo bear children eroded all the rest. This problem became the main cause ot Mwanaidi's divorce.

Another lesson is that although a wife would go as far as identifying a co-wife, that was no guarantee that they will always be in peace with each other. In Mwanaidi's case polygamy became the main cause of conflicts between the husband and wives. Another lesson learnt through Mwanaidi's experience is that divorce in most of the African Communities has not given a woman a fair share of her contribution to the marriage. Mwanaidi had stayed and toiled in building their home, in developing and maintaining the farms; but when the chief granted her divorce, no mention was made of giving Mwanaidi anything as her contribution to the family wealth. She went back to her father empty-handed (except for some clothes). As if this was not enough, her father was instructed to return the bridewealth. Mwanaidi was aware that she had been both exploited and oppressed through her marriage but she proudly stated that such injustice "opened her eyes".

Taking up Employment in Dar es Salaam

Mwanaidi stayed with her parents for a few years before she finally decided to go away to do something for her life. After studying the environment at her father's home she could not think of herself being comfortable there. Her father kept on marrying and divorcing wives and step-mothers would sometimes report to their husband allegations against Mwanaidi. Mwanaidi said that her father married five more wives after her mother, but all of them,. except the second wife (married when Mwanaidi's mother was there) were eventually divorced. Mwanaidi remarked that her father was very harsh to his wives. For instance, he used to inflict beatings on them as a matter of routine. This was the environment at Mzee Salehe's home. It was just impossible for Mwanaidi to put up not only with his father's behaviour, but also with that of her step-mothers.

There was yet another reason which made Mwanaidi go away from home. Some men were coming to her to make proposal for marriage. Mwanaidi had already established that she could not bear a child. Moreover, a child being so significant to any marriage, she was not ready to enter any marriage ties lest she suffered another social blow.

Mwanaidi left home and went to live with her cousin (aunt's son – on the father's side) in Arusha Chini in Moshi. Mwanaidi's cousin used to work in the Sugar Cane plantation. Mwanaidi asked her cousin to look to the possibility of her getting employed. The Sugar Cane Plantation in those days had very limited employment opportunities for women. All manual work like sugar cane cutting was done by men. However, Mwanaidi's cousin managed to secure employment for her. Mwanaidi was employed as a baby sitter/domestic worker for one Indian family in Moshi. Mwanaidi was employed with a starting salary of thirty shillings a month. She therefore moved from her cousin's house and went to live with the Indian family. Her main job was baby-sitting. Her employer was satisfied with her service and behaviour.

In 1954, the Indian family moved to Dar es Salaam to establish some

160

business. Because the Indian family were very much satisfied with Mwanaidi's performance, they asked her to accompany them to Dar es Salaam. Having no objection to this request, Mwanaidi moved to the City where she was destined to stay and live for the rest of her life. The Indian family settled in Upanga and Mwanaidi stayed with the family in the same house, looking after the three children devotedly for eight years.

When the children grew up, she automatically found herself redundant. However, because her work was highly appreciated, the Indian family wrote her a very good certificate of performance so as to enable her seek employment elsewhere. Mwanaidi had not yet acquired any City life experience because she mainly stayed indoors looking after the children. Even with the good certificate given to her she would not know which way to go looking for employment. However, in 1960, the Indian family found her a job with a European family in the same area, Upanga. Mwanaidi was to continue with baby sitting work. The European family was paying her *80/-* shillings per month. When her first European employer went away he gave Mwanaidi another certificate of performance. The family also arranged for her employment with another family residing in Oysterbay. Mwanaidi worked with the family for six months only because the lady of the house (*Memsahib*) was very harsh to her. Mwanaidi left the family and found employment with another white family. This lived around Victoria area along Bagamoyo Road.

Mwanaidi was to reach a turning point when she secured employment with one French family working at the University of Dar es Salaam. Mwanaidi was no longer finding a problem in securing domestic employment because the certificates given to her by previous bosses spoke by themselves. Mwanaidi was now leaving in her small grass thatched hut *kibanda* at Makumbusho area when she was employed by the French family. Mwanaidi had taken the initiative to put up a hut *(kibanda.)* This step vindicates Mwanaidi's strive to become self-reliant and her desire to live her own life. She often used to ask herself "how long shall I continue living with white bosses?" Mwanaidi continued to live in her hut even after securing employment with the French family.

The French boss appreciated Mwanaidi's services as a result of which he took interests in knowing where she was living. One day the French boss left with Mwanaidi to see where she was residing. The Frenchman was dissatisfied with the standard of the hut. He was going to help Mwanaidi to put up a better house. At that time Makumbusho area was being surveyed and people were being moved out. The French boss having learnt of this problem asked Mwanaidi to look for a plot elsewhere as he intended to finance the construction of a house for her. This he would do over and above Mwanaidi's salary. Moreover, the French *Memsahib* used to give her free meals.

When Mwanaidi got a plot in Manzese area she reported to her boss who was ready to supply money for the purchase of building materials as and when requested. Mwanaidi requested the following amounts from her boss – TAS 50 for the plot; TAS 800 for building wood; corrugated iron sheets TAS 1,000; Construction TAS 500, clearing the plot TAS 150; earth filling and plastering TAS 150; and cement plastering TAS 150 shillings.

One day the French boss decided to go to the site to see the house he was financing. He drove to Manzese with Mwanaidi, only to find that the house was not of the standard he had expected. He expected that she was building a cement brick house so that it could be fitted with electric wiring. He disclosed to Mwanaidi that he had planned to give her a refrigarator and an electric cooker. His plans seemed to have been tempered with, now that the house was not up to his expected standard. All the same, to Mwanaidi the house was a mansion and she simply could not understand why her boss was so disappointed.

Furthermore, the French boss whom Mwanaidi still remembers for his generosity assisted her in opening a bank account. He took Mwanaidi to a bank in town and directed her on how to deposit money and how to withdraw money from her account. Since then Mwanaidi became sensitized over the importance of having a bank account. Henceforth she has kept a bank account and cultivated the practice of deposting money in it regularly.

The French boss left the country and rewarded Mwanaidi TAS.2,000/-. The Frenchman entrusted Mwanaidi to another boss, who was also working at the University of Dar es Salaam. This was 1965. The French boss asked the newly acquired boss to see that Mwanaidi secured permanent employment at the University of Dar es Salaam. This was the time the National University was being established out of the East African University. Then, many Africans were being recruited for University service, particularly in the low cadre posts. In this way Mwanaidi found herself being employed in the Female Students' Hall of Residence (Hall III) as a Cleaner, in July 1966, a job she was to do until when she retired in 1985.

While working in the house of the last boss at the University, Mwanaidi was given a servant's quarter. This gave her the opportunity to rent her six room house at Manzese. Fortunately enough, when she got employed at the University she continued living in the servant's quarter. Her motto had been that of striving hard and she has continued with the motto. When Mwanaidi looks back she concludes that life would have been very difficult for her had it not been for the motto she had set for herself. In her conversation she kept on asking "Who would have hosted me today?".

When Mwanaidi started working at the University of Dar es Salaam her starting salary was TAS.240/-, an increase of forty shillings from the salary she was getting as a domestic servant. Getting employment at the University of Dar es Salaam put Mwanaidi in a completely different type of life. Mwanaidi had once been a typical peasant woman, then she became a domestic servant for about thirteen years. Domestic work kept her indoors under the control of foreign bosses. In my discussions with Mwanaidi she did not complain of ill treatment by her white bosses as a domestic servant, but I am not in a position to deny her being oppressed. Even with her peasantry background Mwanaidi somehow managed the new life. Under formal employment at the University, Mwanaidi entered public life. She was now going to meet many people and learn to follow formal employment regulations.

On top of that under formal employment Mwanaidi had to become more self-reliant. She had to take care of her accomodation and food. This was not the case when she was working as a domestic servant where she normally stayed with the families she worked for and was supplied with food. Nevertheless, Mwanaidi did not take time to adapt to the new life. She had decided to rent her six-room house in Manzese so that she could realize an extra income. She did this even after knowing that she was not going to be allowed by the University authority to continue living in the servants' quarters.

Before long Mwanaidi had acquired a plot in the outskirts of the University where she constructed another house. She moved into her own house and went home to collect her brother's children whom she lived with. This step put Mwanaidi in a more self-reliant position. She was not going to pay any house rent nor pay for bus fare to and from the University. She was doing gardening around her plot and this supplemented her food requirements. Soon afterwards, it came to her notice that she had to move from the newly acquired plot. The University was expanding and it had to acquire most of the land surrounding its campus. All the people whose plots fell under the new University boundaries were given compensation. Mwanaidi was one of those evicted but with a compensation of TAS.600/-. Mwanaidi had already inculcated in her mind a sense of investing. She still planned to construct another house elsewhere.

To overcome the housing problem Mwanaidi rented a room in a house located at Mlalakuwa. During this time she was searching for plot to erect a house. She did not believe in renting a house. It was too expensive to do that.

163

Before long Mwanaidi purchased a five acre farm in Makongo area, another risk she took for acquiring a plot in an unsurveyed area. She paid TAS 260/- for the Makongo farm. Mwanaidi had to do a lot of work to develop the area. She built herself a mud house in the Makongo farm and moved there.

Mwanaidi was a busy worker. She managed to execute her work at the Hall ot Residence well and still managed her extra activities after office hours. Mwanaidi said that all through her employment period at the University of Dar es Salaam she was never reprimanded for indiscipline or neglect of duty. She was not even transferred to another section – meaning she worked in Hall III as a Cleaner for nineteen years. Due to her good performance and conduct Mwanaidi used to get her promotion in accordance with the University regulations and procedures. She retired in September, 1985 when she had attained the post of Head Cleaner with a monthly salary of TAS.1600/-.

While working at the University of Dar es Salaam, Mwanaidi joined several Organizations. She was a member of the Worker's Organization (NUTA) and later on (JUWATA). She joined the Organization expecting benefits but up to the time she retired she had not gained anything tangible benefit. She also joined the Women's Organization (U.W.T.) Branch at the University. Under this branch she participated in an income generating project, selling Khanga/Vitenge and drinks. The project did not last long and members never received any dividends. In spite of this, she joined the famous University Consumer Co-operative Society. This was one of biggest Co-operative shops started in Dar es Salaam in the 1970s. The Co-operative which initially became very prosperous deteriorated to zero point. All members lost their ruling shares. Mwanaidi also was a member of the National political party (TANU) and she is still a member of the Chama cha Mapinduzi (CCM), the sole ruling political party in Tanzania today.

Educationwise Mwanaidi was not left behind. When the University started literacy programme for its workers, Mwanaidi was among the first students who enrolled. Mwanaidi knew how to read and write but she wanted to up-grade her literacy skills and gain more knowledge.

With regard to Mwanaidi's relationship with men friends after marriage, she had already acquired a stand not to marry. Mwanaidi commetec that "Children is what makes a marriage in her community, and without them a woman may be working for nothing". With the understanding that she was unable to bear children of her own she had decided not to enter another marriage contract. However, this does not mean that she never had any relationship with a man. She told the researcher that after she had established herself at Makongo, one man, a Chaga by tribe approached her for

164

friendship. Mwanaidi agreed on the proposal as far as she was not going to move out of her house and that the man was willing to come and live with her. Mwanaidi told the man from the beginning that she did not intend to marry.

The manfriend (name withheld) was working as a plumbing technician with Silent Inn (A famous bar in Mwenge Area). Mwanaidi said that in the initial period they got on well with the man and Mwanaidi used to serve him more or less like her husband. Later on the man started coming home very late in the night, drunk. Mwanaidi suspected that her friend had found another woman somewhere else and since she could not tolerate the behaviour of her manfriend coming home late she asked him to quit. Mwanaidi said that there was no question of compromise, the man had to leave and since he was staying in Mwanaidi's house he had no demand to make to her related to property sharing.

The researcher would not like to leave the readers with the impression that since Mwanaidi had no children, she had less responsibility. This is not true. The prime responsibility which occupied most of Mwanaidi's time was that of making her life tolerable if not enjoyable. Mwanaidi realized that she had nobody to depend on. So she had to work very hard to prepare for her life after retiring. This is reflected in Mwanaidi's own remark:–

> So long as I did not have my own children, it would have been a grave error on my part to rely on the children of my relatives. Moreover, had I banked my hopes on the people's claim that I was as beautiful as a woman from the Comoroes, I would have reached nowhere. Who would have been my host today?

No doubt Mwanaidi was forward looking. At the time she retired she had constructed several houses; one in Manzese (six rooms), one in Mwananyamala (six rooms), one in Mwenge (10 rooms) and another one in Mlalakuwa area. She also has a two acre farm in Makongo, which she acquired after her previous five acre farm had been taken and compensated by Ardhi Institute. Mwanaidi had to pull down her house and move to one of her houses. She is now living in her house at Mlalakuwa where she resides with her tenants.

Mwanaidi has always been strong and able to cope with situations as they come. Added on her work and her life struggle was the responsibility to look after her brother's children. Mwanaidi had one brother (born of the same mother and father) – Ibrahim Salehe. Ibrahim took from his father the tendency of marrying and divorcing (like father, like son). Mwanaidi narrated that her brother had married four wives and now at the age of 60 he is staying with none. Each wife has born Ibrahim some children and most of the women left their children behind when they were divorced. The first wife bore five children – three are living. The third wife bore ten children – eight are surviving and the fourth wife, a very young girl who was discontinued from school at class six as she was made pregnant by Ibrahim, when he was working as a driver at the *Usafiri Dar es Salaam* (UDA) bore three children – all of them surviving. The fourth wife left Ibrahim when her third child was only one and half years old. She did not take any child with her. Mwanaidi lamented that her brother is very irresponsible as he does not care for his children. For example, right now he is not staying with any of his children. Mwanaidi felt obliged to raise some of her brother's children. During the time of the research Mwanaidi was staying with four of her brother's children, one of which was a three year old girl. From the researcher's point of view the children have been a good company to Mwanaidi. Mwanaidi however cautioned that she was not looking after her brother's children because she expected certain returns. On the contrary she was only fulfilling a duty:–

"I am not taking care of them so that they may take care of me in future; I would like them to grow up and see the world".

Mwanaidi was also vested with the responsibility of taking care of her old and sick mother. We learnt in Mwanaidi's earlier narration that her mother had been divorced. Later on however, Mwanaidi's mother re-married and bore four children. Unfortunately, the second husband died leaving her a widow. It was also unfortunate that when Mwanaidi's step brothers grew up they did not bother to look after their mother. Due to poor health and poor diet, the old woman's health deteriorated, eventually she became half blind. When Mwanaidi went to collect her in 1973, she found her in a very poor state. She brought her to Dar es Salaam. Mwanaidi attended to her mother for thirteen years, till she left for Ugweno in 1986, to see her children and relatives. It is a tendency of most old people to long to go back to places of their origin no matter how much comfort is provided to them in foreign places.

Mwanaidi has also been very helpful to his brother Ibrahim who for a long time had been living and working in Arusha. It seems that Ibrahim was not as sensible as his sister Mwanaidi, and had made a mess of himself. Mwanaidi took the responsibility of settling Ibrahim in Dar es Salaam. She has assisted him to put up a house at Mwenge. Ibrahim takes most of his meals at his sister's place.

There are several lessons to be drawn from Mwanaidi's experience when she was in wage employment. Mwanaidi entered domestic servant employment because at that time domestic work was by far the main employment which existed for African women migrating to town. The Asians, the white businessmen, the bureaucrats and the elites of course needed such people. Mwanaidi's discipline and conduct gave her a good reputation, whenever she worked. It is through such reputation that Mwanaidi received good certificates of performance which enabled her to find subsequent employment. Mwanaidi was also self-reliant and determined to build and prepare for her life. It is after seeing her effort of becoming self-reliant that the French boss offered to assist Mwanaidi in building a better house. This leads me to conclude that some employers are concerned with the welfare of their workers.

Mwanaidi's work as domestic servant opened opportunity doors for her. It was through such employment that she secured permanent employment at the University of Dar es Salaam We also have to learn from Mwanaidi's struggle – as well as to appreciate the way she managed to cope with her employment and extra activities after working hours. Lastly, we have to learn from Mwanaidi's sense of enterpreneurship. Although Mwanaidi had opened a Bank account in the early 1960s she did not keep all her money in the bank. She invested some of her money in houses and farms. Mwanaidi's words suffice as a lesson to us:

"Money saved in a bank, generates interests once in a year. On the contrary, money invested in a house generates interest continuously".

Retired and a House Lady

Mwanaidi retired in September 1985 at the age of 60. Although she is still energetic, according to the country's labour regulations, a worker is compulsorily retired after a given age. In Tanzania a normal retiring age is 55 years for women and 60 years for men. Mwanaidi retired happily knowing that she had already prepared herself. Consequently, she did not anticipate problems after retiring. The following statements certified this:-

"Work hard when you're still energetic and reserve something for the old age".

Mwanaidi received all her retirement benefits (amount of which she did not disclose). She deposited some of her money in her bank account and invested some in maintaining some of her houses. She gets quite a substantial income, approximately TAS.11,000/- per month, for renting her houses. One observation is that Mwanaidi invested money in constructing houses in unsurveyed areas. There is no single house of hers built on a plot with land ownership title. This is a single great risk but since squatters are still allowed in the outskirts of Dar es Salaam, she still will continue to get income from her houses. However, Mwanaidi will have to improve her houses (e.g. by installing in electricity) if she is to realize a higher income. Right now, no single house of hers has electricity.

Observing where she is living at present, the researcher noticed that Mwanaidi had reserved four rooms for herself-three bed-rooms and one very spacious sitting-room. She had rented the rest of the rooms. She has modern furniture and a well arranged and decorated sitting room.

At the age of 62 Mwanaidi is still very active. She cooks, she washes her clothes and does many other tasks. She also farms in Makongo where she grows vegetables, cassava and sweet potatoes, she keeps few animals at her residence – 12 goats, 16 ducks and five chicken. Mwanaidi administers her tenants making sure that they follow her renting policy and they pay in time. She is often called to settle conflicts among her tennants. Some take her as their mother. The case of Manzese certifies this. She has in the Manzese house some people whom she started with in 1965. These people are now her close acquaintances. She has fixed a relatively low rate of T.Shs.200/- per room compared to renters in the houses paying up to T.Shs.500/-. Monitoring and administering her houses is quite a task to Mwanaidi.

Mwanaidi's story after retirement teaches us one basic lesson – what you become after retiring is a result of what you did for yourself when you were working.

Footnotes:

1. Kimambo, I. Political History of the Pare, (Ph.D. Thesis) University of Dar es Salaam 1967.
2. Breast feeding mothers often offered to breast feed siblings whose mothers had died. The researcher's mother once breast-fed a baby whose mother had passed away. The baby was born more or less the same time as the author. Children feeding/sucking from the same mother had a very close connection with the children of that mother and they grew up not only as friends, but as comrades.
3. The young girls were very shy when demonstrating the ngoma to the researcher and so it was not possible to transcribe the song. Mwanaidi was also reluctant to have the ngoma song cited because she was not sure of it's meaning in Kiswahili.
4. "Mshenga" is a suitor's go-between in the marriage negotiations. It is normally a man. His role goes beyond marriage arrangement. He is also consulted even after the marriage.

CHAPTER EIGHT

Overcoming Cultural Barriers to Modern Life: The Experience of Paulina's Socio-Economic and Political Life

Paulina with Bertha Koda

Preface

Paulina Makarios was born in 1922 in Lilambo village, Peramiho area, Ruvuma Region, Southern Tanzania. Both her parents were peasants. She is a Roman Catholic, ex-class IV leaver who is married with two children and six grandchildren. Presently she resides in Mbezi, a village near the University of Dar es Salaam. Her immediate family includes her husband, the elder son who is 31 years' old, and her four grandchildren. She lives in a small hut one of which is the kitchen and food store. Her son uses the second hut while the third which has two small bedrooms and a sitting room is for herself, the husband and the grandchildren. The huts are constructed by poles, plastered by mud and roofed by corrugated iron sheets which were purchased by Paulina's husband's pension – money. Paulina cooks with the three stones (open firewood stove) but occassionally uses charcoal or paraffin-oil cooking stoves. Her common cooking utensils are the alluminium cooking pans although she also uses clay pots when she is not in a hurry.

Paulina's furniture include four modern wooden chairs, a small wooden table, several three legged stools, three banco beds (modern beds), two string-woven beds, two sponge matresses, several hand woven mats, one cup-board, a mortar and pestle. Her son makes some of the family furniture as he is a carpenter. In the kitchen she has several alluminium cooking pots of different sizes for purposes of boiling tea, cooking stiff porridge, cooking vegetables and rice, etc. She also has several bowls and plates made of tin, or China-ware, spoons (both iron and wooden) China-ware and plastic, cups, mugs and glasses for drinking water, 2 buckets and clay pots for keeping water and also for cooking. Paulina believes that there are certain foods which taste better when cooked in clay pots, while other types like tea taste better when cooked in alluminium cooking pots.

Paulina's eating pattern of three meals per day.has been maintained although she admitted that she can no longer afford balanced diet due to the family's meagre income coupled with the ever rising prices especially of pro-

169

tein food. Even with her efforts to keep a few chicken, ducks, and goats her family has not been able to have a regular balanced diet. For a retired teacher like her it is very painful when her family can't afford balanced diet as she knows the value of such foods. Despite the financial constraints however, her husband, her son and herself are good cooks.

Paulina's dressing habits are moderate, that is, she wears clean dresses and wrappers when she goes to public gatherings including the church and the (locally brew) beer clubs but at home she dresses differently. The black cloth which she usually puts on when she goes to the farm or the kitchen is usually accompanied by an old dress or wrapper.

Her three huts which are usually kept clean are decorated by bougainvillaea flowers grown in the court yard where there is also a drying place of utensils (kichanja) and a drying line for clothes. At the back of the kitchen there is a reserve of firewood collected by either her husband, her son or herself. Totting water from the wells is also a shared role among the family members including the grand children, two of whom are in primary school. Infact all the production and the household chores are a shared responsibility especially between Paulina and her husband. It is partly because of this sharing of roles that Paulina has been able to participate in both the political and public life.

At her present age of 65 years she is still active in political life especially in the women organisation's (UWT) activities. Paulina is among the many Tanzanian women who have and are still fighting for women's rights although her history has not yet been recorded anywhere. Her life history is therefore being presented here as an inspiration for the young generation to continue with the struggle which she and many others have started to gain their rightful position in society.

PART ONE

Growing up in Lilambo Village

1.1 *Introduction*

Paulina Makarios is the first born in the family of five children, three of which were girls. Her parents were peasants (they are all dead now) from a Ngoni tribe. All her parents, sisters and brothers are dead. Her mother died in 1931 when Paulina was only nine years old. Her father died 26 years later. Her only surviving sister died in 1986.

Paulina's life as a young girl changed abruptly after her mother's death. When her mother died, Paulina, as the first born and a girl for that matter had to choice but no take care of her young brothers and sisters until she was married in 1942, at the age of 20. Since some of the sisters were still too young (the last one was 11 years) when she got married, she continued to stay with them in her new home and her husband became very cooperative not because he was a gender-sensitive man but rather because of his love to Paulina and faith in Christ who usually advocated for brotherly and sisterly love.

Paulina spent all her childhood in Lilambo. Her village life as a young girl was very hectic and less exciting given the fact that she was busier than most of her age-mates. Narrating her early childhood, Paulina correctly remembers how hectic the life was:

> "I spent most of my time between the kitchen and the school. I had to cook for the family, clean the house, wash the children, pound millet or maize or cassava … actually greater responsibility of the household chores was carried by me with some assistance from my brothers. Remember that I also had to go to school."
> (translated from Swahili)

Paulina did not enjoy the childhood plays as much as she would have preferred because she seldomly had time for that:

> "Sometimes I envied my age-mates when they were playing in their compounds. At times my friends helped me with the domestic chores so that I could join them and play after all the work is done."
> She narrated.

Even with such periodic assistance from her brothers; Paulina still felt that she deserved more time for play while at the same time she felt committed and duty – bound to taking care of the family. Her religious upbringing also helped her to sacrifice most of her rights and privillege for the welfare of her young brothers and sisters. She was baptized in 1922 as a Roman Catholic and ever since she was known as Paulina rather than Sewaku which is her other name inherited from her grandmother.

1.2 *Educational background*

Paulina had an advantage on matters of formal education, being a daughter of a Christian family. During her childhood it was not common for girls to go to school. Even some boys, especially those from non-christian families were not sent to school by their parents for lack of school fees. It was considered more beneficial for children to assist their parents in the farms and at home rather than sending them to school. It was indeed expensive to send children to school – buying school uniforms, paying school fees, missing their labour input etc. All these were factors to be considered before making the choice of educating children in formal schools. Each parent had therefore a variety of excuses for not sending their children (especially girls) to school. One such excuse was the fear that investing heavily in girls' education is not worth-it since after all girls eventually get married and are then more useful to their husbands' families who monopolize their labour input. As the Ngoni culture (like in all patrilinear societies) stands, after marriage the woman's life is controlled by her husband and the in-laws, while much of her socio-economic relationships with her own family is greatly reduced. All the material gains would then be enjoyed by her spouse and in-laws. Most parents therefore preferred to send sons rather than daughters to formal schooling with the anticipation that sons would take care of their parents at old age.

With the introduction of Christianity however, parents, especially the Christians were very much encouraged or rather forced to send both their sons and daughters to school, otherwise in the case of Lilambo village and Peramiho area in general parents were punished by being excommunicated /or being subjected to hard labour (involving cutting heaps of logs for the missionaries for cooking purposes) if they failed to send their children to school. According to Paulina although the missionaries promoted girls' education, their interests was only limited to providing girls with four years' primary education after which girls either got married or become nuns (if they were Chistians). Paulina was lucky in the sense that her parents were Chrstians who did not want to take the risk of being excommunicated.

Girls and even boys from non-Christian families were however at a disadvantage because they were not allowed to enter mission schools. There were the so-called "bush" schools run by the missionaries with the objective of preparing catechist teachers. Then there were ordinary schools run by both missionaries and the native authorities (N.A. ie. local government). However the force from government was not as strong as that from the church and therefore most of the non-Christian parents somehow managed to ignore the pressure to send girls to school. It should also be noted here that girls started school late and majority got married even before they completed primary school education. Marriage was a good excuse used by most parents for not sending girls to school. Paulina's education environment can be enriched by the following information:

> – Up to 1945 formal education mainly constituted bush schools and lower primary schools standard 1 to 4. The majority were mission schools. After 1945 there was an expansion of middle schools or upper primary education. By 1954 distribution of schools in the District was as follows: 106 schools were lower primary schools out of

which 98 were mission schools and the rest government schools and 7 N.A. schools. The total number of children attending these schools was about 13, 877, the majority of which were boys; middle schools were 15 out of which 1 was a government, 11 were missions and 3 N.A. There was only 1 government secondary school. (source: Songea District Annual Report 1959).

Paulina started schooling when she was 11 years old. She went to a mission school at Peramiho where she took six subjects including Religion, Reading, Writing, Geography, Health (Afya) and Arithmetic. Although she couldn't remember the ratio of girls to boys in her school, Paulina observed that there were fewer girls than boys and all her teachers were males.

Paulina went as far as class four and then left school to continue assisting her father in caring for her young brothers and sisters. But even during her school time she used to take the youngest sister along when nobody was at home to take care of her. The double roles she had to play (i.e. taking care of children and schooling at the same time) however, did not discourage her nor did it drastically affect her performance at school. Although she was not top in her class, she was among the best pupils hence she was approached by her community later in life to assist in teaching adult education classes. Paulina attributes her good performance to two things: Firstly, she was highly motivated by the urge to prove that even girls can perform well in school when given chance, and secondly she wanted to show a good example in her family since she was the first born. She actually feared that if she didn't perform well in school, that would be a bad precedent which might bias her parents (or other parents) not to send her young sisters to school. She also believed that to be a good Christian one has to work hard and perform better in life thus proving that God has all the powers to make one what she or he is. Paulina is actually one of those good Christians who never missed Sunday/church ceremonies/functions without proper reason. Like most village girls, Paulina had very few ambitions since childhood. Her main ambition was to become either a teacher or nurse, the two popular vocations for girls at that time and probably even today. Paulina also aspired for a life better than that of most of the villagers around her including that of her parents. No wonder she was attentive and hardworking in school.

It should be noted here that the system of education by then allowed class repeaters until one reached the standard required. One could thus stay in one class for two or more years. Pupils also started school late, hence some were already adults (18 years and above) by the time they completed class IV.

173

The co-education system through which Paulina passed was very much instrumental in her struggles for life. Getting used to having boys around for instance later on helped to remove her shyness in fora of mixed gender. Her determination to perform as good as boys could also be associated to this co-education which allowed for gender competition in class. The co-education system can also be said to have instilled in pupils' minds a sense of gender cooperation/togetherness which was later on practised by Paulina's family. Paulina nurtured this spirit of cooperation in her family and sometimes fearlessly reminded her husband of this cooperation whenever he tended to behave like patriarchs.

Apart from the formal schooling, Paulina also acquired different knowldge and skills related to agriculture, childcare, homecraft, weaving, traditional medicine (curing minor ailments e.g. stomach-ache, headache, wounds etc) through the informal education of learning by imitating and doing. Paulina for instance knows how to weave a variety of handicraft products e.g. mats, baskets, drinking cups (visonjo) using special reeds (matete or majani ya ulezi). Such skills were common in her home village except for mat making skills which she acquired from a Zaramo friend of hers when she moved to Kawe, Dar es Salaam in December 1950.

Paulina also knows different types of grass, roots and tree barks from which a variety of medicine can be derived. She once lamented that although such medicines are in high demand even today most of the appropriate sources here in Dar es Salaam are inaccessible because the forests which used to accomodate appropriate trees or shrubs are no longer existing. Some valuable shrubs however, can be seen at Kawe and Mbezi-One (the areas she is most familiar with in Dar es Salaam). Paulina is of the opinion that traditional medicine is very helpful in countries like Tanzania, where shortage of foreign exchange limits importation of modern medicines. She cautioned however, that since traditional medicines is usually administered with no precision, more research should be done to determine the right dose so as to minimize under-or over-dosing the patients. As Paulina correctly observes, in the past people were not worried about either over-dose or underdose or possible harmful side-effects. Indeed some of the medicine worked perfectly. Paulina also proudly admits that she never goes to the hospital for minor ailments which she can cure by traditional medicine. She however expressed fear that there is a danger for traditional medicine to disappear if deliberate efforts are not made to pass down the knowledge from the old to the young generation. The need for preservative measures for the valuable trees and shrubs was also expressed by Paulina who also appreciated the role played by the Department of Traditional Medicine at

Muhimbili Faculty of Medicine but was of the opinion that collaboration with the traditional medicine women and men should be made more aggressive.

Already Paulina feared that traditional medicine-women especially those in remote areas might be by-passed by researchers resulting in not knowing a lot of important and useful medical knowledge which is a woman's domain. This fear is aggravated by the fact that most knowledgeable old women are often regarded as witches and hence might not be contacted by the usually young researchers. The challenge was finally thrown first to the youth whom Paulina said should demand from their elders the right to inherit this wealth of knowledge and second to the researchers especially females to keep up this matter more seriously.

PART TWO

Paulina's Marriage

Paulina's marriage can not be understood in isolation from the Ngoni culture, especially as pertaining to issues related to initiation ceremonies (preparing youth for adulthood), relationship between wife and husband and wife and in-laws, courtship, bride-wealth, property relations at family level, custody of children and family planning.

Indeed the Ngoni culture is not different from that of other patrilineal societies in Tanzania where specific social institutions were used (and are still used although to a lesser extent) for "adulthood" education. Initiation ceremonies, for instance, were widely used to educate young boys and girls on their social roles in adulthood, and since such roles were gender-biased the training was also gender-specific. Girls, for instance, were taught to observe certain behaviours and qualities such as gentleness, chastity, modesty, beauty, submission, passiveness and ab-negation. The moral qualities constituted a veritable code that a woman could't transgress for fear of being an outcast from her society. Paulina and other girls were thus taught that a woman is in-complete without a husband. Marriage was therefore a primary objective for a girls' life in society. Girls were taught how to please their husbands during love-making as the main portion of sex education. Other aspects included things to observe when making love or when in menstruation period, pregnant, lactating etc. The aspect of cleanliness was all along being stressed.

In short, most of what was taught during the initiation ceremony was family-life education, including sex-education. Unlike other ethnic groups circumsicion was not part of the initiation ceremony for either boys or girls except for the Moslem boys whose religion obliged them to be circumsized.

As Paulina put it, the Ngoni woman's first role as a wife is to feed her husband and children. The Ngoni saying that a wife should look at the stomach and not the face because the latter never gets thin ("Tazama tumbo, usitazame uso – uso haukondi kamwe") clearly demonstrates that a woman could be ridiculed if her family went hungry. Young wives were often reminded to feed their husbands well to avoid neglect, for, husbands would resort to looking for women who could feed them well. Indeed other young girls were being prepared for their future social roles and obligations in both production and reproduction. Boys on the other hand were taught to be brave, strong, shrewd and strong-willed. Language, songs, and the work of art were used to ensure that both boys and girls acquired the necessary qualifications that were related to their socially designed and gender-specific responsibilities.

Usually the girl was secluded both during the initiation ceremony and thereafter until she got a suitor (which can take years) but as for Paulina, it was slightly different. Because she already was too busy looking after her young sisters and brothers after her mother's death, and as she was already in school, Paulina did not stay indoors after the short period of the initiation ceremony. By then of course Christianity had been introduced in her village and the cultural practise of initiation ceremony was being discouraged by the Missionaries. Despite the spread of Christianity however the tradition guiding courtship did not change. Girls were not supposed to choose their partners. It was the parents' duty to choose partners for their children. In the case of school-going Christians like Paulina, the potential/aspiring in-laws used to seek for advice/opinions from the school teachers (most of whom were males), whose recommendation as to whether the girl in question had good manners was highly valued. Teachers therefore had power to influence the choice of partners.

When the potential in-laws are satisfied with their choice, then they proceed with the subsequent cultural traditions of sending somebody to inform the girl's parents of the intention. Usually the girl's parents have their own criteria for either refusing or accepting an 'offer (e.g. they have to know whether there is no communicable disease like leprosy with in the boys' family etc) but surely the age difference was not considered as a major concern. Fortunately for Paulina the age – difference between herself and her spouse was only 3 years. Paulina was also highly rated by her primary school teacher as a hard working, polite and good Christian.

After the teacher's recommendation the function which followed was for Paulina's aspiring in-laws to send a message accompanied with presents for her father, mother and aunt. Such presents included beads for Paulina, a hoe for her father, a white piece of cloth for her aunt and two shillings (shs. 2/-) for either her brother or father. The message and all its accessories informed Paulina's relatives that their daughter has been chosen as the future wife of the aspiring spouse. Paulina's parents accepted the presents and informed the go-between (mshenga) that they needed time to consult her other relatives especially on matters concerning bride-wealth. Of course as custom demanded, the girl had no say in all such matters. She was brought up to accept without challenging. To that effect she could not refuse the parents' choice even if she had no love for the man. Indeed the primary purpose for marriage was not love but promoting continuity of a clan. Love was just secondary. While it can take years before all the necessary consultations and preparations are completed, for Paulina it took only two years before she was finally handed over to her husband in 1942. Paulina's marriage ceremony was both religious and traditional; the marriage vows were made in church while all the cultural marriage rituals were also performed accordingly.

The bride-wealth of four cows had to be paid to Paulina's relatives. In compliance with the Ngoni culture, one cow went to Paulina's mother but since she was dead, it went to her maternal aunt. The rest of the cows were distributed among the relatives of Paulina's father. According to Paulina, nobody dared to question the rationale of paying bridewealth by then. It was taken for granted that a girl should not be surrendered to a man free of charge. "Mtoto asiende bure" it was said in Swahili language. (Its Ngoni equivalence is "Mwana Chiyaga buri"). As Paulina correctly recalled, the point is that the girl was virtually taken away to the boy's clan. She was somehow torn physically and even psychologically from her family and was thereafter under the control of her husband and in-laws. Since her parents lost almost all powers over both her productive and reproductive roles; it was somehow justified that a girl should therefore not be given away free of charge. Paulina finds the whole arrangement unfair to the girls who must suffer psychologically and are generally treated as minors and sometimes mistreated.

Elaborating on the issue of restricting meetings between the young people intending to marry each other, Paulina thought that after the introduction of Christianity and formal schooling, boys and girls met freely in church and at school, hence relaxing the tight customs related to courtship. The boy could visit his girlfriend but with his parents' consent and after giving prior-information to the girls' parents. He also had to bring his male friends along. The girlfriend on her part invited her female friends and a cock was killed, food was cooked by either the aunt or grandmother and they all shared the food, talked and got acquinted to each other. However, in no way was a boy and a girl left alone. Besides, they were forbidden by both Christianity and the traditional culture to sleep together before marriage Paulina thought that probably the fear of losing virgnity and getting pregnant was the main reason for not allowing young boys and girls to make love before marriage.

Chastity, abnegation and repression of pleasure were the sine-qua-non conditions to which a woman must submit in order to reflect a good moral standing. In the old days a girl lost all the social respect and lowered her dignity if she lost her virginity before marriage. Getting pregnant before marriage was therefore culturally regarded as abhorrence, followed by severe punishment with curses casted upon the partners who disobeyed the warnings. Consequently therefore very few cases of children born out of wed-lock were known, but not because the teen-agers were making free sexual choices or had full control of their sexuality but rather because they highly respected the teachings of the old generations. Absenteeism was therefore the best way of avoiding pregnancy before marriage. It is also said that there were ways of repairing reptured virginity (hymen) which are still in use today. A girl could therefore have sex and then repair the hymen before getting marriaed.

Paulina however warned on the danger of thinking that there were no unwanted pregnancies in the past. In discussing the issue of contraceptives and unwanted pregnancies, Paulina explained that during her village life in Lilambo, she learnt about how unwanted pregnancies were gotten rid-of. Crude methods were used for abortion. A sharp object for instance was inserted through the vagina right to the womb to disturb the whole mechanism and cause abortion. Of course some women died during the process. Another method used when one no longer needed a child was to overturn the womb (kapindua kizazi) with bare hands of local expert in midwifery (wakunga wa jadi).

As for Paulina, the only family planning method she ever used was the absenteeism. All her five children were well-spaced (not less than two years interval as a traditional standard). Nobody was very much worried about having a large family. Infact the more children one had the better. Children were needed not only as potential labour force but also as a social security during parents' old age. Parents and to that effect society at large were therefore more worried about spacing the children and not about the large size of their families. It should also be noted here that at that time (early days of colonialism in Tanzania) it was very possible to produce enough food for even a large family. The soils were still fertile and there was enough land for everybordy. The Ngoni people are also reputable for being very good at preserving soil fertility and moisture using the system called "kilimo cha Ngoro." They build ridges, make compost manure and when possible leave the farm fallow for some years before farming it again. The demand for cash was also limited by then and therefore it was relatively cheap to maintain a large family. Paulina observed however that under the present conditions when the soils are in fertile, the demand for cash is high and children's labour is divorced from the production (and to some extent reproduction) sector (because they spend most of their time in school) it is actually difficult and not advisable for one to have a large family.

Paulina however is of the opinion that absenteeism as a method of child-spacing cannot function effectively if there is not cooperation between the couples. She fears that under present conditions when both men and women tend to be more selfish and don't want to sacrifice much of their entertainments it is not easy for this method to be effectively used in isolation from other methods. She therefore recommends that while women should be encouraged to use it, it needs women's self-determination and sacrifice (because the selfish men will always demand for sex whenever they feel like having it). She also feels that women should be exposed to other alternatives (choices). She also strongly supported the idea of teaching family – life education in schools since initiation programmes no longer exist.

Other customs influencing Paulina's life were those related to childbirth. Paulina correctly observed that a woman in the traditional setting has no control over her body or sexuality. All the time virtues were demanded (of woman) which call for a constant vigilance over oneself, a renouncement of the pleasure of vanity and flesh, a sacrifice of the basic instincts. Either the husband or older members of society controlled her sexuality. To start with, a woman had no choice as to who should make love to her. The husband, for instance, with whom she was allowed to make love was chosen for her. Family planning methods were also chosen by older members of her society. One would perhaps want to know how the partners managed to stay for so long without love-making. On the one hand women were supposed to suppress their sexual urges while men could find other ways of meeting their sexual needs. Of course customs also controlled his behaviour, but cases of adultery were often discovered and the man was fined and if he becomes too notorious for adultery he stood the danger of being killed by the spouse of his female friends.

Child bearing was one big obligation for women. If a long time passed before a married woman gets pregnant some traditional medicines were applied to her. The belief in witchcraft was also strong in Paulina's society.

A barren woman could therefore be taken to the local medicine-woman or man for fear that perhaps she had been bewitched. A woman was incomplete without children, and since child bearing out of wedlock was never entertained every woman was therefore supposed to get married if she wanted to have sex and children and the sooner one married the better because if all her age-mates are married then she won't have peers to socialize with.

As soon as Paulina got pregnant she had to observe certain rituals. (For every major step in life there was an accompanying ritual). Paulina remembers very vividly the day her first pregnancy was four months old. She and her husband were escorted by her mother-in-law and a few old men to the bush where they spent the whole day performing informative rituals.

> "... when a young married woman's first pregnancy is between four and six months old, a woman is forbidden to sleep with her husband, for fear that the unborn baby will be dirtened by the liquid residuals which might block the nostrils and ears thus making the baby uncomfortable and even distract breathing."

(Paulina narrated what she was taught while in the bush).

She explained further that the pregnant mother was forbidden to greet anybody she found working in the fields. Instead she should grab the production tools, work silently for a few minutes and then leave without uttering a word. The objective according to Paulina's understanding was to ensure that those with bad intentions are not given chance to harm either the unborn child or the pregnant mother with witchcraft.

The ceremony at the bush ended in the evening when the whole band returned home after staying hungry for the whole day. A cock was then killed, cooked and eaten with stiff porridge (ugali) made from either maize, cassava or millet-flour as a concluding ceremony after which the couples promised not to forget the seriousness of the rituals.

Divorce was very much discouraged by both the Ngoni and the Christian cultures. A woman was expected to persevere but if the husband was a thief, then the wife was encouraged to divorce him. However, cruelty on the part of the husband, was inadequate cause for divorce. The wife could however run away to her relatives if beaten. The husband was then severely reprimanded. Paulina observed that the majority of women were mistreated by their husbands and suffered a lot but stayed-on just for the sake of their children. "Ilibidi wavumilie shauri ya watoto", she said, and commented further that others were afraid of showing their discontent for fear that the husband might maliciously make it appear that it was a woman's fault and that he was actually performing his patriarch duties of correcting her bad behaviours. "Mwanamke ni budi aelekezwe anapokosa" Paulina recalled her elders teachings. Paulina believed that even men should be corrected when they go astray. "There will be no justice if I leave my husband uncorrected when he goes wrong" Paulina said. In actual fact she always tells her husband whenever he goes wrong.

Paulina's married life has two phases: phase one is when they were living in Peramiho and the second phase is her life in Dar es Salaam at Kawe and Mbezi-One. Although part of phase one has been discussed above, it is still important to discuss Paulina's economic and social activities. While in Peramiho, Paulina gave birth to three boys who later died mysteriously. Paulina still claims that she has not been able to understand the cause of her sons' deaths except some suspicion that it had to do with her breast milk which she thought had some form of poison because all the three boys died a few days after feeding on her breast milk. The belief that these deaths had to do with lactation was shared by her in-laws and many other people including Paulina's husband but with different interpretations. Her husband for instance said it had to do with witchcraft. Although the accusation on witchcraft was not directly pointed at Paulina, some villagers blame her for the death of her sons, especially after connecting the deaths with Paulina's breast milk.

Since the death of her sons, Paulina's good relationship with both her husband and in-laws was very much shaken. To that effect the main responsibility of sending her to the doctor for her breast disease was taken by her father and not either her husband or the in-laws. It appears that Paulina's in-laws lost some interest in her while her husband ran away from her immediately after the death of the third son.

While in Peramiho Paulina lived as a peasant. She and her family produced maize, millet, cassava, beans, pumpkins, peas, green vegetables, groundnuts and fruits. Theirs was predominantly subsistence economy although her husband worked at the Roman Catholic mission occassionally to get money. The food crops like pumpkins were also occassionally sold at the mission to feed the pigs. Although the income was meagre Paulina's family had a happy life (before the children died and the husband disappeared) because her husband cooperated with her in almost everything. Even budgeting for family's basic needs was shared between the two of them.

Life for Paulina's family started to change after the sudden death of their first born in 1944, and things became more serious when the second and third born also died within a short time after delivery. Paulina found herself being blamed for the death of the children as if she was the killer. The fact is that whenever something bad befalls the children, it is usually the mother who is blamed as if she has the power to cast away misfortunes. More misfortunes be-fell Paulina's family when she suddenly fell sick with a terrible breast disease which was un explainable and as it is typical with some traditional culture, anything of that sort is immediately connected with witchcraft. Paulina was blamed on grounds that probably she did not observe some of the traditional rituals and that is why misfortunes were befalling her family. The belief in witchcraft in most ethnic groups in Tanzania is common especially when a phenomenon which can not be explained befalls the family or community.

Paulina's illness added more confusion to her husband which culminated into his disapperance from home early in 1948. By then Paulina was too ill to worry about the whereabouts of her husband. Left alone with neither children of her own (all the three children were dead) nor the husband, poor Paulina managed to get some assistance from her relatives who sent her to a traditional medicine-man in Nyasa who administered medicine which worked well. After one year she was able to return home after paying three goats to the doctor for his medicare.

It should be noted here that before the introduction of cash – economy, medical services from the traditional healers were free of charge but as some demand for cash increased every service was to be paid for. However, for the highly respectable traditional healers, the amount demanded as payment was just a token. There are others however who have turned the service into business and demand high charges. According to Paulina, some payment was justifiable especially where both treatment, food and accomodation was provided by the doctor. As for the three goats which she paid, Paulina said that was nothing really compared to the happiness she and her family felt after the cure of her notorious and mysterious disease of the breast.

The search for her husband (late 1949)

After the cure of her disease Paulina had very little to live for at Peramiho, having lost all her children and her husband. She wasted no time. As soon as she returned to Peramiho from Nyasa, she immediately thought about tracing her husband. She did not see how she could live alone among her in-laws and neighbours. Life would not be normal. She vowed that she will search for her husband no matter what others think of her. At the same time, her father who sympatnized with her for all the misfortunes which be fell her encouraged her to do so.

All this was happening during the colonial times. Cash economy was introduced and existed side by side with subsistence economy. Plantations of sisal, coffee, tea etc. were opened in the country and some employment opportunities were being created. Men migrated from all corners of Tanzania to the places where employment was available. The main employment opportunities were in the plantantions. The British colonial government at this time (1949) had already established a mechanism which allowed for continuous supply of labour – force for the plantations. The Sisal Labour Bureau (SILABU) established then facilitated for recruitment of labour from all regions especially from the so called "labour reserve areas" where no cash crops were introduced. Ruvuma region where Paulina and her husband come from was one of the so called "reserve areas,"

In the process of establishing labour reserves in Tanganyika Songea District was the third, following Tabora and Mwanza. Songea District was drawn into the labour market immediately after the Maji Maji War in 1907 as punitive measure on the Ngoni people who had fiercely fought against the Germans; Songea District was the first to be drawn into labour market in Southern Tanzania South of the Central Railway line, and by 1924 annual labour migration from the District was 6 to 7 thousand people and by 1948 the percentage of male population between the ages of 17 and 50 who were outside the District on labour migration was 40% (Source: Tanganyika Government, African Census Report 1957). Songea had been leading in producing migrant labour up to mid-1920s when it was by-passed by Kigoma Region.

Mr Francis (Paulina's spouse) managed to migrate from Songea to Dar es Salaam which was not only a sisal producing area but also housed a big harbour which was a potential place to offer employment opportunities. In Dar es Salaam there was also the Meat Processing Plant called Tanganyika Packers which offered employment opportunities. Of course before the search for her husband Paulina was not aware that Mr. Francis was in Dar es Salaam.

Male migration from rural to urban areas was common while female migration was very much discouraged by both the African culture and the colonial government. Women contributed more to the colonialists by concentrating on subsistence to subsidize their husbands' meagre incomes from wage employment in towns and plantantions. Of course it was cheaper to maintain a single man whose family is in the rural areas producing food to feed itself independently from husbands' meagre salaries, the so called 'bachelors' wages.'

However, at the time when Paulina was searching for her husband, the situation had changed a bit. A few women had already migrated to towns. That was after the second word war when the colonial government felt safe to allow for wives to follow their husbands to towns. The introduction of formal education to giris like Paulina also changed the traditional migration pattern tremendously.

The phenomenon of female migration to towns is well known globally. While some women migrated to follow their husbands, others migrated to search for jobs in order to meet the growing cash needs or search for better social services. Others still migrated to towns as an escape from the rural patriarchal family relations. In the case of Paulina she not only wanted to escape from the patriarchal family relations which were operating against her wishes but was also searching for her husband without whom she thought life would be too difficult to bear.

In the late 1940s however the male: female population ratio in towns was not favourable. There were for instance 260 males for every 100 females in areas with wage employment in Tanzania. (Gulliner P.H. 1955) The ratio went down as days went by as indicated in Table 1:

Table 1: *Males per 100 Females, Urban areas Tanzania*

	1948	1957	1967
Arusha	110	106	104
Dodoma	165	128	115
Iringa	121	150	102
Kigoma	197	101	120
Mtwara	128	124	121
Lindi	142	124	109
Morogoro	128	127	110
Mbeya	133	121	101
Musoma	—	122	107
Moshi	168	167	129
Tanga	146	137	119
Tabora	111	113	101
Mwanza	139	140	120
Dar es Salaam	141	131	123

Source: R.H. Henin; 1967 Population Census of Tanzania: A Demographic Analysis. Bureau of Resource Assessment and Land-Use Planning, Research Paper No. 19. October, 1972. (as quoted by N. Shields 1980.)

Until 1971 the majority of migrant women were still married women following their husbands. In 1971 the National Urban Mobility employment and Income Survey reported that 66% out of total women interviewees from 7 selected Tanzanian towns indicated to have followed their working husbands in towns. Only 9% came directly to seek for wage employment. Men on the contrary, singled out the search for employment as the driving force for them to migrate to towns, see table 2.

Table 2: *Migration Population, Main Reason for coming to Town, by Sex Tanzania:*
Urban Areas.

Reasons	Male %	Female %
To seek employment	70	9
To attend school	6	2
To live with parents or other relatives	6	73
To visit	10	11
Others	7	4
Total	100	100

Source: NUMEIST, 1971 (quoted in Nwaganga Shields, 1980).

With the expansion of women's educational opportunities, unmarried
female migrants increased. Between 1950 and 1952 for instance the unmar-
rieds formed 13% and between 1970–71 they were 33%. Table 3 clarifies this
point, while tables 4 shows that the majority of those with relatively more
education came to town to seek for wage employment.

Table 3: *Migrant Population: Marital Status on Arrival by Sex and year of Arrival*
(Urban Tanzania)

	Males		Females	
	Unmarried	Married	Unmarried	Married
	%	%	%	%
1970–1971	64	36	33	67
1964–1969	67	33	25	75
1953–1963	60	40	26	74
1952 and before	58	42	13	87

Source: Numeist, 1971 (quoted in Nwaganga Shields, 1980).

Table 4: *Female Migrants – Main Reason for Migration by Education (%)*

Education	To seek employment	To attend school	To be with parents and other relatives	To be with husband	To visit others
None	4	—	8	69	19
Std. 1–4	5	—	6	77	11
Std. 5–8	18	7	8	53	14
Forms 1–6 plus	20	11	7	45	17

Source: Numeist, 1971 (quoted in Nwaganga Shields, 1980).

It was also reported that in 1974 migration rates to Dar es Salaam for women with standard 1 to 4 education was 2.3 times greater than that of males, while those with standard 5 to 8 it was 1.6 times greater. In terms of actual numbers however, there are as many women as men in towns although the former has less employment opportunities.

It appears that the uneducated rural-urban migrants originate from poor rural households, and since such migrants are unskilled, they meet lots of risks as soon as they arrive in town. Usually there is a longer timelapse for them before they are eventually employed.

Prior presence of relatives and/or friends or husband in towns is almost essential to a migrant woman's successful adjustment to town life-style. One has to get both material and moral support in terms of accommodation, food and sometimes pocket-money from someone-else before she gets employed.

Married women however can survive without wage employment. In 1974 for instance, Sabot found out that in Dar es Salaam where Paulina migrated to in 1950, sixty two per cent (62%) of the unemployed women were married. In 1951, labour census show that women comprised 5% of total labour force. However, only 20% of all employed women were in the non-agricultural sector (offices, industries and other service sectors). In 1971 again, only 21% of the urban female population was employed in both formal and informal sectors (Sabot 1974). Infact unemployment rate (excluding subsistence income earners) for women in Tanzania increased from 7% to 20% between 1965 and 1971, while for men there was just a slight move from 6% to 7% within the same period, (Sabot 1974).

Although there has been an increase in women labour force from 7% in 1969 to 12% in 1978 to 15% in 1981 (Jaspa 1980, Mbilinyi 1982) female employees are still underpriviledged and are employed in unskilled/semi-killed service-oriented jobs.

Paulina – a courageous woman

It was not easy for one to travel from Peramiho to Dar es Salaam and it was even harder for a village woman to overcome all the cultural barriers and manage to travel from Peramiho to the city of Dar es Salaam. Even making a decision to travel alone and search for a lost husband needs great courage and determination.

The few happy years Paulina spent with her husband at Peramiho motivated her to search for her husband. She saw great hope and vision of good life ahead if only she found her husband. She was still young and hoped to get more children. She also honoured her Christian marriage of one husband. Searching for her husband was very comforting and exciting, but its implementation seemed to be very complicated and Paulina feared this adventure. First of all she had to find an excuse to leave home unchallenged by her in-laws. Secondly she had to guess where her husband might have gone to. Thirdly she had to mobilize the little courage and material resources she had which might help her on the way. Lastly she had to take courage and give a deaf ear to all the bad things which might be said about her when her disappearance is discovered. However, her knowledge of Geography and Swahili language and a bit of socialization experienced at school gave her confidence and illusions that all will be well. She also prayed to God to guide her in her search.

The approach she chose was very interesting. First of all she posed as someone interested in fish trade (fish monger). At that time there was lucrative business in fish trading in Peramiho but fish had to be collected from Mahenge. Big caravans of both men and women used to ferry fish and Paulina grabbed the chance. She told her in-laws that since she had no small child to care for she would join the caravan. Of course the in-laws had no cause to refuse although it was not common for women to join such caravans. They allowed her to enter into the fish business. Note that Paulina had no freedom to make her own decisions without the consent of her in-laws.

Prior to making this plan, Paulina had been informed by her father tha a certain man working in Kilosa who had come to collect his wife had mentioned that Mr. Francis (her husband) was also working in Kilosa. The man volunteered to take Paulina to her husband. With encouragement from her father, Paulina agreed and the three joined the caravan going to collect fish from Mahenge and since there was no reliable transport the caravan took several days to reach Mahenge. When the caravan reached Mahenge Paulina and the Kilosa man and his wife went on to Kilosa via Ifakara.

It was true that Mr. Francis had stayed in Kilosa during the last part of 1948 but at the time of Paulina's arrival he had already left for an unknown destination. In desperation, Paulina wrote letters to the nearby District councils seeking for assistance. She believed that the District councellors had information about her husband who might have gone to their SILABU offices to register for employment in sisal plantantions. The Kilosa district council on its part put up the announcement which came to the attention of one of Mr. Francis' uncle who was staying at Kilosa. He then went to meet Paulina at the 'Kilosa man's home. The uncle informed Paulina that her husband had left for Morogoro. He then took Paulina to Mvumi where another uncle was staying. From Mvumi they proceeded to Morogoro where one of their relatives informed them that Mr. Francis had left for Dar es Salaam after staying there for one farming season when he grew rice and harvested

9 bags. Paulina and her uncle returned to Mvumi and happened to meet a friend of her husband who assured her that her husband was staying at Kawe and that he was working at Tanganyika Packers. Mr. Francis' friend offered to take Paulina to her husband but since the uncle did not completely trust this friend, he himself decided to escort her to Dar es Salaam.

The trip to Dar es Salaam by train did cost Paulina, her uncle and the friend T.sh. 20/- each as train-fare. When they reached Ilala, they stopped and stayed with an aunt before going to Kawe. They first wanted to send Mr. Francis a message that his wife was around. Unfortunately Mr. Francis was on safari but returned home after two days and got the message which requested him to urgently go to his aunt at Ilala. The tactic of sending a message first to the husband to announce the arrival of a wife was used to allow the husband time to prepare for the visitor. For some men that tactic was done in solidarity so that in case there is another woman (mistress) the husband is given ample time to get rid of her. In case of Mr. Francis however it was believed that there has never been another woman in his life apart from Paulina. The few years of his stay in Dar es Salaam before Paulina's arrival were said to be spent in solitude. There was no evidence however to prove that Mr. Francis had no occassional female visitor for it is common knowledge that many African husbands tend to have mistresses in towns while their wives stay in the rural areas.

The meeting of wife and husband was very dramatic. Mr. Francis arrived at his aunt's home and found someone sleeping on a mat. Although he was informed that the person on the mat was his wife, he didn't believe it until he looked at her feet and recognized them as his wife's. That was in January 1950. It was from that same day that Paulina's search ordeal was over and a new life began.

Life at Kawe

Paulina said it was like a dream thinking that she had managed to travel all the way from Peramiho to Dar es Salaam without major problems. Mr. Francis on his part could hardly believe that the woman infront of him was his wife. There was a big celebration after recovering from the excitement. A cock was killed, rice was cooked and neighbours friends and relatives were invited. After a good meal both the husband and wife narrated the life experiences they had been undergoing.

They moved to their residence in Kawe and stayed there until 1954 when they moved to Mbezi-One village. It was at Kawe that Paulina learnt the truth as to why Mr. Francis (her husband) abandoned her in 1948. As a matter of fact, it was not only the death of their sons and illness of Paulina which confused Francis and led him to abandon his wife. Other misfortunes

188

like the deaths of Francis relatives which occured consecutively forced Francis to believe that somebody was bewitching his family. This scared him that he might be the next victim. As for his wife, he thought she was going to die too. The reason for his disappearance therefore, was partly to search for a traditional doctor (mganga wa kienyeji) who could solve his problems. That partly explains why he didn't bid anybody farewell because according to most African traditions, one searching for care of a witchcraft – related illness should not bid anybody farewell because the witch might know and apply more witchcraft to mislead the victim and make him forget his original mission of looking for a doctor. Asked why he didn't take his wife along, Francis sincerely answered that he was too confused to remember that. He was however glad that both wife's and his own life were saved from death and they thereafter remained as good Christians.

Paulina's life at Kawe was both exciting and challenging. The mere fact that all her neighbours were not from her own culture was a challenge of itself. She learnt the Zaramo culture and even learnt some skills like mat-making, cooking food with coconut milk instead of groundnuts etc. For the four years they stayed at Kawe, Paulina was longing to get a child but in vain. It was while they were at Mbezi One that she managed to get two sons, the first one born in 1956 is an albino called Michael. William was born three years later.

It was all shock to herself, her husband and even neighbours when Paulina gave birth to Michael. It was the first time for them to see an albino. Being good Christians Paulina and her husband did not show their disappointment only and inwardly they prayed to God that all stays well. Paulina felt ashamed to expose her child in public because he was so different. She didn't know the cause of such abnormality on the child's skin but had a feeling that something went went wrong somewhere. She thought that may be it had do with her diet when she was pregnant but then she clearly remembered that she always followed the advice given by the Sewahaji clinic (in Dar es Salaam city) nurses where she used to go for ante-natal clinics.

Paulina wanted to know why her child was an albino but feared and even felt ashamed to ask. She was however consoled by her neighbours who told her not to hide the baby because it is God's will and nobody's fault. They even consoled her that Michael would help her when he grew up and indeed that is exactly what is happening now because it is Michael who is now taking care of his parents at their old age.

Paulina's experience confirms the importance of health education to mothers, especially on certain illness and abnormalities which might very easily be related to witchcraft, bad omen and could actually lead to killings of the abnormal persons as it used to be in some ethnic groups in the past. Fortunately for Michael his parents were Christians who accepted him as God-given, and always assured him that his skin wa just different in appearance but was otherwise O.K. whenever he asked them why he was different from his brother. In Tanzania there are many albinos who have their own association to which Michael belongs. William, the second born is normal and is working in a different town while his three sons and one daughter stay with their grand parents and uncle. Although Paulina no longer stays at Kawe, she usually visits her friends there and stays for weeks. To her, both Kawe and Mbezi-One are her homes.

Paulina is one of those women who are envied by their neighbours because of the cooperation she gets from her husband. Theirs is a very interesting couple. They share all the household chores including cooking. When they feel like having beer, they go to the beer-clubs together. They also go to the farms together. The secret behind this success is not known but Paulina seemed to correlate it with the good upbringing (on the part of her husband) and the fact that they never had a daughter therefore the husband felt obliged to assist his wife in all roles. The other secret is that Paulina never hides her feelings from her husband. She never feared her husband. She treats him as a partner regardless of the fact that he paid bride-price for her. The other secret might be that the larger part of their life was spent in foreign land (Dar es Salaam), very far away from relatives who might regularly remind them to behave like typical products of patriarchal society. Isolated from the Ngoni culture and mixing with the Zaramo of Dar es Salaam and a bit of the European culture (the husband was an employee at some stage) might have put Paulina in a better bargaining power when it comes to discarding those cultural norms which were detrimental to her development. There is no doubt that the cooperation between Paulina and her husband was greater in Dar es Salaam than at Peramiho. Can that be a product of the proletarianization process, given the fact that both of them were now alienated from their traditional cultural relations?

When in 1968 the women of Mbezi-One had to ask for permission from her husband to allow her to teach in "adult education women programme" Mr. Francis had no reason to refuse because he knew that his wife had all the potentialities for such a job and that the benefits acruing from such an effort will be shared among his family members. Paulina's experience seems to suggest that the secret behind a happy married life is having certain principles and abiding to them. Paulina for instance belived that girls are as good as boys. She also believed in being open-minded, sharing roles and responsibilities between husband and wife and also in fighting for one's rights consciously. She never believed that women are inferior to men nor did she believe that husbands should have a monopoly in making family's decisions. Mr. Francis' understanding of married life also seems to be different from that of most of the Ngoni and other patriarchs. It also seems that when both wife and husband share same interests and believe in same or similar principles, married life can be very joyful..

PART THREE

Paulina's Socio-Economic and Political Life

When Paulina married Mr. Francis in 1942, she knew that she was marrying a peasant and therefore theirs would be a peasant life, and they were both prepared for it. In Peramiho therefore, Paulina lived like any other peasant woman, with the double roles of production and reproduction. Paulina worked on her husbands' land where she and Francis grew maize, beans, cassava, pumpkins, millet, green vegetables and fruits to mention only a few. She was not worried about appropriation of the surplus she created because with the primitive tools they used (the hand hoe, panga etc) what they could produce was only for subsistence. Moreover, the understanding which existed between Paulina and her husband did not allow for any fear that her husband might exploit her.

The cash income provided by her husband by selling his labour to the missionaries and from selling some pumpkins etc. to the mission whenever a little surplus could be realized did not allow for either of the two to spend money lavishly.

Paulina concentrated on farming and made sure that her family was never hungry. She often remembered the Ngoni saying which reminded her to look at the stomach and not the face because it is the former which gets thin and not the latter. She also remembered the warning she learnt at the initiation ceremony that the best way to keep your husband to yourself is to feed him well. With the cooperation of her husband and the assistance from her younger sister who was staying with them they produced enough to feed her small family.

Paulina's migration to town in 1950 was not motivated by the wish to have paid employment. She was only looking for her husband who had neglected her in 1948. When she reached Dar es Salaam however, she found herself staying almost idle as a housewife. Having no children, even the household chores were not many, given the fact that life at Kawe was not as hectic as the village life where one has to collect firewood, fetch water, go to the farms, pound with a mortal and pestle and cook not only for the nuclear family but also for the relatives. At Kawe life was easier because she was responsible to only one person, her husband.

It should be remembered here that most of the women who migrated to town had problems in getting wage employment even if they had acquired some formal education. Paulina for instance was an ex-class IV leaver and if she were a man she could stand a better chance of getting wage employment. As a woman it was not easy to be employed and being a married woman, she was not in a hurry to seek for employment. Marriage was a security because by then she could live on her husband's income, unlike the single women who had nobody to depend on for their livelihood. There were very few employment opportunities at Kawe and the few that existed were monopolized by men. Paulina once had an ambition to become a teacher but there was no school at Kawe by then where she could teach.

While at Kawe Paulina learnt mat-making skills but she had no idea of using that skill for income generating. Her life at Kawe therefore remained simple and dependent, but not too enjoyable. To a person like her who has been used to hectic life (farming, fetching water, earning an income etc) this life-style was boring. She however managed to survive for the four years before they secured a farm at Mbezi-One village in 1954.

Life at Mbezi-One village was similar to the village life in Peramiho. As soon as they were given land by a certain Mzee Salehe, Paulina and her husband began growing cassava, pineaples, pawpaws, peas, coconuts, pumpkins, groundnuts etc. In those days the weather was more reliable, the soils were still fertile and although the production tools were still primitive, farmers more often produced surplus which they sold to meet cash demands. Paulina even managed to buy her TANU (Tanganyika African National Union) Party card from the sale of surplus food crops. Of course her family was still small. Farming remained their main occupation until her husband got employed at the Kimara Matangini by the Water Department as a day watchman in 1966. He stayed with his job until 1980 when he retired.

Mr. Francis' wage employment brought some changes in the life pattern of his family. Formerly he and his wife used to go to the farm together, now it was Paulina alone with her children. That in a way changed her daily work schedules. As soon an her husband left for work at about 6.00 a.m., Paulina made tea or porridge for herself and the children (the second one was born in 1959) after which she and the children left for the farm (which was only a few yards away) and worked until 10.00 a.m. when she returned home because it was already too hot for the kids. At home she prepared lunch (e.g. stiff porridge made of maize or cassava flour, with beans, or pumpkin or peas or cassava leaves or fish). After lunch Paulina rested until evening when the husband returned from work to assist her with the kids or pounding or fetching water and firewood.

In actual fact the time used for farm work decreased and consequently the yields also dwindled. As a result part of the husband's income had to be used for the purchase of food. However, Paulina went and still goes to the farm whenever she has time. She is now an old woman of 65 years but still does some farm work. She work with her husband in their farm and although they are less strong they still manage to grow some sweet potatoes, cassava, peas, pumpkin and pineaples. They are also enjoying the coconuts (which they planted about thirty years ago) some which are occassionally sold "to get some cash for salt" as Paulina puts it.

Under the present conditions, the income from their farm is so meagre that they can hardly survive without extra assistance from their two children, Michael and Willy. The latter however, has his own family to care for and his assistance to his old parents is very occassional. It is the older boy therefore who puts all his efforts to make sure that his parents eat, dress and get medicare. He is still single at the age of 36 years.

Paulina's family never went hungry even when they depended solely on agriculture for subsistence. The regular cash income from her husband before he retired was however a good security especially during the later years of 1970s when the weather was very unpredictable and farmers incomes were uncertain.

Paulina's Political and Public Life

Formal education is very important for one interested in political and public life. Researchers in women's political status in Tanzania for instance have shown the correlation between education and level of political participation. As for wage employment, of course there is no doubt about the correlation between education and type or category of job one can get.

Paulina's formal education was a great asset which she used ever since she was young. It was that education for instance which gave her self-confidence to look for her husband when he disappeared from home in 1948. The same education and especially the mastery of Swahili language made it easier for her to mix with the Zaramo people when she moved to Dar es Salaam. The same education again landed Paulina into a teaching job in 1968 at Mbezi-One village.

Paulina is not a trained teacher and her fellow women who chose her as their teacher in 1968 knew very well that she had no teaching certificate. However, without hesitation the Women of Mbezi One wrote a letter to Mr. Francis asking him to allow his wife to teach them needlework, domestic science, reading, writing and dancing (ngoma).

The women of Mbezi One were already organized in a group. As for Adult Education classes, Paulina was not their first teacher. The former teacher who was also a woman had left because she was called to her home village to attend her sick parent. Paulina, a dedicated member of the women group of Mbezi-One was considered the best alternative to replace the former teacher.

Mr. Francis could not possibly betray the 'women-cause' by refusing to allow his wife to enlighten her fellow women using her talents. After permission was granted, Paulina started teaching under a Cashewnut tree because there was no proper classroom. Under normal circumstances in Tanzania, primary school buildings are used for Adult Education classes. However, since Mbezi-One had no primary school then, the best alternative was to conduct classes under the shade of a tree. However, as the rainy season approached, both the students and the teacher became worried. They held various meetings to discuss this issue but the main problem was lack of building materials, especially roofing materials. Eventually they found a solution when the University Primary School changed location (in 1971) in which case the old iron sheets were donated to the women of Mbezi-One. These women contributed building poles and their husbands, especially Mr. Francis, assisted them in building one room. More corrugated iron sheets were donated by a group of Danish women staying in Dar es Salaam by then. It was then possible to complete roofing of a big room which, except for lack of benches, was fit to accomodate all the 100 students.

Paulina recalled very vividly the enthusiasm expressed by her students and if it were not for the eagerness her students showed in learning new knowledge, she wouldn't have the stamina to go all the way to Kigamboni government office every now and then to collect teaching materials including chalks, notebooks, pencils as well as her salary of T.sh. 100/- per month.

Apart from academic teaching she also encouraged learning by doing (practicals) especially in domestic science. In order to do this effectively, the idea of opening a group farm was discussed, endorsed and a plot was acquired from the village commmunal land. A three acre farm was cultivated for three years where rice, bananas, pineaples, green vegetables, peas (kunde), maize and pawpaws were grown and sold to earn the group a cash income. At one time the group decided to co-opt male members but abandoned the idea after realizing that male attendance for the farm-work was very poor.

During the three years of operation the farm provided ingredients for the domestic science lessons as well as food for the group members. However, the income from the farm decreased year after year because the women could only afford to spend a few hours on the farm due to the many roles they had to perform daily. They had to care for their own private farms (all were peasants), care for the children, perform the domestic chores and on top of all that attend the adult education classes to which they all were very much committed.

As for Paulina, she had to change her life pattern again. The teaching job fully occupied her and therefore she had to employ casual labourers to take care of her farm. Fortunately enough her children were already in primary school so she was at least not occupied with childcare.

Paulina taught until 1977 when TANESCO (Tanzania Electric Supply Company) nationalized the school area with a compensation of T.sh. 4,100/- because TANESCO had to install its poles at that area for distributing electricity to the Zanzibar island.

Narrating her teaching experience, Paulina said she very much enjoyed her work and was satisfied witn her efforts and when she stopped teaching in 1977 her son Michael took over the teaching of adult education classes. Visitors from both the government and the foreign diplomatic missions (the Danish) used to visit her to see her job and at one time a sewing machine was donated to her group and a few women managed to learn sewing skills before it was stolen a few years later. The Danish women in collaboration with the University nursery school administration assisted Paulina's group in running a nursery school at Mbezi-One which operated for 3 days a week and only in the afternoons. Although the time was short, that service was very much appreciated by both the parents and the young kids who enjoyed the socialization process and even learnt a few letters and some songs. Paulina's classroom was used by the kids for this purpose.

Indeed the cooperation between Mbezi-One women, the University Nursery School and the Danish Women was highly appreciable and to demonstate this, at a farewell party organized by the Mbezi-One women for the Danish Women in 1977 a donation of T.sh. 300/- was given to Paulina's group.

The cooperation with the UWT University branch was very much enhanced by the first chairperson of the University branch who saw the need to work together with Mbezi-One women on political and economic issues. Joint functions were organized. Mbezi-One women were usually invited to entertain visitors with ngomas and songs. The Danish women also used to assist Paulina with transport in taking her students for study tours at Urafiki Textile Mill, Dar es Salaam Airport, National Service Campus at Mgulani – Dar es Salaam etc.

Paulina's political life on the other hand can be measured by using a few indicators such as her active roles in UWT, TANU, CCM etc. She joined UWT on 4th September, 1968 and TANU in 1975. She is also one of the foundermembers of Chama cha Mapinduzi (CCM).

It has been explained elsewhere that in a developing country like Tanzania where women's workload is too great, and coupled with the belief that politics is a man's domain, it is very difficult for the average woman like Paulina to take active part in politics. Although the political system in Tanzania gives chance for women to compete with men for both electoral and nominated political posts, Paulina, like many other women preferred to restrict her formal political participation to membership in the political party (TANU and later CCM), paying the party dues and attending the party meetings. It is very interesting at times to know why people join political parties. As for Paulina for instance, her interest in TANU was not a mere gesture for political participation but rather a calculated measure which was aimed at leading her to various destinations, one of which was her dreamt vision of a society where both men and women share same social, economic and political status. Note that she joined UWT before joining TANU.

However, the experience she gained through her participation in UWT taught her that no matter how active UWT members are, the liberation of women cannot be brought about by women alone. There were issues which UWT could not resolve but which could be dealt with by TANU. Policy making for instance could not be handled by UWT alone. It was TANU which made major policies including those affecting women's lives. It was basically after that realization that Paulina felt the need to join TANU so as to be able to participate directly (as a member) in TANU activities. She hoped that since TANU allows membership of both sexes, it is one of the best institutions where both men and women can sit together thus overcoming the cultural barrier that politics is a man's domain. Women could therefore take part in decision-making at public level. Paulina encouraged most of her fellow UWT members to join in TANU with the outcome that today at Mbezi-One CCM members are mainly women.

Paulina was more active in UWT where she was not only a member of the branch executive committee but also one of the chief advisors to the branch. Her teaching job had influenced so many of the Mbezi-One women that whenever there was need for major decision-making for UWT, she was always consulted. Paulina can be said to be a charismatic leader who is aware of many developmental issues and very articulate as well as convincing when she wants to drive a point home.

The activeness of Mbezi-One women owes much on Paulina's determination to improve the lives of women and their families. Paulina had a lot to say about the liberation of women when she was first interviewed in 1987. Trying to explain how she understood the concept of women liberation. Paulina expressed that while general liberation to her means reducing and eventually overcoming all the hardship in life, women liberation means not only overcoming all the hardships but also effecting gender equality on issues related to access to production resources, ownership rights, equal distribution of recources, goods and services and equal sharing (with man) in decision-making at both household and public level.

In short Paulina thought that women's liberation means that women should have equal power and equal benefits on matters pertaining to socio-economic and political (cultural) development. That is precisely why she devoted most of her life working with women and trying to contribute to their well being. Asked how best that goal can be achieved, Paulina had different strategies in mind. Expressing her experience in sharing decion-making, she thought that was the starting point. Paulina then expressed the need for UWT and mothers in general to be more dynamic in mobilizing themselves and change the out-modelled child-upbringing which is gender-biased. She also thought CCM could play a very big role in conscientizing its members on the need for a new culture where roles-sharing between men and women should be extended to the domestic chores also. To her, the ten cell unit is also a strategic organ to effect a lot of changes towards women's liberation since it is a grass root organ which can mobilize, energize and encourage individual households to change out-modelled culture and replace it with a revolutionary one.

Paulina's experience has shown that leaders for the women's emancipation should be the women themselves. She however cautioned that not every woman can lead the revolution. There are those who are just interested in self-aggrandisement. And yet there are some who are not yet gender-sensitive although they have all other leadership qualities. Another very important point raised is that since the purpose is to liberate the whole society, women have also to mobilize the male allies and fight together. The process of gender-sensitization should therefore be extended to both women and men especially the youth, although strategically women should be sensitized first.

Paulina was also of the opinion that women struggles can be launched at all times in all places, and that every woman is actually participating in these struggles in her own way although the degree and form of participation differs. Paulina for instance correctly observed that the struggles she participated in when she was growing up in Lilambo differ in form from the current struggles she is participating in, but all the same she sees them as one and the same struggle.

Paulina seem to have decided to settle in Dar es Salaam until her death. She and her family have no plans to return to Peramiho except for occasional visits.

"We are more attached to Dar than to Peramiho now, for we have spent most of our life time here. After being away for so long, we shall feel less at home in Peramiho... No.. We shall die here in Dar and be burried here in our farm."

said Paulina on behalf of her family in her concluding remark.

PART FOUR

Lessons Learnt from Paulina's Life History

A renowed social scientist once said that "Experience is the best teacher." Indeed Paulina's experience has taught us a lot. Through-out Paulina's life we have witnessed the development of feminist consciousness. Her attempt and determination to perform well in school for instance has taught us how in those days girls struggled to prove that they have same mental capability and can compete with men if given equal chance, the fact which is widely accepted after an increased number of girls managed to jump from one grade to another up to the University level. More and more girls are now taking subjects like Engineering which were once a reserve for boys. We also see how the co-education system has moulded Paulina's political and feminist consciousness. From her experience it has been shown that gender inequality can be discouraged if boys and girls are allowed from young age to mix freely, and cooperate in all matters pertaining to their socio-economic and cultural lives. The education she received opened the way for more participation in the development process. Indeed, part of Paulina's success in her life owes much to both the formal and informal education she had passed through.

It is however disappointing to note that as far as health education is concerned, to some extent the type of knowledge imparted to the youth was incomplete. The scientific way of explaining causes of disease for instance was lacking. The only explanation provided for most disease was in relation to spirits, gods and witchcraft. Under modern medicine on the other hand the colonialists tended to put more emphasis on curative rather than preventive, and although causes of some of the diseases were known, such information was not given to patients and the society at large. The same trend continued even after independence. It is no wonder therefore that the cause of albino abnormality was not known to Paulinà and all the people around her. However, todate the Tanzanian government is trying her best to educate the masses on health issues through various ways including campaigns, radio programmes ętc. Mothers also get some health education when they visit clinics and hospitals. The question which remains to be answered however is: "How much of the health education should be imparted by the formal schooling and how much should be learnt from the informal education?" Paulina's failure to challenge some of the cultural norms such as the payment of bride-wealth however shows how effective the traditional informal education and training was. Students seem to have undergone through a learning experience where one was forced to accept and believe whatever was being taught. Challenging or criticizing was regarded as an act of disobedience which was liable for punishment. As for Paulina, she didn't even think of criticizing the practice of bride-wealth because by then she thought it was properly done. It was only much later that she had time to think about it and concluded that it perpetuated the oppression of women. There are many women like Paulina even today. There are those who still think it is degrading to be married without bride-price. Women with such ideas cut across all social groups including the elite. There are also those who hold the opposite view but as individuals have no power to end the practice under the present era. Their major contribution in the struggle against bride – wealth is limited to making sure that their daughters are not purchased with a bride – wealth when they get married.

In Tanzania today the effects of bride-wealth are seldomly being discussed. In 1975 when the former President, Mwalimu Nyerere was inaugurating the International Women's Year and participating in celebrating the International Women's day (March 8th) he correctly pointed out bride-wealth as one of the stumbling blocks to women's liberation. The payment of bridewealth is known to be greatly restrictive on women's freedom, reducing them as legal minor's. The Swahili phrases such as "Akili ya bibi ni sawasawa na ya mtoto mdogo" ("A woman's brain is like that of a child") clearly show the low status women were given in society. In terms of acquisition of property during marriage, bride-wealth paid seemed to give the husband all powers over his wife's economic contribution. A wife had little control over the wealth she produced or over the children she produced and raised. During colonialism, even with the introduction of Christianity bride-wealth payment was left intact. It was only after the Marriage Act of 1973 was adopted in Tanzania that this issue was positively addressed to. Of course the Marriage Act does not forbid the payment of bride-wealth but transforms it into a private contract between the families of the potential spouses and hence non-payment does not affect the validity of the marriage, (A.K.H. Weinrich, 1982). Paulina's change of attitude about bride-wealth can therefore be taken as a challenge to the Tanzania feminists who should tirelessly launch campaigns against bride-wealth. If people are made aware of the negative effects of bridewealth, then it is possible to win them as supporters of the campaign against it.

Bride-wealth can be linked with what is regarded as "presents" given to the bride's family. Paulina's family for instance was given a hoe, some money and clothes while Paulina herself was given beads. There are various interpretations of the significance of such presents. The hoe and money which is given to the bride's father and brother could symbolize the fact that the girl's economic contribution to her family which was under the control of her father/brother will no longer be forthcoming. The father therefore should take back the production tool and think of who should next use it in his family. The white cloth given to the bride's mother/aunt could symbolize the fact that the mother was expected to have made sure that her daughter is pure, and has her virginity. Besides, she will no longer enjoy the material benefits which used to be provided by her daughter. The beads given to the girl just reminds her that beads are an important asset for a young bride to wear at the hips. It is believed by the Ngoni tribe that when the husband plays with the beads at bed-time, it adds more sexual excitement to both partners. Note that women are given consumer items (beads and cloth) while men are given tools of production. This tends to symbolize that it is men who control the economy.

Paulina's village life has also informed us that being a girl at times forces one to play more roles than boys and yet both are expected to perform well in those roles which they share. Paulina for instance had to resume the domestic chores which her mother used to perform (before her death) while at the same time she had to go to school and was expected to do well in school. This means that with the little time she had for school work, she had to work extra hard in order to reach the acceptable standards. Despite all that of course, we have seen her successfully completing her primary school education.

Paulina's experience in this case has been shared by many women in Tanzania who also have to play the double roles (housework and office or farm work) even after completing their studies. The unequal gender division of labour designed by society has very much to do with this. It would be interesting however to compare the state of women during the colonial period with that of pre-colonial period given the fact that the colonial period was characterised by complex sex division of labour. One could therefore argue that the subordination and exploitation of women was greater during the colonial than the pre-colonial era. In any case, the socialization process has to be revolutionized to create a new culture where role-sharing between sexes is reinforced, especially in a country like Tanzania which is aspiring to build socialism. The sharing of both domestic and production respon-sibilities demonstrated by Paulina, Francis, their children and grandchildren regardless of sex has given us some hope that gender equality in all spheres of life is possible but only if the concerned parties work for it consciously. The secret behind this success lies in socialization, which tends to be a women's responsibility.

One important element which had tremendous impact on Paulina's life is the belief in witchcraft/superstition. Her husband ran away because of it. Her children died and she herself almost followed suit, partly because she and her people believed in witchcraft and did not seek medical help until much later and not from a hospital but from a traditional healer. Indeed this fact should be born in mind when talking about the problems of women in Africa today. Already in some areas in rural Tanzania such as Shinyanga old women are being killed as victims of this belief in witchcraft. They fall victim due to continued use of firewood and cow-dung for cooking which make their eyes red, – one culturally accepted indication of a witch. Sadly, these old women are hated not only by neighbours but also by their children espe-cially sons some of whom are even said to have taken part in suspecting their mothers (of witchcraft) and even in killing them. Indeed women are once again paying dearly for the poor technology used in the domestic sphere which has caused the health hazards (red eyes) which are misinterpreted by the misinformed local people as indicative of witchcraft. Perhaps witchcraft should be top in the agenda of issues to be researched on and discussed by African feminists in the immediate future.

Paulina's attempt to look for her husband (when she was abandoned) and the correct strategies she adopted affirms a force of protest against some of the cultural norms which are detrimental to women's freedom and development. Paulina's experience has posed as a conscientizing process which can be subdivided into four themes: (i) Women as victims of culture, (ii) women as victims of circumstance, (iii) culture as a dynamic process and as an aspect of the development process and, (iv) Human being as a social animal and an active controller of social development.

Paulina's life experience is a lucid reflection of all these themes and especially of a Ngoni Cultural reality and myth which together support and perpetuate a secular tradition of African women's submission. With her experience one sees how the individual life fits within the social context and portrays the problems an African woman faces in real life, the struggles she has to undergo, the strategies she can adopt and the possible results one can achieve. Probably Paulina's "success" is an illumination of the bright future awaiting women if and only if their struggles for liberation are fought through correct strategies.

Her correct understanding that liberation has to be fought for and not prayed for; that women should demand for their rights and not beg for them is a clear indication that even the old generation has a role to play in women's liberation. Her efforts not to allow women's subordination in her home as indicated in part two clearly give one a transformation strategy aimed at ending subordination in the home. Of course it is not enough to persuade or convince a husband that it is in-human to subordinate his wife. Besides the completely new ideology which is called for, isn't merely a question of Legislation; for, if it were so, Tanzania with all her progressive laws or U.S.S.R. with her socialist ideology would not still be blamed of gender inequality in the home today (because their national policies clearly speak against gender inequality). Experience has shown that both legislation, education, persuasion, convincing arguments as well as social opportunities and material conditions are prerequisites to put the ideology into practice and ensure gender-equality.

Throughout her life, Paulina's struggle gives a sense of both psychological and mental development emanating from her intergration into the social dynamics. Her life in Dar es Salaam and especially her role as a teacher and to some extent a political activist clearly cultivates that psychological and mental development in both herself, her pupils and fellow villagers as well as the co-author of this life history and probably the readers too. Indeed a human being is a social (being) animal.

It is clear from the four parts that throughout her life Paulina has been trying to overcome the cultural barriers which have tended to limit women's participation in many aspects of life. Sometimes Paulina has consciously fought to overcome such barriers while there were also times when she unconsciously did so. It is not possible to list all aspects of the cultural barriers she has fought against but it is important to mention that her rich experience in socio-economic and political participation in itself shows how successful she has been in overcoming most of the cultural barriers to modern life.

Her life therefore remains a source of inspiration, which, by its penetrating and centralizing power can contribute to the revolutionary gains for women's total liberation and that of the whole society. Aluta continua.

References

1. Gulliver P. (1965): *A Report on the Migration of African workers to the South from the Southern Highlands Province with Special Reference to the Nyakyusa of Rungwe District.*

2. Jaspa 1982: *Basic Needs in Danger A Basic Needs Oriented Strategy for Tanzania.* ILO Publication Addis Ababa.

3. Mbilinyi Marjorie 1980: *"The Problem of Sexuality and Fertility among Female Youth".* Paper presented to IDS Staff Seminar series, UDSM.

4. Ophelia Mascarenhas and Marjorie Mbilinyi 1983: *Women in Tanzania. An Analytical Bibliography.* Scandinavian Institute of African Studies, Upsala, SIDA Stochholm.

5. Sabot T.H. (1979) *Economic Development and Urban Migration. Tanzania, 1900 – 1971* London Oxford.

6. Shields, N. (1978), *Women in the Urban Labour Market: The Case of Tanzania.* Washington D.C., World Bank Staff Working Paper No. 380.

7. Susan Geiger: *Life History Research,* Workshop paper published as WRDP Papers No. 1, 1985.

8. Weinrich A.K.H. 1982: *Changes in the Political and economic roles of women in Zimbabwe since Independence.* Article reproduced from Cultures – dialogue between the people of the world published in Women – from witch-hunt to politics. (Unesco publication 1982).

9. Wright Marcia (1975) "Women in Peril: A Commentary of the Life Stories of Captive in Nineteenth – Century East – Central Africa." *African Social Research,* 20 (December).

10. Various files from the Archives on Migration, political economy of Dar es Salaam, Sisal Production, Tanganyika Packers etc.

11. Tanganyika Government, African Census Report, 1957.

CHAPTER NINE

Conceptual and Legal Issues

1. The Fundamental Question of Democracy

It is difficult to deal with the question of gender relations without coming up against the fundamental question of democracy and freedoms which are demanded by modern states. Women are determined to denounce false theories of democracy and freedom which usually mean the democracy and freedom of men. Throughout history, democracy tended to mean better conditions and space for the dominant classes. The French revolution of 1889 for example, and all social systems (modes of production) including even socialism as exhibited in Europe today, were ushered in and manipulated by dominant interests. The majority of the producers and reproducers were simply regarded as an underclass. The privileges of life, the rights to properties and freedom of expression were reserved for the few who represented a dominant group. In this situation one notices that women were facing double subordination due to their class positions and more significantly as a gender. It is therefore necessary to problematize the issue of gender relations and democracy in specific contexts in order to capture the reality of each cultural setting. One cannot have an ideologically accepted gender subordination and yet claim to be democratic or socialist. It is popularly believed that there can neither be socialism without democracy nor democracy without socialism. Since women form the majority of our population and remain an underclass, democracy is still questioned.

In Africa, the gender subordination is more significant because after the colonial era, there arose all sorts of socialisms which would have led one to expect quick emancipation of women. However, what happens instead, is the assumption that poor women are satisfied with their conditions even in the so-called socialist countries to the extent that the call by educated women to change various cultural aspects is sometimes dismissed as unrealistic or an imitation. This is not awkward in Tanzania alone but in various African countries as well although world opinion has been stronger on the recognition of women's lives as burdensome. African female scholars have clearly brought out this contradiction, and have even gone further to highlight on how society has chosen to inform women through education.

Indeed, society should also give a chance to educated women to liberate their lot instead of disregarding their contributions. Thus African people have to try and understand how their societies are composed and the social relations therein.

History fortunately is full of literature which directly or otherwise has spoken for women among the category of the poor (although a few women are rich). The Marxist literature, although incomprehensive about the condition of women, especially African women, still provide a platform from which to explain the conditions and positions of women as well as the way out. Some African philosophers like Frantz Fanon (1978) should be recognized here for their contribution on the theory of alienation which not only discusses the method of colonizing Africans but also the implied overall impact of colonizing, enslaving and degrading women not only as a gender but also as a disadvantaged group. Consequently bourgeois feminists in 1970s introduced the gender approach in academic literature as an analytical category along with class, race, and ethinicity. African women agree as to the usefulness of the gender analytical category but it is noted that for African reality" it has to be posed together with the problems of colonization and underdevelopment. In other words, the African women experience a triple oppression as a gender, first under colonialism and its effects, secondly under neo-colonialism and the continued process of underdevelopment and class formation and thirdly as a gender in the national and household boundaries.

Women have gone through different epochs or modes of production with their men but it is obvious that each mode of production has given more and better bargains to men than to women. As a result of this unequal development, there has not been a clear projection of how to remove the gender-gap without resistance. Bebel (1971) suggested that women of the future will become free when the kitchens and childcare facilities become liberated and transformed into public utilities. Bebel sounds like the utopians of the 1850s who spoke of the good ideas of socialism without a clue as to how it would be realized. While such ideas have a place, the question is to liberate men from false consciousness and to educate them on the alienation processes as explained by Fanon, as well as cautioning them on the power of evolution which is going to catch them unprepared while women are consciously pushing on with their survival mechanisms as well as development strategies. For, just as modes of production overtake one another, human species may also begin to challenge each other among young and old, female and male, non-schooled and schooled etc. It is therefore not defeatist to begin to acknowledge forms of resistance put up by women, and forms of resistance put up by society to women's efforts. Indeed, all these show that at stake is the fundamental question of democracy. Is it to be given, bought or fought for?

Resistance abounds in African cultures when educated women suggest positive cultural changes which acknowledge and take care of women's burdens. It appears that the educated women in Africa will also need to find protection for their right to practice new values which the new education has inculcated in them, especially freedom, democracy and participation. Indeed these women have changed and have adopted critical, analytical and sometimes radical perspectives towards solving women's problems. One major impediment which still discourages the efforts of such women is the accusation that they identify and underline problems which are far-fetched and are not supported by 'typical' Africa women. This book has answered this polemic by giving a chance to ordinary women to speak for themselves thus giving a chance to the "doubting Thomases." Individually, women have posed their oppressions and conceptualized them according to their understanding. Co-authors have in many instances in this book refused to make interpretations to avoid imposing a seemingly academic flavour. For example, Bibi's later life (ch. 2) is presumably influenced by Arabic cultural diffusion which characterise coastal history and is reflected in Bibi's later life style showing transformation characteristics from feudal relations into capitalist relations of production. Co-author Patricia refused to take it further avoiding being embroiled in political economy of Islam - because as she correctly points out, the "life speaks for itself."

We note how Marjorie (ch. 6) led Kalindile to conceptualise in some detail the role of Christinity and Kalindile's leadership role within it. The life historian was also led to deal with the issues of bride-price and women's reactions to male behaviour. Mama Koku (ch. 5), Mwanaidi (ch. 7) and Eva (ch. 4).dealt at large with issues of income, property and self reliance in the lives of women, while Paulina (ch. 8) as well as Kalindile brought out clearly the issues of women's groups and organizing as well as adult education activities for women. Indeed these discourses are as clearly posed and have underlying philosophies just as other literature has posed them. The issues are not, therefore, farfetched but reflect on how women are tolerating the oppressive situations and the responses they adopt when they answer back. Some of the dominant themes have been picked to elaborate a bit more on women's lives and reflections.

a) Rural – urban migration
The theme which women demonstrated without words is the rural – urban

migration. There was nothing abnormal about it at least as far as the women were concerned. However, it is read elsewhere that the colonial authorities were never happy with women who were leaving their husbands to go looking for livelihood in towns because this trend would cause court cases of men claiming repayment of bride-price (cf Mbilinyi, 1984; Swantz, 1985). It is clear that the statistics of urban women have gradually risen from few numbers to an almost equal ratio as indicated in chapter eight (Paulina with Bertha). This proves the claim that women are entitled to urban space as much as men are, provided the urban setting can make adequate provisions to tap women's productive potential than leaving them as lumpen proletarians as argued by Ngaiza (ch. 5).

b) Bride-price

The other theme which attracts our attention is the question of bride-price. As the histories presented in this book dealt with the old generation except for Anna (ch. 3), there was no chance to expect that the practice of bride-price, much as it was problematic, would be denounced. Both female and male were proud of it. Eva (ch. 4) talked of the process of courtship and change of husbands as if bride-price was not an issue. It was a societal norm dogmatically imposed and mystically accepted like a fetish. Kalindile and her daughter Sambulika (divorced) did not mince their words in educating us (ch. 6) that even if bride-price "enslaves" it was in order. For, a woman to just marry off like that is unrespectable and ridiculous! Even educated women like some co-authors in this book admitted that they supported the principle provided it did not entail unbelievable implications. Even if the bride-price is just a "needle" it is better than no price at all, for women feel small and humiliated if no token of bride-price was paid. In the circumstances, then, it is merely a matter of time and changed circumstances before bride-price is completely abolished.

We note the efforts in the 1950s and 1960s (cf Cory 1962) to streamline and unify bride "price" among ethnic groups sharing similar traditions all over Tanganyika. This effort was not supported (respected) within respective customary laws because it emanated from above and missed the philosophy of the people regarding bride-price. It has remained the same today. A lot of expressions have appeared in the newspapers calling for unceremonized courtship and an end to bride "price." In short, the old generation still holds the upper hand and the young generation has to bow down to their culture.

In order to change that philosophy, it must be understood and an enabling enviroment created to show that women can be respected without having to pay-bride "price" for them. Ironically, when relations break down, respect is not guaranteed by bride-price. For that reason a correct process to address bride-price has to evolve from the traditional settings in order to reassess the guiding philosophy and to make new democratic decisions which should involve women.

c) The Institution of marriage

The foregoing necessarily leads us into the controversial institution of marriage. Somewhere there is peace while elsewhere there is mistrust, divorce and polygamy. Much as these have become the facts of life as seen from life experience, the question of what is to be done still looms large. It has become clearer than before that neither the history makers nor their co-authors are too radical about the institution of marriage. They all share a liberal approach. Note for example that their suggestions include changing property relations, improving village life, revolutionizing women's upbringing into self reliance vis-a-vis false expectations of depending on males, educating fathers, providing legal aid to women and improving women's art of manipulating men or perseverence.

The life histories are so revealing and moving that one would have expected less liberal conclusions from the authors. Let us take the question of marriage as the most glaring example. Almost all the stories depict the institution of marriage as an oppressive snare that imprisons women and sucks their vitality and humanity. From this, the obvious conclusion would be either to call for the abolition of marriage or at least to question its very basis. Yet this is not what happens, rather we get a call for reform and improvement of the institution. While marriage and the family lend themselves to criticism as the most effective fetters of the women, yet this is, indeed, the most obvious factor that regulates the relations between men and women. All the forms of marriage existing in Tanzania (matriarchal, patriarchal, levirate, monogamy, concubinage, polygamy, etc) need an updated examination to see how they affect the man and the woman today and how they can be regulated.

The answers to the above problematic are not simple. Women did not speak of dismantling marriage or the family institutions because they believed in their importance and necessity. They believe as argued by Kalindile (ch. 6) that the problem is lack of democracy, freedom and justice generally. Above that, women are still alienated as ably taught by the African Philosopher, Frantz Fanon (1968) and echoed correctly by Emmanuel Hansen (1978). Consequently the problem of female-alienation has to be addressed to enable them to recognize their true self. In the same manner, men have to be empowered to be confident by understanding and accepting the true-female images. Alternative responses to oppressive marriages from other cultures have not met the admiration of African women. For example, the existence of lesbianism and gayism in western cultures is one kind of response or revolt against oppressive male-female relations. Refusal to enter into marriage is also not acceptable to African Women as it under-mines and underestimates society's power to correct the mistakes which are socially perpetuated in marriage but which can be done away with.

In otherwords, the collective answer is not to run away from it as this is an escapist and coward reaction, but to force society through pressure groups to redress the family which is aknowledged as a natural space for adults. Collective bargaining is necessary because it may lead to changing the cultural ideology on gender and the family, while radicalism is simply a minority survival strategy for the fittest and it breeds undue misunderstand-ings.

In Tanzania, there is a strong belief that women have the power to make life better if they were given a chance. For 23 years after the Arusha Decla-ration, which introduced "ujamaa" in Tanzania, women painstakingly expected reasonable change at household level as a result of the transition to socialism. The declaration indirectly warned however that:

> Socialism is a way of life, and a socialist society cannot sim-
> ply come into existence. A socialist society can only be built
> by those who believe in, and who themselves practice the
> principles of socialism.

Arusha Declaration Feb. 1967

It is no small wonder then that today, Tanzania's transition to socialism is beset by many problems, some of which are very obvious at household level. Thus dictators at household level cannot turn into socialists in the public domain. In the circumstances the struggle by the oppressed has to take all possible forms especially through organizing. Besides learning about the moving accounts of the women's histories, expected outcomes are first of all that a more focused and meaningful family code within the customary law and statutory law would be demanded.

A second expectation is that men of good will from all walks of life and professions may begin to form "family clubs" as opposed to "beer clubs" in order to deal with these hard facts of life. It is realized that women have found strength from all sorts of solidarity which men can also explore. Thus any attempts to deal with the family will find success through enhanced democratic measures which provide for basic freedoms and justice. More education and training to women liberates them from alienation, while educating men should liberate them from the false consciousness of superiority and other exaggerated power egoes.

d) *The Household Economy*

In essence the household economy also needs an elaborate discussion. In African circles it is believed that lack of food and money are the major causes of disharmony (not lack of democracy and freedoms). Thus if the household economy can be improved to provide enough subsistence, then harmony could prevail (basic needs theory). But evidence exist to suggest that women's oppression goes beyond subsistence. It includes reproductive rights, rights to family property and children, rights to uninterfered shelter and rights to social, economic and educational opportunities as well as social security. All these rights are conditioned by the patriarchal relations (to which older women are unconsciously part of). It is these patriarchal relations in Tanzania which hold back the potential of a household's progress. This is exemplified by the evidence that once women are left free to pursue independent un-inhibited economic activities, they do what they could have never thought of. Some of them are capable of creating reasonable income as well as creating securities for their dependants. The women in these life histories except for Kalindile and Paulina (who stayed in matrimonial bonds), changed from poor propertyless women to happier, propertied and responsible women taking care of themselves and their children in the business world without demanding that they should be "equal" to men.

The above examples mainly suggest that the way out is to get out of marriage. But not all the women in question chose to be out of marriage. It was by mere coincidence that where partnership could not hold or the husband passed away, the women naturally had to be alone. In summary we are reminded by the forergoing chapters that the way out is not sporadic responses but a concerted effort to sort out all strategies and come up with an agreeable formula. It should be remembered that our life historians found that: education, divorce, cooperation, economic activities, religion, prostitution, formal employment and appealing to authority were all methods leading to good life after struggle. While these strategies are posed, they are individually difficult to pursue. Take for example the case of prostitution and its dangers; cooperation without adequate skills; economic activities without enough credit, and divorce without shelter, economic and moral support. Even appealing to authotirities individually may victimize women. In what society considers acceptable situations, the persuance of all the above strategies amounts to resistance or revolt by "bad" women, and as a result, there is little or no support from many people.

210

2. The Legal Provisions

The stories, indeed, speak for themselves but they have to be subjected to the legal provisions of Tanzania. The intention here is to demonstrate that women acknowledge the national efforts (cf. Msumi, H 1988 and Appendix A.) but that they recognize also that it is the oppressed who should prescribe the rules of the legal game, for as it stands, the oppressed are still the losers. Without exaggeration for example, the early life history of Anna X (ch. 3) on school girl pregnancies leaves our society guilty of default to use the law to defend the unbelievable numbers of school girls who found themselves pregnant prematurely. Other cases of pillage as argued by Bibi (ch. 2) are also numerous and not to mention Mama Koku's story. The issue however from the legal point of view is that failure to know or use the law is no excuse.

The customary laws in many African societies more often than not discriminate against women, and especially so in patriarchal families. This being the case, women were brought up to accept whatever customary laws dictated to them without arguments. Males have the final say in almost everything, be it economic, sexual, educational or emotional. In traditional society, this was an acceptable reality and one cannot blame women for the dominant ideology of the time in which many of them were participants. Women were brought up to accept customs regardless of whether the same were oppressive to them or not. Taking the issue of bride wealth for example; nearly all women marry after it has been paid, some knowing very well that the same is the cause of many women's suffering. Most of the women, even today, think that bride-price validates marriage and gives respect. Women have not yet realized that the act of paying bride-price reduces them to legal minors with no power over themselves, their labour power and over the property they acquire. The *Law of Marriage Act 1971* attaches no importance to bride-price and as such non payment of it does not invalidate a marriage.

Lack of awareness of legal rights is another problem faced by many African men. Until two decades ago, nearly all women in the traditional setting had their husbands chosen for them. This was so because most African societies believe that an African marriage is an alliance of kinship groups or families, and marriage is a means whereby one kinship group obtains a new member of another group through a recognized procedure. Normally a could-be wife is neither consulted as to whether she would like to be married by the chosen husband, nor is she involved in the bride wealth negotiations. The Law of Marriage Act makes consent to marriage mandatory and imposes a sanction to any person who forces another to marry. In spite of this provision some parents, due to selfish reason and disrespect for the

211

interests of the female gender, still trade off their young daughters. African women in the traditional setting are denied access to many rights even those specifically provided for under the constitution. They are denied access to education, access to property ownership, right to a just pay for their labour, and freedom of movement to the extent that women who went to towns in search of means of livelihood were usually branded as prostitutes. In some cases women were and some still are denied rights to engage in income generating activities by their husbands who did not sometimes care to provide for the family. This is tantamount to denying someone a right to life.

3. Legal Issues Arising from Tanzanian Women's Experiences

There are numerous legal issues ranging from matters relating to marriage, ownership of property, inheritance laws, and security of employment to access to economic resources. The issues can be divided into 4 main groups: a) Access to Economic Resources; b) Matrimonial Relationship; c) Violence Against Women and d) Access to Education.

a) *Access to economic resources*

Many women play an active role in taking care of their families. Some of these women start this at a very tender age and even after marriage they are still the major service providers and income generators for their families. Yet under customary laws they can own nothing, since everything, including a wife belongs to the husband. This is not only unfair but discriminatory and hence against the constitutional provisions providing for equality of all citizens and residents and the right to own property and engage in lawful gainful employment. In some cases husbands go as far as preventing wives from engaging in income generating activities as they fear that economic independence will make women arrogant and less submissive. The traditionally accepted view that all property belongs to the husband even though acquired by the wife, makes it impossible for women to have access to loans. Many of the lending institutions require security in forms of land or title deeds before one can borrow. The land or title deed is usually in the husband's name and he may be unwilling to even stand as a guarantor of his wife to allow her utilize the title deed as a security.

Some of the women, while struggling along, manage to acquire some property. A few manage to build several houses but usually in squatter areas. Such areas are unsurveyed and as such legally they have no good title and therefore their houses can be demolished any time. Although the owner of a demolished house is given some compensation, it would be difficult to build again taking into consideration the ever rising price of building materials and other problems.

b) Matrimonial relationship

Here we shall refer to polygamy, maintenance, and acquisition of property. Polygamy is practised by many ethnic groups in Tanzania. Although the *Law of Marriage Act 1971* allows polygamy, it is a big problem. It reduces a woman's status and creates insecurity in the woman and the home, imminently threatening any meaningful development in the home. Many women marry in accordance with customary law rites which allow a very wide room for polygamy, so that a good number of them find themselves in a polygamous situation. Women are happy to be the first wife as there are some rights and privileges not only to herself as a first wife but to her children too. Idealy women do not want co-wives although chances to escape these situations are rare unless one marries a Christian who abides by the Christian marriage tenets. It is unfortunate that although statutory law allows only one wife in monogamous marriages, some men keep concubines. The effect of this is destabilization of matrimonial peace, and a lot of hardship arise as the man would neglect his family and concentrate on the concubine. In such a situation, the only legal remedy available is for the aggrieved spouse to sue the concubine for damages. This remedy, however, is not a solution to the problem as it may aggravate the situation and make it worse to the detriment of the wife and her children.

There is a lot of confusion as regards presumption of marriage as provided for by the *Law of Marriage act 1971*. There is a provision stipulating that when a man and woman live (co-habit) as husband and wife for a period of 2 years or more, then there will be a rebuttable presumption that they were duly married. This presumption applies only to those people who have no encumbrances, such as monogamous marriages. It should be clear that wives should not be harrassed by concubines even if wives choose to accept male promiscuity as a reality.

Although customarily a man has a duty to *maintain* and care for his wife and children, in terms of cash needs, many a man have shunned their duties leaving women to struggle on their own. Many women find themseleves in this predicament and as a result they grow food for both consumption and sale so as to provide for the family. In fact a good number of households are de-facto being supported by women. Some husbands have given up providing for children as if they are exempted from that responsibility. This poses an unresolved legal problem for urban women who may be homemakers or working in low income jobs. Available options such as Counselling, divorce on grounds of neglect or desertion are usually humiliating to women. Even when it is the women who take care of the family by providing food and other necessities and even education for the children, under the same customary law there are no clear cut rules as to what will be her entitlement in the event of divorce or separation from her husband. Infact she is entitled to nothing, even her children, and her husband is not duty bound to support her. Under statutory laws, the right *to own private property* is recognized and this is very important for each partner. The same law allows the wife to pledge her husband's credit for basic necessities if the wife has no independent income. The law also provides for division of matrimonial assets, maintenance and custody of children in the event of divorce.

If a woman is seeking for the division of matrimonial assets she must prove contribution towards the acquistion of the assets. This contribution need not be in the form of money. Contribution includes even taking care of children and housework. The law seems to provide for urban conditions because the rural conditions would need a different legal provision in the event of divorce. In case of maintenance, the court can order the husband to maintain the ex-wife until she remarries.

If a woman wants *custody of the children* she may get it regardless of whether bride-price was paid or not. Statutory laws does not entartain the traditional belief that children are the property of the husband. Decision as to who should be awarded custody is based on the welfare of the child principle. The court will consider the best interests of the children. The affluent parent may be refused custody if it is shown that it won't be in the best interest of the children to live with such a parent. A parent may be a drunkard or one with moral turpitude etc., and the court will not give such a parent custody of children, no matter what the custom says.

c) *Violence against women*

The problem of violence against women features in the lives of many African women. The violence takes many forms, such as domestic violence and sexual harrassment, desertion, and child denial as seen from several precedents. According to traditions and customs, women are under the control and authority of their husband. Like the father, the husband is given a 'legal' and moral right to manage and control a woman's behaviour. *Wife beating* is permitted as a way of chastising the wife, and women are instructed not to fight back. This violence could even result in death, but the customs pay no due regard to it. It is only with the coming of colonialism that wife beating and wife murder were prevented and controlled by law and as a result men became afraid as they could be hanged for murdering their wives. Several laws try to prevent these acts of violence by providing punishment of assaults, battering, murder, harm etc. *The Penal Code Cap 16 of the*

214

Laws of Tanzania imposes punishment ranging from life imprisonment to even hanging in the case of murder. However, in many instances women do not report such acts of violence for fear of reprisals from their husbands and in-laws. This is possible through organized pressure and support groups.

Female *circumcision* is one of the acts of violence against young women. Although the government condemns it, some "tribes" still practice it under the influence of ill-informed beliefs as well as male interests. It is through education and persuasion to the communities and the girls that such practices can die away. A legal code of conduct on reproductive rights should be provided which will give people the right to decide on circumcision at the age of marriage (20) and such operation if desired should be done by qualified hospital staff.

Looking into the question of rape and sexual harrassment as faced by an increasing number of women, the law is very clear. When a person has carnal knowledge of a woman without her consent, he will be liable to imprisonment of seven years. So the misconceived notion that once a man offers a woman (barmaid) beer and the woman has then to pay through sexual favour is wrong and thus punishable. However, such relations are bargains between adults but care has to be taken where bargains are turned into assault. It has also been noticed that in practice booking rapists and proving cases of the rape has become a big hurdle. Women are best advised to organize around this problem and set their terms.

d) *Access to education*

Women are generally denied access to secondary and higher education. Traditionally it was thought that formal education was not for girls. Where they were allowed to get education it was either as an after thought or the women themselves were vigilant in pursuing it. Some parents believed that education was just for boys. It was feared that girls would get pregnant while in school and embarrass their parents. The legal position as it stands now is that primary education as per the *Education Act of 1978* is compulsory for both boys and girls between ages 7–13, and parents are liable to punishment or fine if they do not take their children to school. There are instances where school girls get pregnant. The law has provisions to punish the older men who impregnate school girls. *The Penal Code* makes it an offence and imposes a punishment of imprisonment term for any one who has sexual intercourse with a girl under 14 years even if the girl had agreed to the act as this is an offence of defilement of girls under 14 years. The social intervention currently available is to give family life education to schools so that girls can understand the risks of their gender. In the past, quite a number of school girls were spoilt by other men but only a few men were booked. Even today, tne school dropout rate suggests pregnancy as the major cause. Therefore women should persue this issue.

4. Areas in the Current Laws which Need to be Revised/Changed

Although already there is an ongoing effort to revise inadequate laws affecting women, it is proper that some of the issues which need to be addressed be put on this record.

a) *The Law of Marriage Act of 1971*

This piece of Legislation, though it tries to safeguard the interest of women, needs to be amended in some of its provisions. To start with, the minimum age to marry should be increased from 15 years for girls to 20 years. The provision as it stands now conflicts with other pieces of Legislation. It defeats the purpose of education for all children, boys and girls. At 15, the youth more often than not would still be at school and in rural areas they would be in primary school. Healthwise, a 15 years old girl is still a child and if she marries and gets a child, it will be a child bringing up another child. She is also at risk during pregnancy and child-birth. Knowledge wise, she has not been exposed to health education and child development and therefore she is premature. Even to enter the marriage contract which is so complicated and yet fluid needs more maturity and preparation than it is done today.

Under the same *Act,* bigamy should be made an offence. In this way a husband under a monogamous marriage who marries under the guise of customary law or who keeps a concubine will be liable to a penal sanction and this will act as a deterence. This habit, which at the moment is rampant, can be checked. More so, leaders need to observe decency and to be a good example to the youth.

The law of Marriage Act 1971 should include a specific provision with summary procedure whereby a wife and children who are not provided with necessaries for life can seek for court order so that a part of the husband's income can be deposited in court to maintain the children. This is necessary because at the moment the procedure to get maintenance is too cumbersome and too bureaucratic, hence women do not see the point of seeking relief in court. The problem of broken homes, deserted mothers and children is a researchable question to create data for more problem analysis. However in the spirit of responsible parenthood, fathers should get the approval of their wives to collect their incomes just in case they are not responsible.

b) *Education Act 1978*

The punishment imposed on a person who does not enroll his/her child in school should be a fine of 20,000/- and above, instead of the one imposed currently which does not exceed 5,000/-. In this way parents will feel the pinch after parting with such an amount. Mostly, parents remove children from school so as to marry them off and get money from bride-wealth which in most cases does not even amount to 20,000/-. Such parents will not resort to marrying of their children and hence risk parting with 20,000-!!

Men responsible for impregnating school girls should also be punished heavily. This means the Education Act must be amended in such a way as to impose a stringent sentence on men with such loose morals. Pregnant school girls should not be expelled from school.

c) *The Law of Inheritance* should also be amended and made uniform and applicable to all persons regardless of religion, sex or "tribe." In this way customary laws which discriminate against women won't leave any room for such manouvres. At the moment there is a project working towards reformation of Laws of Inheritance to which women can make a contribution through the Law Review Commission.

d) *The Affiliation Ordinance* should be amended so that a putative father can be ordered to pay a reasonable maintenance and education insurance scheme to an illegitimate child instead of the unrealistic sum of 100/- a month which is not enough to buy even one litre of fresh milk.

e) *Employment Ordinance.* Amendment can be made so as to arrest situations like those whereby bar owners use tricks to deprive barmaids of their wages. There should be some form of security of employment which enable bar maids to pursue their rights without fear of losing their jobs.

f) *The Strategy:* Women themselves should use the existing laws to fight any evils done against them. There are many laws in favour of women but women either fear using them or are totally ignorant of their existence. So the enlightened women must help their sisters and the law enforcing institutions should be sensitized so as to understand the problems facing women. It is in this way that women will forge cooperation with other institutions and law enforcers than is ther case now, when even policemen hesitate to entertain complaints about wife beating, rape or assault due to existing negative attitudes. The efforts initiated by the Law Review Commission as listed in Appendix A is a beginning towards a collective effort to change the Laws.

REFERENCES

"The Arusha Declaration" in *Ujamaa Essays on Socialism* by J.K. Nyerere 1968 Dar es Salaam Oxford University Press, p. 17

Babu, A.M.; 1981

    African Socialism of Socialist Africa. Dar es Salaam, TPH.

Bebel, August; 1976

    Society of the future. Moscow, Progress Publishers.

The Constitution of the United Republic of Tanzania 1977 as amended in 1984

Cory Hans;

    The Unification of the customary law of the Bantu tribes of Tanganyika. (47 answers on bridewealth by District Commissioner, Tanga Rural District). Tanga 1962 (MSS)

Education Act 1978: United Republic of Tanzania.

Fanon, F.; 1978

    Social and Political thought by Emmanuel Hansen. Nairobi, Oxford University Press.

Law of Marriage Act 1971: United Republic of Tanzania.

Marx and Engels;

    Basic writings on Politics and Philosophy edited by Lewis S. Feuer New York, Anchor Books, 1959.

Mbilinyi, M.

    "Runaway wives of Colonial Rungwe" *International J. of Sociology of Law,* 16:1, 1988.

Msumi, Hamisi; (Hon. Justice)

    "Law and justice in Women's Development" *In Joint Seminar of* members of the National Executive Council, Ministers of the Government of the United Republic and Members of Revolutionary Council of Zanzibar concerning the Place of Women in Economic and Social Development in Tanzania, Dodoma 7–10 May, 1988.

Penal Code Cap 16 of the Laws of Tanzania.

Swantz, M.;

    Women in Development: A Creative role denied? London. C. Hurst & Co.

218

LAWS TO BE EXAMINED ON LEGAL RIGHTS AND STATUS OF WOMEN IN TANZANIA

S/No.	Title	Act No./Year	Ordinance
1.	Adoption Ordinance	—	Cap. 333
2.	Affiliation Ordinance	—	Cap. 275
3.	Age of Majority Ordinance	—	Cap. 431
4.	Age of Majority (Citizenship Laws)		
5.	Act " "	No. 24/1970	—
	"	—	Cap. 512
6.	Business Names (Registration) Ord.	—	Cap. 213
7.	" (Amendments)	Act. No. 4/1975	—
8.	Business Licensing Act	No. 25/1972	—
9.	Children and Young Persons Act	No. 15/1980	—
10.	Chidren and Young Persons Ord.	—	Cap. 13
11.	Companies Ordinance	—	Cap. 212
12.	Day Care Centre Act	Act No. 17/1981	—
13.	Employment Ordinance	—	Cap. 366
14.	" Amendments	Act No. 1/1975	—
15.	" Amendments	Act 20/1975	—
16.	" Amendments	Act 7/1979	—
17.	Election Act Amendments	—	—
18.	Human Resources Deployment Act	No. 6/1983	—
19.	Hire Purchase Act	No. 22/1966	—
20.	" GN 3/2/66	Act 7/63/1966	—
21.	" GN 3/2/66	—	—
22.	Immigration Act	Act. No. 8/1983	—
23.	Immigration Amendment	Act No. 8/1983	—
24.	Interpretation of Laws and General Clauses	Act 30/1972	—
25.	Industrial Promotion and Development Fund (Establishment and Management) Act	No. 11/1984	—
26.	Labour Laws (Misc. Amendments) Act.	No. 25/1982	—
27.	Land Registration Ordinance	Act 12/1981	—
28.	Law of Contract Ordinance	—	Cap. 433
29.	Land (Law of Property and Conveyancing)	—	Cap. 114
30.	" " Amendments	Act 28/1970	—
31.	Law of Marriage	No. 5/1971	—
32.	Laws of Inheritance GN 436/63	—	—
33.	National Education Act	No. 25/1978	—
34.	Marriage, Divorce and Succession (Non-Christian Asiatics)	—	Cap. 112

35.	NPF Act	—	Cap. 564
36.	NPF Act Amendment	Act No. 26/1978	—
37.	Occupational Diseases (Amendment)	Act 17/1983	—
38.	Parastatal Pensions Scheme	Act 14/1978	—
39.	Pension Ordinance	—	Cap. 371
40.	" Amendments	Act 5/1971	—
41.	Public Officers (Age of Retirement)	Act 28/1981	—
42.	Security of Employment Ord. (Amend)	Act 1/1975	Cap. 574
43.	Severance Allowance Act	—	Cap. 487
44.	Widows and Orphans Pension Ord.	—	Cap. 54
45.	" " Amendment	Act 5/1971	—
46.	Workmen Compensation Ordinance	—	Cap. 263
47.	" " Amendments	Act 41 of 1969	—
48.	" " Amendments	Act 5/1971	—
49.	" " Amendments	Act 17/1981	—

Source: Judge Hamisi Msumi *Op.cit.* 1988 P.58–59 (The author is the Judge of the High Court of Tanzania. He is also the Chairperson of the law Reform Commission of Tanzania).

CHAPTER TEN
Lessons Learned

A selective approach has been adopted in this chapter to highlight on the issues which are considered urgent and strategic on the women's agenda. This does not mean that we have ignored others which many respective readers may consider equally critical. For that reason, it is advisable that individually these materials should provide a basis of analysis of various issues.

The lessons are drawn up from the various phases in women's lives, including upbringing, formal and informal education, preparation for marriage, bride-price, expectations from marriage, the role of the husband, motherhood and health, divorce, widowhood, the need for economic independence and self-reliance and the struggles for change. Since these issues are all interrelated, they will be discussed in general without itemisation.

It has been recorded that, all the women in the life histories were born into patriarchal family relations in which power was concentrated in the hands of the father, followed by other adult male members of the household. This team could use the power either to make or to unmake the lives of the rest of the members of the household who were either daughters, wives, and even mothers and workers. Where these groups of the led lived, and what they did for their future was basically determined by the controllers of the means of production, the men, both within and outside the household. The men decided who went to school when and for how long, and what they did after that, including who married whom and when. The role of the women actresses in their own life's drama or that of their daughters, was originally that of a supporter or complier. All these aspects have emerged clearly in the life histories.

All the women in the life histories were brought up, being moulded at every stage to conform, in varying degrees, to existing power relations. Their mothers were entrusted with the responsibility of ensuring that the girls walked in their footsteps, because in the absence of the mother, the girls have to bear the burden. They thus fully participated though not necessarily consciously, in the perpetuation of the exploitative power relations in the patriarchal set up. The exploitation or over use of some of the women started at very early stages as in the case of Mama Paulina who assumed

221

responsibility for the running of the family at the age of 9 (Chapter 8), although delegation of these tasks to her was by fate and not by design. Kalindile's case (chapter 7) is also another female childhood treatment that lends itself to many questions while suggesting at the same time issues of adolescent female protection.

The major lessons learned in these studies concern the struggles by the women at various stages in their lives to disentangle themselves from dependency on men which in most cases was deepened by women's unfounded original moulding to depend on their male providers for life instead of preparing them for life as independent persons. There are also lessons of women accepting certain oppressive norms.

We have seen that the women in this book were drawn to the city mainly as a result of marriage processes. They only differ in the means by which each came to the city. Only Kalindile (chapt. 6) in this collection is a rural woman who did not perhaps face circumstances which could drive her to the city. One notices also that she is typical of the rural women moulded by christian values. Regardless of the means by which the women found themselves in the city, the picture that emerges from the life histories is that the need for cash cuts across all ages, all ethnic origins, all marital status and levels of education. The increased need for cash income was spurred off by the sudden realization by the women that they were independent personalities with responsibilities to fulfill and tasks to perform. The latter were clearly spelt out for the women by the thorough non-formal education which is traditionally imparted to girls during their early childhood. The best examples are provided by Mama Paulina (Chapter 8) whose mother died when she, the first born child, and a daughter, was only 9 years old. So she assumed households tasks and chil care at that tender age. At the same time she had to attend school. Thus her double roles were clear to her from early in life. She seems to have had a supportive father, but the fact that did not remarry was a major constraint on Paulina who had even to take her youngest sister with her to school, for constant care.

Her father's commitment to his children is also somewhat watered down by the fact that when Paulina got married at the age of 20 she had to take her 11 year old sister and other older ones with her for care. This incident points out to the inescapable fact that women survive alone with children when their spouses depart while men fall victims to the revelation that they cannot stand alone and care for children. They have to re-marry as soon as possible. Paulina is also lucky in having a supportive husband who shares the household chores with his wife to give her time to participate in political and public activities. He is also proud of his wife's ability to teach and assist other women in developing their skills. He thus recognises and appreciates her responsibilities as a wife and also as an individual member of society.

Bibi (chapt. 2) was also lucky in having a husband who supported her to continue educating herself. She thus attended Adult Education classes and also taught other women in the Adult Education groups and in the women's economic project to which she belonged. Kalindile also had no complaints on interference with her education and adult teachings through women's groups (chapt. 6). Another supportive man was Bibi's uncle (ch. 2) We know little of her father, but her uncle supported Bibi's efforts for self education early in her life. Perhaps this early support encouraged her pursuit of education thoroughout her life. Typically, there are male patners who have liberated themselves and do not find any power struggles with active women. Such men are mature and confident so that they are apt to respect individual democracy.

All those men made a contribution in shattering the myth of the male as a patron of the household, the rest of the members being seen as his clients. And this is one of our main areas of emphasis in this discourse, that is, women should fight to bring about changes which will educate husbands on the fact that when they "allow" their wives to participate in self-advancement classes or economic activities, they are not giving them a privilege but a right and privilege for the family. Men should see it as their duty to give women the necessary resources to advance themselves. In contrast to Mama Paulina's and Bibi's husbands, (chapt. 8:2) Mama Koku's husband (chapt. 5) was threatened by his wife's success and she lived in constant fear of him as he could beat her up any time even when, for example, she made a positive suggestion that they should build a house.

One can briefly conclude here that the relations between them and their fathers at an early age gave them hopes and expectations for similar relationships later with their husbands. Any contrast to their hopes creates new consciousness and so women begin to question their rightful conditions and positions. They question their dependency and its justification as well as beginning to explore what they can do. It can be said that women like Mama Koku and Eva Anna (chapt. 4,5) Mwanaidi (chapt. 7) could not have changed their behavioural patterns without oppressive stimuli. Although Anna's father is furious at her stupidity in getting pregnant while at school yet he was also reassuring and after delivery he found a school for her while providing all necessities for the baby.

The original reaction of Anna's father, upon receiving confirmation of his daughter's pregnancy, was more a result of his embarrassment at the "shame" brought upon his family by his daughter. It is this "shame" which led him to ban the male culprit from associating further with Anna. Another less broad – minded parent would have financially milked dry the boy or his family, making a fortune out of what was seen then as his daughter's misfortune in order to avenge himself. This though, is not to condone Anna's father's total dissociation of the boy from Anna's troubles. He should have taken legal measures which one could consider appropriate to Anna's right.

In contrast to Anna's father, we have Eva's father (Chapt. 4) who forced his daughter to marry a man whose best quality probably was the fact that he or his parents could cough up 26 cows and 20 goats for the bridewealth. The paradox of bride price is a matter of time within changing socio-economic formations. Kalindile and her daughter Sambulika (Chapt. 6) have left no doubts on their position on this issue which must have shocked Marjorie. They have an unwavering support for bride price ".. even if it enslaves.."

Eva's father realised too late that he chose the wrong suitor for his daughter and thus encouraged their divorce. But he was still the beneficiary from this divorce since he retained all the brideweath while his daughter went off empty – handed to form other liaisons. He did not demand bridewealth from the second suitor until the man had stayed with Eva for seven years and they had a son.

The positive roles played by the parents and an uncle in the three case studies previously cited and the belated guilt felt by the father in the third case are all evidence of the fact that the man, even as an individual, has the power and ability to redirect or change cumbersome customs. Anna's father swallowed his traditional pride and took care of his daughter while Mama Paulina's father built up a relationship of confidence and trust with his daughter. There is thus a need for mothers to develop in boys gender awareness from the start and positive attitudes towards their sisters. This would assist them later in relating positively with their wives and children. Here is a necessary cultural revolution which needs to be ushered in by the women themselves through transforming the household labour as well as the women's attitudes towards themselves.

In these life histories, spelling out the tasks for girls was very central in their upbringing to such an extent that even Mama Koku (Chapt. 5), who was not too much bogged down by household chores, still was clearly aware of what was expected of her as a girl. In fact, Bibi (Chapt. 7) saw this as a central function of her childhood activities. What was not clearly spelt out for the girls was the fact that they were individuals and were expected to bear responsibilities. Nobody told any of the girls before they got married or entered into all kinds of relationships the fact that being a mature woman more often than not means being on your own whether you are married or not. A woman has to bear full responsibility for herself and for her family and not just perform routine tasks.

The women in the life histories found out this rather late. They were not prepared for the tough lessons. However, Kalindile (Chapt. 6) is rather different. The Nyakyusa by then had serious puberty rites and Kalindile by her personality wanted to show off that she was tough, daring and independent. She reconciled herself with the social system.

When Anna (Chapt. 3) had her first baby at the age of 14, her parents were very supportive and provided all the moral and material support for her and her baby. But after the imprisonment of her father and uncle, her life changed drastically. She had to go back to her mother in Ruvuma and fend for herself. That is when she matured. Later she got married, excited at the idea of getting away from the tough conditions in the village and ready to make a "good wife" for her employed husband, and having a home of her own, but without knowing the full implications of those presumed achievements

The lessons that were traditionally provided to Anna and the other women in the life histories were mainly on how to perform their roles as wives but not as individuals. Thus the contents of puberty ceremonies covered behaviour, beauty and general respect and obedience to the husband. The girls were also taught cookery, food preservation techniques and sometimes handicrafts. These two were also taught at school. These hand skills have been used by women like Eva (chapt. 4) and Mama Koku (chapt. 5) and Kalindile (chapt. 6) to generate income, but primarily they were imparted for the immediate benefit of the husband, that is "to decorate for his pleasure." All the other activities such as production and income were by the way. Her earlier education and that of other women had not given them a fuller picture of what constitutes a marriage. Education was meant to improve household performance. Anna realized these after seven years of marriage when life became difficult and expensive, leading to her being sent back from Mombasa, with her children, for good on a single ticket. She herself admits that it was then that she realised that she had to shoulder the burden alone. She says: "I had never worked out of home all my life and I realized I had to look for a job to support the children."

By being abandoned by her husband she was forced to jump on the band wagon of cash earners inspite of her inadequate education. That's how she moved to Songea and finally to Dar es Salaam working as a barmaid-cum-petty trader. She neatly summarises her move from a financially dependent daughter and housewife to an inadequately financed barmaid as a traumatic experience. The trauma is deepened by the fact that she was not prepared for it like all displaced women. Anothe woman who was forced into economic maturity was Mama Koku (chapter. 5) Mama Koku was brought up neatly, almost shielded from life's brutalities like shamba work, inadequate family provisions, ignorance and similar deficiencies. At 20 she got properly married and like Anna she was ready to become a "good house-wife to her employed husband." Life changed abruptly in 1968 when they came to Dar es Salaam city where the "big city syndrome" was probably too much for her husband, who in turn became too much for her in terms of call-ousness, but too small for her in terms of family maintenance and support. Consequently she had to start learning to be self-reliant under very difficult conditions and untold hostility from someone with whom she was supposed to be one. This alone, reduced her memory of other happy events like having children.

Mama Koku summarises the lesson she learned almost belatedly: "I have realized that women cannot only be contented with dishwashing and taking care of the husband, rather women should think of tommorrow right from the day they contract a marriage. Even in the villages women need to see these dvelopments and change the economic status." Kalindile is injured by the life of her daughter Sambulika who "owns nothing and never will" because she is a woman (chapt. 6:2). She appeals to Christian values of self reproach to mean that it is the self which is responsible for problems (chapt. 6:19-20). Bibi (Chapt. 2) on the other hand was better off in the sense that she was active in economic projects throughout most of her mar-ried life, and was in fact a partner to one of her husbands in his trade. Nonetheless, she stated that such economic independence was a new phenomenon which bettered the status of women. We can conclude, there-fore, that we also need protection of women's rights over property and economic resources and gains earned during women's active life as they spend their labour in the service of the household.

From these cases it is demonstrated how women are shocked into the realization that bearing the financial burden is part and parcel of their maturity. Consequently researchers and disseminators of information con-cerning women have also learned that ways should be found as a matter of priority to implement the suggestions made by Mama Koku (chapt. 5) and the other women whose life histories form this document. These include the fact that girls should be taught from an early stage to be self-reliant and not to embark upon married life "empty-handed." The stories have demonstrated that even an employed husband is not and has never been a secure and permanent assurance of a good future. Indeed, the voices of

226

these women make the best consultancy available on the positions and conditions of women in Africa and specifically the Tanzanian experience.

The main snag here is the fact that some men block women's way to economic independence, correctly fearing that this will diminish the women's subservience to them. But if parents taught children of both sexes from early ages the importance and inevitability of each one as an individual to be self-reliant this would go a long way towards diminishing both the problems of a woman being shocked into self-reliance at a later stage and the man fearing an enterprising woman. This points to the need for strengthening co-operation between the formal and informal education sectors so as to give the youth, especially the girls, a balanced view of their future. The women in the life histories have embarked on the right path by providing education to their children including the daughters. They themselves either missed out completely formal education or their education was interrupted by various social forces. While others failed to find alternative means of educating themselves, others like Bibi (Chapt. 2) attended Adult Education clases. Bibi's struggle for self-education and improvement is typical of an increasing number of women left out of primary school who then seek education through adult education programmes. A number of women who feel they are too old or too busy to attend classes still see the importance of educating their daughters and they have made possible efforts to do so.

The government could do better to assist them to achieve their targets by introducing several measures in the formal education sector, including the provision of family life education in schools, the non-expulsion of girls whose education is interrupted often by unscrupulous older men who make them pregnant and abandon them.

The government also faces challenges of a low level development of science and technology in transforming economic and social services in rural areas. The establishment of Vocational training centres for girls to widen their chances of learning trades for income-generation to enable them to be self-reliant as youths and later on as adults with added responsibilities, is long overdue. This training should be linked with the improvement of living conditions in the villages so that youths are not enticed by cheap jobs and other attractions in the city. The current existing gap between rural and urban areas need to be abolished. The poor village production facilities like the hoe, or services like pounding grain with mortar all wear out girls and women. They need total transformation to facilitate and ease the work burden of the women.

The women's organisation, UWT has also a positive role to play in intergrating the two sectors of education. This is clearly exemplified in the working relationship that existed between the Mbezi One Village Adult Education group to which Mama Paulina (chapt. 8) was a teacher, the nursery school and the UWT branch at the University of Dar es Salaam. This kind of network and cooperation is essential not only for giving women adult education but also for engineering unity among the various classes of women as a first step in the fight for gender equality.

The Mbezi One Women's group also demonstrate the supportive role small women's groups provide for their members. The women learned and farmed together. This unity is a strategy which one cannot abandon today even in the face of the ideology of private enterprise since there are benefits to be gained by the poor in group dynamics. Kalindile (chapt. 6:20) has displayed the role of church groups and village women social support system both of which suggest positively the place and role of groups for women.

Bibi (Chapt. 2) also belonged to a women's development group which shared skills and resources. She recognized the advantage of such groups and has continued to participate in political, economic and educational groups throughout her adulthood. In fact, if Eva (Chapt. 4) had had an opportunity to belong to such a group her economic struggles would have borne more tangible fruits than merely enabling her to survive in the city. It is only a few women like Mwanaidi (Chapt. 7) who could achieve self-reliance largely on their own.

Talking of tangible fruits in the form of material wealth and financial security does not necessarily mean that we are advocating that women should embark on the acquisition of property at break-neck speed. Our advocacy is centered around the fact that tradionally most girls enter marriage empty-handed as they do not own land or other property in their father's home unless they inherited it upon the death of their fathers. And for those whose marriages fail, they walk out or are pushed out only empty-handed but also drained of their energy and youthfulness. In all the cases studied which involved separation and divorce (chapt. 2, 4 and 7), the question of who gets what did not even arise because at the most what women could take with them were their very personal properties including a few pots. Anna's case (Chapt. 3) was even worse because she stepped out of her marital home in a foreign country taking nothing but her children and personal belongings and even leaving a second house they had built together. She did not sense that it was the last time she would see that home. She did not attempt to claim either child maintenance or a share in the property acquired together. The feeling that women do not own property and therefore cannot claim property is deeply inculcated in both men and women's minds.

An ironic situation arises with Mwanaidi (Chapt, 7) She was "victorious" in her divorce in the sense that unlike in most cases, she walked out in "peace" with a divorce certificate testifying to her good behaviour and tolerance: but her good behaviour did not erase the fact that she produced but did not reproduce for her husband, thus failing to fulfil one of her main roles as a wife.

Women have a lot to Learn from Mwanaidi in that she has worked hard with determination and has managed to convert her abstract and unreal victory into concrete success, as shown in her story. She learned early in life, on her own, to redirect the energies left over from toiling to produce material wealth for her husband, into working hard to build a secure future for herself and for dependants of her own choice.

In the other two cases (chapt. 3 and 5) the women were left with children to support but with no child support whatever from their husbands, nor were they aware of legal provisions available for child maintenance although one must point out that even if they claimed the 100/- per child per month this is not enough compered to the current prices. These are the issues which have been addressed to the legal arms of the government through various bodies, especially the Law Reform Commission. The provision of legal aid and counselling for women as proposed elsewhere is very central because many women miss their dues because of ignorance of the law relating to such issues. Kalindile's story on marriage rites of "washing" with a husband as a sign of "understanding" sounds like a coustomary legal contract (chapt. 6:10). However these types (chapt. 6:10) of marriages provide for a one-way-ticket, perhaps to insist that marriage is for-ever.

In the case of widowhood (Chapt. 5), Mama Koku's share in her husband's property was not automatic. She had to fight with determination to secure some government recognition of her contribution in the maintenance of one of its senior employees, her late husband, whom she had toiled together for all the 25 years of her married life; with no returns. It is true that luck was with her in that her appeal fell on a sympathetic ear but not all women can adopt such high level techniques in demanding their rights! In fact, such approaches may also turn the provision of a right into granting a privilege, which is not what women want. Bibi (Chapt. 2) is also a widow and her recounting of the process of acquiring her current home was vivid, partially because, as a recent widow, it was quite possible that their house would be taken from her by her late husband's relatives. Thus she was insistent on her ownership.

Women's liberation requires that the legal, political and socio-economic channels be open so that women can make use of them, to exercise their rights. However, much more so, there is urgent need to make women aware of this process and their obligation to utilize services provided by the nation to protect vulnerable groups as well as maintaining peace and justice in families. This position however does not totally disagree with Kalindile's tactics (chapt. 6:37) who challenges us with the question later that ".... is the court a woman?"

The final conclusion one observes is that women's oppression is a universal phenomena. We do not for example delienate serious differences in the women's lives which reflect on the political economy of Tanzania with particular reference to the districts where women belonged. Women have similar problems as if they are in the same or similar forms of production and socio-economic settings. There are oppressions for young women just as there are for the old, the formally educated and the non-formally educated as well as those women with children and those without; the rural and the urban women. That women's "acceptance" of 'dependant status' is a myth, has been proved beyond reasonable doubt. It is clear that women are ready to adjust due to different circumstances as shown in these experience.

Lastly, women have shown different forms of struggles and resistance. Each one has an answer. Kalindile and Mama Koku (chapt. 5,6) seem to represent the most common forms of response to family problems, that is, silence and manipulation while Bibi, Eva and Mwanaidi (chapt. 2,3,7) are acting as per Islamic code. On the other hand, Mama Koku, Paulina and Kalindile (chapt. 5,8,6,) are also acting as per christian code. All these reactions seem to suggest that this is how life is in the families in Tanzania now and in the past. The disturbing problem is that much as life means struggle, Tanzanian women are sent into it from the wrong premises –.and that is where the answer to women's emancipation lies.

Even when one's entitlements are clearly spelt out, the implementation process is often hampered by how ready one is to share the cake with relevant officials. The situation has been worse for women who are on their own and have no "connections" with officials who are either close relatives or are the exceptional few who perform their duties without demanding an illegal "handshake." These hard facts point to very important ramifications about the need to re-examine the institution of marriage and to rectify family legal procedure. One should be reminded as pointed out in chapter 5, that women did not choose to be refugees at any point of their marriage contract. In that case, serious regard should be made to the effect of lack of immediate personal and private shelter to displaced women. In other words, family law should provide automatic redress for homelessness to displaced women accordingly.

The legal Section above (Chapt. 9) tells the women that every problem has been provided for by the statutory law. Surely, that is not true because as we learn from the swahili sayings, "mzigo wa mwenzio ni kanda ya sufi" or "it is the shoe wearer who knows where it pinches most." The legal sector in Tanzania has been operating within the dominant culture of corruption which evolved slowly since the late 1970s. As a result, women who honestly attempted to resolve the matrimonial abyss and other gender conflicts through the court system found it an uphill struggle. Whilst this legal approach is indeed logical (idealy), the majority of women, besides lacking the means and the wits to avail themselves of the legal facility, have politely challenged the legal system. In unequivocal terms, a peasant woman Kalindile (chapt. 6) demonstrates to us that the women's "silent" struggles are far superior than the legal process and she says: "Is the court a woman?" Kalindile certainly meant much more than that, she implied that a woman offended by a man would be granted justice only if the court system was of the woman's making, conscious and aware that the women and children in most cases would be the wronged party. Indeed, Kalindile's statement would hold some truth if only the would-be female systems were free of corruption to set a living example. In other words, every approach, legal, political, cultural, social, economic and personal has to be given a chance to regulate matrimonial peace. Mama Koku (chapt. 5) couldn't agree more with Kalindile, for she suffered under the hand of a custodian of justice (lawyer) to the extent that she could not think at any one moment that the court had a place in her circumtances. And if all wronged women and children and men were to go to court what would the courts do?

From all the lessons learned through the wisdom of the few women in this book, it can be said that women need to know more about respective gender systems. Women take men for granted as well as the social systems around them so that when things go extremely wrong, they do not know what to do because they are not prepared. It is also note worthy that women should organize and struggle to shape and influence the laws while at the same time exercising their personal powers of bargaining and manipulation as part of household politics. We thank the women for their life stories. The prize to the life-history makers is for the Women activists to take action after reading this book. For men they should not take women for granted, while for leaders, women's lives pose a challenging task by questioning democracy.

ABOUT THE CO-AUTHORS

Alice-Nhoma-Wamunza is a Senior Librarian and a Sociologist at the University of Dar es Salaam. She is a former Convenor of WRDP (1985–1988). She has authored and co-authored a number of articles on women in development and librarianship.

Anna Nkebukwa is a Senior Librarian and Political Scientist at the University of Dar es Salaam. She is a former WRDP Secretary (1985–1988). She has authored useful articles on women and librarianship.

Assey Muro is a Principal Resident Tutor at the Adult Education Correspondence Institute. She is a founder member of WRDP. She is currently a Project Officer at UNICEF in Dar es Salaam. She has written many articles on Education and Women in Development.

Bertha Koda, an Interdisciplinary Social Scientist, is a Senior Lecturer at the Institute of Development Studies, University of Dar es Salaam. She has authored and co-authored many articles on women in development and gender issues. She was the first Secretary of WRDP (1980–1983) and the first convenor of the IDS based Women Study Group.

Magdalena Ngaiza, an Interdisciplinary Social Scientist, is a Senior Lecturer at the Institute of Development Studies, University of Dar es Salaam and a former Librarian. She has written and co-authored several articles on women, health and information. Also a founding member of WRDP, she is currently Assistant Convenor.

Marjorie Mbilinyi is Professor of Education in the Institute of Development Studies, University of Dar es Salaam. Marjorie is a leading author of many published articles and several books on gender-related issues and on Education, Women's health and employment. She is a founding member and the first convenor of WRDP 1980–1984.

Patricia Mbughuni is a Senior Research Fellow at the Institute of Kiswahili Research, University of Dar es Salaam. She is currently on leave without pay and working as Advisor to the Women's Desk of Small Scale Industries Development Ordanisation (SIDO). She has written on women and education, culture and economic activities. Patricia is also a founding member of WRDP.